AMERICAN PARENT

BALLANTINE BOOKS   NEW YORK

AMERICAN PARENT

My Strange and Surprising Adventures
in Modern Babyland

Sam Apple

American Parent is a work of nonfiction. Some of the names of individuals depicted in this book have been changed to protect their anonymity. Any resulting resemblance to persons living or dead is entirely coincidental and unintentional.

Published in the United States by Ballantine Books, an imprint of The Random House Publishing Group, a division of Random House, Inc., New York.

BALLANTINE and colophon are registered trademarks of Random House, Inc.

Several brief sections of this book first appeared in different forms in the following publications: Babble.com, *The Financial Times Magazine*, *The New York Times Magazine*, *Parents Magazine*.

LIBRARY OF CONGRESS CATALOGING-IN-PUBLICATION DATA
Apple, Sam.
American parent: my strange and surprising adventures in modern babyland / Sam Apple.
    p.   cm.
ISBN 978-0-345-46504-7
1. Fatherhood—United States. 2. Parenthood—United States. 3. Child rearing—United States. I. Title.
HQ756.A658   2009
306.874'20973—dc22   2009008918

Printed in the United States of America on acid-free paper

www.ballantinebooks.com

9 8 7 6 5 4 3 2 1

FIRST EDITION

Book design by Simon M. Sullivan

For JENNIFER *and* ISAAC,
and in memory of my mother,
DEBRA APPLE

First Comes Love

I WAS TRYING TO STUDY, but it was no use. Ryan wouldn't stop talking about the "juicy" buttocks.

We were in the lounge of our college dorm, and the dorm's librarian had just walked by in tight jeans.

"Damn that thing is juicy," Ryan said.

I nodded and kept my eyes on the book in my lap.

"I mean seriously juicy."

Ryan lived in the room next to mine, and it took patience to be around him. He ogled every girl who passed him in the halls and then made crude comments under his breath. His room was furnished with couches he had stolen from another dorm lounge, and when he wasn't talking about women's body parts, he was talking about the size and power of his bass speakers—a power I could attest to because I felt it vibrating through my floor every night as I tried to fall asleep.

I was hanging around with Ryan out of loneliness. It had been over a year since I'd moved from Houston to Ann Arbor to attend the University of Michigan, and I still hadn't found my niche. There were plenty of nice people around, people who seemed a lot like me, except that they were having much more fun. I wanted to get to know these people but my shyness made it almost impossible. On the weekends I would sometimes go to parties in groups, only to return to my room feeling more alone than when I had left.

At some point during Ryan's ode to the dorm librarian's ass, a beautiful girl walked into the lounge eating a Kit Kat bar. I had noticed the girl once before in the dorm's computer lab and immediately decided that she was much too pretty to talk to. She was tall with strawberry blond hair and her lips were so full and alluring that I couldn't help but wonder what it would feel like to kiss—or at least apply gloss to—them.

The girl was walking in our direction. I prayed that Ryan wouldn't say something gross.

"That's Jennifer. I'm friends with her," Ryan said, the pride visible on his face.

"Whatever," I said.

"Hey Jennifer," Ryan called.

Jennifer smiled. Her Kit Kat was melting and the tips of her fingers were covered in chocolate. "Oh, hey, funny to see you again," she said.

Ryan explained that he and Jennifer had gone shopping together earlier in the day.

I nodded, amazed that a girl who could clearly have the company of any guy on campus had chosen to spend an afternoon with Ryan.

Jennifer sat down and Ryan spoke about his speakers for a few minutes. Then, as though he could hear the voice in my head begging him, Ryan stood up and said that he had to go. I could have hugged him.

Jennifer and I were alone in the lounge, and as we talked, it became increasingly clear that her looks were only a small part of the package. She was a philosophy major and she loved Chris Farley. She played the guitar and painted in her spare time. She shared my love of a good root beer and she agreed that the world would be a better place if we all had breakfast for dinner much more often.

And yet what really struck me wasn't what we spoke about but the sense that Jennifer and I were getting through to each other. Even in conversations with friends, I sometimes feel as though we are not really communicating so much as taking turns saying what we want to say. But from the first moment with Jennifer, her words were making it to that out-of-the-way spot in my brain that absorbs and processes incoming data. I don't think I could already have been in love, but I've since thought that we really only listen, in the deepest sense of listening, to the people we are in love with.

As we parted, I asked Jennifer what room she lived in, the dorm equivalent of getting a number. It was an uncharacteristically bold move for me, but I knew that I would hate myself forever if I didn't at least ask.

"405 Anderson," Jennifer said.

"Cool," I said, as though it was no big deal, as though the hour I had just spent talking to her wasn't already the highlight of my college years, as though I was not going to repeat that number in my head a thousand times until it was safely down on paper and then put the paper in my special box of important things along with my passport and the Bill Bradley rookie basketball card that I'd once believed was going to allow me to retire at a young age.

The next night, after spending an hour in the dorm bathroom trying in vain to pat down my poofy hair, I made the journey to the fourth floor of Anderson Hall and knocked on the door.

I waited for a full minute, as terrified as if I'd just stepped on a mine, but Jennifer's door never opened. Nor did it open the next night. Or the one after that.

Had I known that Jennifer was not in her room because she was at Disneyland with her thirty-year-old boyfriend, I probably would never have gone back that fourth time, that fateful night when the door finally opened and Jennifer stood before me talking on the phone in a faded yellow sweatshirt.

"Hey," I said.

Jennifer asked the person on the phone to hold on.

"Hey," she said.

"I'm Sam, the guy you were talking to the other day in the lounge."

"I remember," Jennifer said.

She remembered me. It had been less than a week and yet it seemed miraculous. This is the paradox of profound insecurity: The slightest acknowledgment of your existence is a great affirmation.

I waited for Jennifer to end her call, and then we walked through the dorm's narrow halls, side by side, like a young Victorian couple on a first courtship stroll in the park. I was nervous and walking at full speed. Later Jennifer told me that she was practically running to keep up.

As we made our way around the dorm, Jennifer made a crucial admission: She didn't like Ryan, either. She had gone shopping with him that day only because she too was lonely, she too had found that turning eighteen and being dropped off in southeastern Michigan among thousands of strangers could be a harrowing experience. Jennifer said that after shopping for pants with Ryan, they had gone out to dinner and that Ryan had ordered exactly what she had ordered and then timed his bites to coincide with hers.

"That's really freaky," I said.

"It was terrifying," Jennifer said.

It was another year and a half before Jennifer cut off all ties with her older boyfriend in her hometown of Cincinnati and became my girlfriend. But while the waiting was hard, I never let my frustration get in the way of our friendship.

Sometimes Jennifer and I went to parties together, but mostly we sat around the dorm sipping coffee and talking. We shared a love of bizarre hypothetical questions, and we would stay up late into the night posing them: Would you still be my friend if you found out that I genuinely believed that the eighties sitcom *Perfect Strangers* was the greatest achievement in Western drama? What if you found out that I had an enormous walnut collection in the closet of my dorm room? A yes never ended the line of questioning. What if I told you that the walnuts were my best friends and that I sometimes sang to them in the evenings? Still yes? What if I were reciting deeply erotic poetry to the walnuts?

In another favorite game, Jennifer and I would imagine what would happen if one of us turned in the most brilliant philosophy paper of all time. We called this game the "bell fantasy" because our visions always began with one particularly crusty professor skimming the paper in his office and then dropping to his knees in shock as he realized that all of the great puzzles of Western philosophy had just been solved. When he regained his strength, the professor would crawl to the corner of his office and ring a cobweb-covered bell that had been hung there decades ago in anticipation of just such a moment. As the ringing echoed through the halls of the Michigan philosophy department, the other professors would rush over, and the game was to imagine their responses to the astonishingly brilliant paper. We probably dreamed up a thousand different scenarios: A professor would faint, or begin vomiting, or glance at the paper once and then dive headfirst out the window, or—my personal favorite—look at the paper without moving an inch, his shock revealed only by the trickle of urine from his pant leg.

For Jennifer, the bell fantasies were a fun diversion from

writing philosophy papers. But the diversions held special importance for me. I'd spent much of my life to that point playing a very different kind of "what if" game. The what-ifs of my youth were the dark hypotheticals that breed in the imagination of the neurotic, the death-centered fantasies that are no less terrifying for their ridiculousness: What if the weird smell on the piece of plastic I have just smelled causes brain cancer? What if the red dot on the muffin I am eating is AIDS-infected blood?

My neuroses didn't disappear when I met Jennifer, but our conversations turned many of my worst instincts inside out. If I couldn't stop fantasizing about AIDS muffins, I could at least also fantasize about happier things. I was learning to take refuge in my imagination. It was an important psychological step.

Jennifer and I became a full-fledged couple during our senior year. Then Jennifer moved to Philadelphia for law school, and I moved to New York to work at a magazine. The long-distance relationship made us both miserable, and we broke up. At least, we told ourselves we had broken up. We stayed in touch over the phone and, when Jennifer moved to New York after graduation, we resumed our relationship. We didn't always acknowledge it—sometimes not even to ourselves—but we both knew that we would probably end up together: We'd never fully lost the connection we'd both felt that first night in the dorm, and there are only so many other people who like to fantasize about philosophy professors vomiting.

A YEAR AFTER we moved in together in Brooklyn, when we were both twenty-six, I decided to ask Jennifer to marry me. I also decided that I did not want to make a joke out of the marriage proposal. I was concerned that the jokes had gone too far. Even saying "I love you" to Jennifer had lost its earnest punch after I fell into the habit of adding that the "you" in question was not Jennifer but rather a Chinese woman named Yu.

I wanted the engagement to be different. I wanted Jennifer to know it was she and not Yu that I loved.

I couldn't help but have a few absurd proposal fantasies. In moments of weakness, I thought of floating the ring in our toilet in a boat made of wooden tongue depressors. I would paint "USS Engagement" on the boat's side and perhaps drop rose petals in the surrounding waters.

I thought of telling Jennifer over the phone that I had pierced my face. I would listen in silence as she expressed her dismay and then return home with the ring Scotch-taped to my nose in such a way that it looked like a piercing.

I thought of burying the ring, diamond and all, in a jar of peanut butter and letting fate play its hand. If Jennifer never craved peanut butter again, then perhaps it wasn't meant to be.

But it was meant to be, and allowing Jennifer's taste for peanut butter to determine our future was crazy. I made reservations at a bed-and-breakfast in Saratoga Springs, New York. Jennifer and I would spend the day taking in the small-town charms, and then in the evening, on the banks of a shimmering body of water (for reasons I can't explain, I was convinced that shimmering water would magnify the seriousness of my intentions), I would ask her to be my wife.

The plan did not go smoothly. In pursuit of a lake I had located on my map, I led Jennifer on a meandering, hour-long trek. As I grew increasingly lost (the trek involved three life-threatening sprints across the same interstate), Jennifer grew increasingly confused. In the seven years we had known each other, I had never once suggested taking a walk. Nor had I ever expressed such great interest in a lake.

"Maybe we should turn around," Jennifer said.

"I just think this lake is going to be really amazing," I said.

When we found ourselves on a dark road with no signs of civilization, I admitted to having no idea where we were. We hiked back to a gas station off the interstate, where the seemingly stoned attendant told me that the lake I was looking for did not exist.

Stranded at a gas station on the outskirts of Saratoga Springs, the diamond ring loose in my right front pocket, my commitment to earnestness began to wither. I would request that the attendant hide the ring in his thick hippie beard and then ask him to ask Jennifer to scratch his chin. I would buy a Drake's Coffee Cake and pretend to choke. When the attendant Heimliched me, the ring would fly out of my mouth amid a spectacular shower of Coffee Cake crumbs.

No jokes! We took a cab back to our bed-and-breakfast and, at a nearby park, I noticed a small pond. There was no shimmering, but it would do. I got down on one knee and asked Jennifer to marry me.

She said yes. It was awesome, and we still had a day left to enjoy the small-town charms of Saratoga Springs. The next morning we headed to a horse show and llama-jumping contest at the local racetrack.

We arrived moments after the last llama had made its last jump, but our disappointment was overshadowed by the dizzying array of horse-themed products for sale. And as we walked hand in hand admiring the hoof trimmers and the galloping mustang collector's plates, I realized how stupid my plan had been. When I was with Jennifer, it was impossible to keep the jokes at bay. She made me laugh and she inspired me to try and make her laugh. I felt lucky. It wasn't a feeling I was used to.

OOO

AFTER A YEAR of marriage, Jennifer felt ready to have a baby. I was less ready. I wanted to be a parent, but I had arrived at something that felt right, and I was afraid of entering a new phase of life with countless opportunities for things to go wrong.

If I wasn't paralyzed with fear, it was probably because I was convinced I'd never be a father—not after all the baths I'd taken.

The bathing wasn't my fault. Our Brooklyn apartment had a Jacuzzi bathtub. When we moved in, a friend saw the Jacuzzi and joked that I would never leave the tub. Two years and an estimated five hundred baths later, the joke didn't seem so funny. But what could I do? I was a writer working from home part-time and our apartment was chilly. It was a perfect storm of bath temptation. I bathed during the day and when Jennifer came home from work, I occasionally joined her in the tub for round two. I bathed until I was dizzy and dehydrated and my skin felt like chewed Bubble Yum. I read and wrote articles in the bath and even did telephone interviews—always careful to be still so that the interviewees would not hear a splash and realize they were speaking to a naked journalist.

It was only after Jennifer and I decided to have a baby that I read that hot baths can lower your sperm count. When I stumbled upon this bit of trivia during a Google search for information on the impact of jockey underwear on fertility, I felt sick. The article suggested that your sperm count could go back up if you stopped bathing, but surely whatever studies had been done had not anticipated the amount of time my testicles had spent in hot water.

I was so sure that I had ruined my chance at fatherhood that when Jennifer walked into our living room holding a pregnancy test strip, I didn't consider that it might be positive.

"Will you look at this?" Jennifer said, handing me the white plastic strip. I looked. At the edge of the strip were two parallel pink lines. One pink line was thick and full, the other splotchy and faded.

"Do you see one or two lines?" Jennifer asked.

"Two," I said.

"Are you sure? Two?"

"Two lines."

"Really?"

"Yup."

Jennifer's doubt about the pregnancy test stemmed from her own fears about fertility. She too had convinced herself that she would be incapable of having children based on flimsy evidence. We were both young healthy adults but in our minds we were as likely to conceive a child as we were to grow new limbs.

"Two lines means I'm pregnant," Jennifer said.

I looked back at the strip of plastic in my hands. The two pink lines were still there.

If someone had asked me how I would feel if I found out that Jennifer was pregnant, I probably would have said "overjoyed." I probably would have said that I would be jumping up and down with excitement. And later I did feel some of that raw happiness—along with my raw panic. But as I looked up at Jennifer, I was too overwhelmed to feel much of anything. Jennifer began to cry, and I held her against me.

THIS BOOK IS ABOUT the questions and issues that I thought about as Jennifer and I made our way into parenthood. Rather than following an outline, I let our own journey dictate the course of my writing and followed my curiosity where it took me. Most of all, I was interested in the latest parenting trends. After Jennifer became pregnant, I began to read baby websites and observe the parents and babies in our Brooklyn neighborhood, and the more

I learned, the more convinced I became that something strange was going on. The signs of this strangeness were everywhere, from the enormous and enormously expensive strollers, to the bizarre baby names, to the growing list of natural birth techniques, to the overwhelming number of new baby products, to the baby classes that seemed entirely unsuited for babies.

As I took in bits and pieces of information about all these different parenting phenomena, I sometimes felt like an anthropologist taking notes on a foreign culture, a culture with its own rites and rituals, its own tools, even its own vocabulary. But unlike an anthropologist, I had no academic remove from my subject. I was going to be a parent soon. I wanted to understand the new world I was entering. I thought that if I looked into enough theories, explored enough trends, and spoke to enough experts, I would be able to find order in the chaos that new parents face in the months before and after the birth of a child.

Now I know better.

Contents

PART ONE
○○○ BEFORE

ONE

Parents and Products

The Rise of the Baby Industrial Complex

BABIES HAVE A LOT GOING FOR THEM. Their big eyes and fat cheeks are cute. Their skin is soft. They will laugh at just about any joke so long as you slap your head and fall down at the end of it.

It's no surprise, then, that parents have always wanted to give nice things to their babies—even the earliest human civilizations had rag dolls and other simple toys. What's surprising is the amount of money that new mothers and fathers in America now spend. Nothing in the history of parenthood compares to it. Part of the spending increase can be traced to the growth of the up-scale baby products industry. Rich parents are now buying $15,000 handcrafted cribs and $1,200 Italian leather diaper bags with faux-fur-trimmed changing pads. Some of them are even scenting their babies with $53 bottles of baby cologne. But it's not just the rich. It's all of us. Revenue from the sale of baby products has almost tripled since the mid-1990s, and the average American child now receives seventy new toys a year.

I had my formal introduction into what journalists and bloggers have begun to refer to as "the baby industrial complex" during the second trimester of Jennifer's pregnancy. Jennifer's parents were in town, and the four of us had gone together to Buy Buy Baby, the chain of baby superstores that has become famous for its overwhelming selection—some locations have more than twenty thousand products for sale.

I had mixed feelings about the shopping trip. There's a Jewish superstition against buying things for a baby before the birth, and I was in no mood to take chances. But I was also in no mood to interfere with all of the hard work Jennifer was doing to prepare for our son's arrival. Prior to the pregnancy, Jennifer and I had been living as similar a life to the homeless as a middle-class couple with a comfortable apartment can manage. We have both always been diligent and organized at work, but we left that diligence and organization at the door when we returned home. We cobbled our meals together at the last minute and ate them standing up in the kitchen. If the pantry was empty and it was cold out, a dinner might consist of nothing but a spoonful of peanut butter dolloped onto whatever stray food item we were lucky enough to dig up behind the expired cans of soup. And then there was the pile of junk next to our bed. At first it was a small pile, but over time it grew so high that we began to refer to it as "Mount Saint Junkmore" and then simply as "Mount Saint." After a while Mount Saint became part of our lives, as though we were powerless to remove it. I even began to take pleasure in searching through it for lost treasures.

I knew that we would have to change our slovenly ways before the baby arrived, but during the first months of Jennifer's pregnancy, I spent most of my time thinking about all of the things I needed to do rather than doing them. Jennifer, meanwhile, was undergoing a dramatic transformation. To my great surprise and confusion, she began to clean even when we were not expecting guests. She bought curtains for our windows and a small soap dispenser for the bathroom. She made lists of items we would need for the baby and more lists of items we would need to get rid of before the baby arrived.

The new hyperorganized Jennifer bothered me when I first

noticed her. I feared I was losing the idiosyncratic Jennifer I'd always known and loved, the Jennifer who had once unthinkingly walked into a college classroom eating beets out of a jar with her hands, the Jennifer who, in the middle of law school at the University of Pennsylvania, had decided to write a long work of nonfiction about colonial impersonators and then spent a semester hanging around an obese Ben Franklin look-alike.

It took me a few months to realize that my fears about Jennifer were misplaced, that there is no contradiction between quirkiness and cleanliness. And when this insight sunk in, I also realized that the new rational side of Jennifer wasn't so new. At work as an advertising attorney, Jennifer picked apart misleading product claims every day. And when I was dumb enough to argue with her, Jennifer picked apart my own logic with equal ease. The linear-thinking Jennifer could be frustrating at times, for example, when she would explain why one of the inventions I had dreamed up would never work. (Apparently there will never be a market for edible Frisbees that serve both as activity and postactivity snack.) But I've also always found it comforting to share my life with someone so grounded. If I am a helium balloon, then Jennifer is both the helium that sets me afloat and the string that keeps me tethered to the earth.

And so when Jennifer said that it was time to go shopping for the baby, I didn't protest. I was fully prepared to be overwhelmed by the experience—having a breakdown at a baby superstore is now a rite of passage for new American parents—and Buy Buy Baby did not disappoint. A friend had given Jennifer a list of items we might need during the baby's first weeks and the list was full of products I would never have thought to buy. I had read that the baby would have a scab where the umbilical cord had been cut, but I had no idea that we needed cotton balls and rubbing alcohol for cleaning the scab. I knew that we would need onesies—the legless leotards with snaps at the crotch that have become the official uniform of the American newborn—but I did not know that we would need both short-sleeved and long-sleeved onesies or that the long-sleeved onesies should also have mittenlike extensions to prevent our baby from clawing his own face. I knew that we would need wet wipes, but I would never have imagined that we would also need dry wipes for the first weeks, when our baby's tush would apparently be so exquisitely sensitive that chemically moistened wipes would pose too great a risk. I knew that we would need a small crib, or co-sleeper, so that the baby could sleep next to our bed, but I am almost certain that I could have spent a week in the store without having ever realized that we would also need small sheets for the co-sleeper.

It took us a solid hour to exhaust all of the items on our list, and our list was just the beginning. We bought baby-safe soap and baby-safe detergent and baby-safe stain removers. We picked out a U-shaped pillow that, though marketed as a device to help floor-bound newborns prop themselves up on their arms, appeared to be little more than an unusually expensive neck rest. Then we picked out a second somewhat larger U-shaped pillow that, though marketed as a pillow for the baby to rest on while breast-feeding, appeared to be little more than an even more expensive neck rest.

I wasn't entirely convinced that we needed all of the items in our cart, particularly the baby toiletries, which have turned into a booming business in recent years—drugstore sales of such items rose 14 percent between 2005 and 2006 alone. But at the time, I was too anxious to question whether normal soap could really be so dangerous. And the line between need and want is murky. At one point—I think it may have been shortly after we picked out the second U-shaped pillow—it occurred to me that, if we really wanted to be resourceful, we didn't have to buy anything: I could sew cloth diapers from my old sweatpants and cut washable wipes from old sheets. If I wanted the wipes warmed, I could moisten them with hot water, or hold them over an open flame. If I wanted an infant bathtub, I could line a cardboard box with a plastic garbage bag. Even pacifiers were probably excessive in a world scattered with smooth stones.

Because we didn't own a car, the one item we could not do without was a stroller. Some of the strollers at Buy Buy Baby looked like what I'd always thought of as a stroller: They had small plastic frames and four small wheels that looked entirely sufficient for the job of wheeling around a baby. But many of the strollers looked nothing like the strollers of my imagination: These strollers were twice as big as the others. They had shiny metal frames and wheels so tall and thick that immigrants who spot them for the first time probably assume that American parents engage in competitive off-road baby racing.

After speaking with a salesman about the prices and functions of the different models, Jennifer and I settled on a Maclaren, a solid, lightweight stroller, by no means cheap at two hundred and fifty dollars, but less than half as expensive as some of the other models.

Jennifer's parents had been generous enough to offer to pay for our stroller, and I was about to thank them when my father-in-law turned back to the salesman. "Just for the heck of it, let's see one of those," he said, pointing to one of the shiny monster-wheel strollers a few feet away.

My father-in-law was pointing to a Bugaboo, a popular brand of Dutch strollers—sometimes referred to as "stroller utility vehicles"—that has become almost synonymous with parental excess. The Bugaboo is to the Maclaren what the Lexus is to the Toyota Camry. It's a nicer item, but you pay the extra money more for the way it makes you feel about yourself than for the improved quality—or, at least, that was my impression when I had first heard about the Bugaboo months earlier.

Our stroller salesman was also a professional actor—I later spotted him on an episode of *Law & Order*—and he was good at what he did. "Oh, so you wanna see a Bugaboo?" he said, shooting us an "Are you sure you can really handle one of those?" look.

We followed the salesman over to the display model where he smiled at us and then began removing and changing stroller parts so rapidly that soon the Bugaboo no longer seemed like a stroller at all but a magic contraption that could turn into any sort of vehicle you wanted. His hands moving with the speed and grace of a professional card dealer, the salesman reversed the Bugaboo's reversible handlebar, then somehow made the front wheels disappear. He popped different seats on and off the frame—a baby bassinet, a car seat, a regular seat—and then reclined each of them at different angles.

Soon a small crowd had gathered to watch the demonstration. Jennifer and I stood a few feet back and shuffled uncomfortably. The salesman was just beginning. He draped the stroller in a plastic rain cover, then replaced the rain cover with a white mosquito net. He inserted a stroller "cozy" that looked like a sleeping bag made for arctic exhibitions and then snapped on a drink holder and a sun umbrella. By the end of the demonstration, I wouldn't have been surprised if he had pulled a lever and transformed the Bugaboo into a hovercraft that could glide over large puddles.

Rather than making me want the stroller, the demonstration had left me thinking that it would be a minor miracle if I managed to figure out how to use it before our son's bar mitzvah. But Jennifer made a good point in favor of the Bugaboo. Without a car, we'd be using the stroller every day, and our baby might appreciate those oversized back wheels when traversing Brooklyn's bumpy sidewalks—especially when it snowed.

"I'll get it for you if you want it," Jennifer's father said.

"No, no," Jennifer and I said in unison. The Bugaboo model we were looking at cost over seven hundred dollars. "We couldn't ask you to do that for us."

"I'm not doing it for you, I'm doing it for him," Jennifer's father said, pointing at Jennifer's belly.

After a few more perfunctory no's, Jennifer accepted the incredibly generous offer and thanked her father. I thanked him as well, but as we moved on to car seats, Jennifer could read the distress on my face. This is the problem with a good marriage. You can hide nothing.

"What's wrong?" she asked.

"Nothing," I said.

"You're upset about the Bugaboo, aren't you?"

"It's just so nice," I said.

I am no ascetic, but I've always been uncomfortable with public shows of wealth, a class-consciousness I inherited from my father, whose own father drove a scrap metal truck. Even if I could afford to fly first-class, I don't think I could do it: The pleasure in extending my legs more than two inches or consuming more than a tablespoon-sized portion of pretzels would be far outweighed by my sense—almost entirely delusional—that I was betraying my working-class roots to mingle with the rich.

"But don't you want the most comfortable stroller for our baby?" Jennifer asked.

I thought hard. On the one hand, I did not want to deny my child the best stroller on the grounds that it did not fit well with my faux bohemian sense of self. On the other hand, it was just so nice.

"I'll deal," I said to Jennifer.

"We can always splatter the Bugaboo with mud and cut some holes in it," Jennifer said.

Jennifer was joking but it struck me as a good idea, at least until I thought about the look on my father-in-law's face when he learned I'd taken a steak knife to the seven-hundred-dollar gift he had just given us.

PLENTY OF THEORIES have been put forth in recent years to explain the rise of the baby industrial complex, and there is probably some truth in all of them: A growing population means more babies needing more things; parents are having children when they're older and have more disposable income; parents who work are busy and exhausted and anxious for products that promise to make their lives easier; it's become increasingly common for mothers to work and manage their own money, and mothers spend more on babies than fathers.

But all of these theories notwithstanding, the single most important factor in the rise of the baby industrial complex might be the most obvious one: The people selling the products have gotten better at their jobs. Marketing to parents has probably always involved false promises and fearmongering—a 1905 ad for "scientific" baby shoes in *Life* magazine warned parents that flat feet "are nearly always the result of improper foot-gear worn during childhood"—but it took marketers a long time to appreciate that nerve-racked parents are the perfect target. Now it can be hard to find a single product that doesn't come with at least one pseudo-scientific claim to "build coordination" or "stimulate natural curiosity." The Learning Curve company's "Lamaze Stretch the Giraffe" plush toy is a fairly typical example. The product's Amazon page notes that the giraffe was developed "in conjunction with child development experts from Yale University" and claims both that the giraffe's rattle and crinkle sounds "help stimulate

and develop baby's auditory skills" and that the doll's large eyes "help calm the baby while supporting healthy eye development."

All of these pseudoscientific claims, in turn, are being delivered to new parents via increasingly sophisticated marketing strategies, from websites that email out monthly, panic-inducing updates on your baby's developmental milestones—along with ads for "developmental" products—to the free diaper and formula samples being given out at obstetricians' offices and hospitals, to the seminars at baby superstores where "experts" lecture new parents on various aspects of baby care and then tell them what to buy.

There were no seminars taking place at Buy Buy Baby during our shopping trip, but not long after we bought our Bugaboo, I learned about a Mother's Day dinner for new moms at a chic midtown hotel. The event, organized by a marketing company called Big City Moms and sponsored by Botox Cosmetic, included predinner shopping at booths set up around the hotel and a presentation by Vicki Iovine, author of *The Girlfriends' Guide* series on pregnancy and parenting. It seemed like a good opportunity to see firsthand how companies market to new parents, and the founders of Big City Moms said that I was free to join them.

Because it was close to her office and came with the promise of a good meal, Jennifer had decided to meet me at the hotel. When I arrived, she was sitting in a large chair in the lobby with her hands on her belly.

"I think the baby is hiccupping," Jennifer said.

"Hiccupping?" I put my hand on Jennifer's belly and felt it jolt. "I think you're right," I said.

"I just can't believe there's someone hiccupping inside of me right now," Jennifer said.

We'd had plenty of time to get used to the strange and miraculous fact that we had created a person, a person who was now

growing inside Jennifer, but every now and then we would stop
and think about it and feel stunned anew.

"You know what's even weirder?" Jennifer said.

"What?"

"There's a butt inside of me right now."

"That is really weird," I said. "You have two butts."

"And four ears," Jennifer said.

We probably could have gone through every last body part and
felt newly amazed with each one, but I didn't want to miss the dinner.

I went upstairs to the mom's event alone—Jennifer had already
checked out the scene and wanted me to come and get her
when the meal was served. The dimly lit hotel halls were packed
with well-dressed women, many of them pregnant. I was the
only man in the vicinity, and it made me uncomfortable. After
admiring the decoupage wipe boxes for sale at one table and
the children's shirts with special patches to detect UV radiation at
another, I headed to the bathroom even though I didn't have to go.

There is not so much to do in a bathroom when you don't have
to go, but it is a dilemma I'm accustomed to. I have been ducking
into bathrooms to escape uncomfortable moments at least since
junior high parties when just the sight of a girl I liked was enough
to send me racing in the direction of the nearest toilet. After pat-
ting my hair down and making my puckered-lip mirror face a few
times—a face that I will never be able to stop making no matter
how many times Jennifer tells me that it makes me look like an
aspiring gay model—I realized that the men's room was empty and
would remain so, since I was the only man around. I took out my
tape recorder to make a few notes, then, when I could think of
nothing else to say, I walked out of the bathroom, tape recorder
still in hand.

Two pregnant women stood staring at me.

I wanted to tell these two women that, contrary to how it might look, I had not just recorded my trip to the bathroom, but I've learned the hard way that any attempt to explain an awkward moment only makes it more awkward.

In need of something to do, I tracked down one of the organizers of the event and introduced myself.

"You must feel like the big stud surrounded by all these women," she said.

I smiled, thanked her for allowing me to come, and headed back to the bathroom.

When I reemerged, the doors to the enormous dining room were open. The new and expecting moms spread out among a sea of round tables, each with a tray of frosted cupcakes in the center. I went to get Jennifer and then we found seats in the middle of the room. In addition to silverware, our settings included a Botox Cosmetic gift bag and a copy of Vicki Iovine's *The Girlfriends' Guide to Getting Your Groove Back: Loving Your Family Without Losing Your Mind.*

I had already eaten a cupcake and broken my complimentary light-up cosmetic mirror by the time the first speaker, a public relations executive from Allergan, makers of Botox, took the podium.

"It's truly amazing to see all of you here," the public relations executive said. "After all, who deserves to be celebrated more than moms—and I say this as a daughter myself."

Waiters hovered around the tables filling wineglasses. "This is really all about taking care of yourself and your skin," the Allergan executive went on. "And this is a topic that's very near and dear to Allergan's heart."

I was confused. I hadn't realized that our dinner would include a discussion of skin care, but there was no time to think. Vicki Iovine was already approaching the podium.

"Welcome everybody," Iovine said, beaming. "I can't believe you all look so pretty." Iovine was *Playboy's* Playmate of the Month in September 1979, and she still had a model's figure. "I love gatherings!" she shouted into the microphone. "Two or more girlfriends gathered in the name of friendship—it really tickles your heart.

"What we're giving ourselves tonight is such a gift," Iovine continued. "And we deserve it! We should do this at least once a month, girlfriends."

A howl of agreement rose up from the seats.

Iovine spoke for several more minutes about the wonderfulness of the evening. Then, even as I was wondering how long she could continue to praise an event at which so little had actually happened, her tone changed.

"The truth is, motherhood is frightening," Iovine said. "Whether it's dealing with the stretch marks, dealing with the gassy emissions, whether it's getting back in shape or how to find a sexy nursing bra, you have to rely on your girlfriends."

I glanced at Jennifer. She did not look amused. "As moms, we are so expressive in our faces," Iovine went on. "Not only do we teach our children everything from face-to-face contact but we also communicate with each other so much with our faces."

Iovine scrunched her eyebrows and flared her nostrils. She looked as though she had just been insulted and was struggling to think of a good comeback. "This is the expression of motherhood," she said, explaining that, when mothers make this face, two vertical lines—"the angry elevens"—form along the sides of the eyes.

Iovine instructed us to remove the complimentary Botox light-up cosmetic mirrors from our gift bags so that we could examine our own angry elevens. Jennifer ignored the request. I took my broken mirror out.

"All together now," Iovine said, "let's make the concerned mommy expression." I scrunched my eyebrows and puckered my lips just like Iovine and then passed my mirror over my brown eyes and along the slight rightward slope of my nose.

"Note the angry elevens," Iovine said.

I was able to locate the lines around my eyes, but I saw no anger in them. I put my mirror down. Iovine was beaming. She said that before Botox got rid of her "angry elevens" she had looked as if she was frowning even when she was happy. "As you move on further down the mommy trail, following in my moccasins," she said, "you will find that you can't lose the expression."

Unless, that is, you inject Botox into your head. Iovine told us that last year she had gone to the dermatologist and requested "the full package." "I got every kind of mole and freckle burned off," she said, as Jennifer and I munched on our salads. "And then, for dessert, I got Botox injections for these lines right here." Iovine pointed to her eyes. "We can live for a very long time," she went on. "The question is: Will we want to?"

"I'm ready to go when you are," Jennifer said.

I convinced Jennifer to stay for the rest of the meal. I'd been out of college for almost a decade and yet the idea of passing on free food still felt fundamentally wrong. Iovine concluded by telling us we were gorgeous and inspiring. "You are hot mamas," she said, "and remember, you deserve to be as hot as you feel."

At the time I assumed that Iovine's enthusiasm for good skin couldn't possibly be sincere, but I later discovered that she is also the author of *The Girlfriends' Guide to Pediatric Eczema.*

After polite applause a dermatologist took the stage. She showed us enormous slides of wrinkled faces and circled the angry elevens. One photo was of a grandfather who she said was using Botox so that his wrinkled face would no longer frighten his grandchildren.

By now the moms had mostly stopped listening and the event's organizers had begun to wander through the room shushing us. When the room temporarily quieted, the dermatologist called a volunteer mom up to the stage, handed her a marker, and asked her to circle all of the places on her face that she thought needed work. The woman made thick black lines all over her cheeks and forehead until she looked like a diagram of an animal that had been marked up to indicate the choice pieces of meat.

The dermatologist seemed pleased with the woman's work. "You would do incredibly well with Botox," she said.

I took a last bite of my vegetables, stuffed a cupcake into my Botox bag, and turned to Jennifer.

"Let's get out of here, girlfriend," I said.

TWO

The Confusion of the New Parent

On Being Björned

THE IDENTITY CRISIS OF THE AMERICAN FATHER might be the longest-running identity crisis of all time. In 1929, *Parents* magazine published an essay by a young father searching for his role in his baby daughter's life. "We know where the woman's place is—in the home. . . . But man! Nobody, no book, has ever shown him where his place is when the baby enters."

The identity crisis might have peaked with the rise of the men's movement in the 1980s, when fathers, searching for a way to be both masculine and decent human beings, thought they might find an answer by running around in the woods together. But it's unlikely that the confusion of the new father will ever disappear. There is just too much for new parents to be confused about—mothers and fathers both. We spend the first twenty or thirty or forty years of our lives trying to figure out who we are and how we got that way, and then, just when we're starting to make some sense of it all, we take on a new role that makes our old selves feel almost irrelevant.

Or at least that's the way I was thinking when my personal fatherhood identity crisis reached its apex in the baby carrier aisle of Buy Buy Baby. The most popular baby carrier in New York at the time was the BabyBjörn—a thick piece of navy blue cloth with shoulder straps and clips that, when properly outfitted over your

torso, allows you to wear an infant. In our Brooklyn neighborhood, Björns were so popular that a baby on a parent's chest
seemed like just one more fashionable accessory—a drool-covered
broach that occasionally smelled of excrement.

The store had a coat stand with a few sample Björns for customers to try on, and, attempting to show that I cared about what
we were doing—I have an inexplicable tendency to drift away in
silence when I shop with others—I took a Björn off a hook and
draped it over my arms. For the next two minutes, Jennifer and
her parents, who had joined us for the shopping trip, stood by pa-
tiently and watched as I tried and failed to make sense of the surprising number of straps suddenly dangling from my torso.

When it became painfully clear that I was never going to Björn
myself properly, my in-laws stepped in to help, and I stood motionless, arms out to my sides, as they fitted the straps around me
and pulled them tight.

It must have looked like an ordinary enough scene—a young father trying out a new infant product—but I understood the significance of the moment immediately: In a fluorescent-lit aisle of a
baby superstore at the beginning of a new millennium, I was taking part in the modern secular version of an ancient ritual. Probably my prehistoric forefathers had gone through something
much more dramatic; probably their in-laws had whipped them
with carefully preserved goat intestines or poked them in the eyes
with the bones of a sacred owl. Probably both. Probably when the
ceremony was over they had to eat the owl bones while the village
elders tweaked their nipples for sport.

However the in-laws conduct the prebirth ritual with the father, the meaning is always the same: Once the ritual is complete,
the man is no longer a father-to-be. He is a father. The arrival of
the baby is almost incidental.

For some fathers the end of the ritual might be a time of joy, a moment to celebrate the good times ahead. And perhaps if I had been in a better mood, I too would have been joyful. But at that particular moment, as I stood in silence with the Björn clipped around my waist and snug against my shoulders, the realization that I was now a father brought more anxiety than excitement.

There are lots of things for a new father to panic about, and I was on top of all of them. I was worried that the baby would be smushed every time something brushed against Jennifer's belly and that the baby would somehow be poisoned whenever Jennifer and I were in a room with a strange scent. I was worried that I would pass out during the birth and that Jennifer's obstetrician would have to stop what he was doing and give me mouth-to-mouth and that—even if I was lucky enough to be revived—I would end up with oral herpes from the procedure. Perhaps most realistically, I was worried that my son would inherit my propensity to worry.

But on that day, as I looked down at the babyless Björn on my chest, it was one of my more narcissistic panics that took hold, the panic that in becoming a father I was somehow bringing my own story to a premature end. Most of the time this anxiety was abstract, less a rational chain of thoughts than a vaguely understood, fear-inducing sensation that I'd had a chance to make something of myself, and now—just as I was getting started—it was time for me to give up the quixotic quest and make something of someone else. But there was also the concrete. I wanted to continue to write, but in becoming a father I was taking on new financial obligations that I feared would force me to put aside my literary ambitions. I wondered if, in choosing parenthood, I had exchanged a future book for a future suit. And though I appreciated that there are much worse things than wearing suits, to an aspiring writer a suit is pretty bad, particularly when you can't tie a tie without it looking so ridiculous that even people you don't know come over to adjust the knot.

Even as my heart pounded in my chest, a part of me knew that I was being stupid—a part of me always knows. My own father had raised my sister and me after my mother became sick and still managed a successful writing career. And in most respects, my adjustment to fatherhood promised to be easier than most. I've always loved playing with children and I had no concern about giving up my nightlife, because I had none. Nor did I have any fear that I would be emasculated by changing diapers, or doing whatever else it was that new parents did—I still only had a vague idea. Since I had been raised by my father, the idea that taking care of small children was somehow unmanly seemed bizarre to me. But my awareness of my own stupidity rarely makes the stupidity— or the accompanying anxiety—go away. This is the problem I've always had with talk therapy. In my own experience, self-knowledge mocks more than it heals.

I'm not sure how long I stood in my sample Björn and panicked about my own demise. It felt like a long time, but probably it was only a few seconds. All I remember is that I was standing in a sea of baby products with my arms out, and that it was Jennifer's voice that brought me back.

"Can you turn around so we can see the back?"

I turned around. "How does it feel?" Jennifer asked.

"Um, pretty good," I said. "I guess."

Not long after our trip to Buy Buy Baby, I saw a flyer for a new-fathers' workshop. I decided to sign up.

The fatherhood workshop was at a birth education center in Manhattan and six other dads-to-be were in attendance. When I walked into the classroom, the instructor, Ron, was sitting with his elbows on a small table at the front of the room. He looked about sixty and wisps of salt-and-pepper hair had been combed across his balding head. His glasses rested at the bottom of his nose.

I expected the teacher of a fathering workshop to be a men's movement type, the kind of guy who encouraged you to cry regardless of whether the thing you were talking about was remotely sad and then gave you a bear hug that lasted for so long that you began to fear for your health. And I thought my expectations had been borne out when Ron asked us to go around and say a few words about our own fathers.

So I was surprised when, several minutes into the workshop, Ron looked up with a glum expression and said, "Let's face it. Taking care of a baby can be incredibly boring."

Ron turned out to be the opposite of the men's movement guy. He was the high school teacher you occasionally see on TV but never in real life, the one who doesn't give a damn about the rules or the meddling principal or the calls from concerned parents. He was the one who tells it to you like it is whether you're ready to hear it or not.

For the next hour and a half, Ron treated us to one coarsely phrased bit of wisdom after the next. On sex after pregnancy: *It will be six weeks before a woman is "ready for reentry," so to speak.* On the importance of letting your kids make their own choices: *If your kid wants to play sports and you want her to play piano, don't bust her balls.* On the neediness of children: *Your kid is sort of like a homeless guy; they're helpless, they're always asking for a dollar.*

After telling us that studies show that men's testosterone drops while they're engaged in child care, Ron paused. "How does that make you feel?" he asked us.

We looked at one another and said nothing.

"You think after doing child care all day you're going to have a boner like this?" Ron spread his hands several feet apart and shook his head. "No way."

Ron said that the secret to good parenting was remembering to see the world from the child's perspective: "When I lose track of how they're looking at things, that's when I become an asshole." To emphasize the point, Ron recalled the look of wonder on his daughter's face when she saw a dog for the first time. "Can you imagine what it's like?" he asked, his voice growing louder. "I mean, can you imagine that? They're thinking, 'What the fuck is that? What the fuck is that?' "

I appreciated Ron's frankness but it wasn't until the end of the class that he said something that made the workshop seem worth the time and money. Ron said that the world as we knew it did not have to end when we became fathers, that we could and should continue doing the things we liked to do. "Something different has happened," he said, "but your life keeps going."

It wasn't the most profound point and yet at the time Ron's comment struck me as almost revolutionary. I had been so focused on how fundamentally different things would be that it really hadn't occurred to me that there might be any continuity between my old life and my new one.

But perhaps Ron was right? Maybe I could be a father and still be me? Maybe my own story wasn't coming to an end? It seemed at least possible.

I TOOK SEVERAL FICTION WRITING COURSES in college, and I was always surprised by the recurring themes I saw in my work. The circumstances would change from short story to short story but the character and themes would end up being more or less the same: A young man, feeling overwhelmed by forces he himself didn't fully understand, would act out in a bizarre way—he would refuse to shave his beard; he would refuse to stop repeating the same inexplicable sentence—until eventually he had driven away everyone who mattered to him. The man would never act out of maliciousness. He himself wouldn't understand why he was doing the strange things he was doing. But he would be powerless to stop no matter how much suffering and loneliness he brought upon himself.

I've had little time to write fiction since college but the character never left my imagination. And while I don't think of the character as my alter ego—I've never wanted to drive away the people who love me—sometimes when I think about a specific moment from my life, like the time my in-laws dressed me in a BabyBjörn, I know almost instinctively what the man's bizarrely self-destructive response would be.

Once his Björn was secured around his upper body, the man would refuse to take it off. His wife and in-laws would be confused and then angry, but the man would shrug off their protests and wear his Björn right out of the store like a new pair of shoes. In the following week, the man would respond with a maddening nonchalance to the pleas of friends and relatives to remove the Björn. "I just like how it feels," he would say. Or, "I'm going to be a father," as though that were any reason to be wearing a baby carrier without a baby in it.

With each new day, the man's behavior would grow more and more strange: He would begin to coo at the empty Björn. He would take sponge baths instead of showering so as not to get it wet. After two weeks, his pregnant wife would leave him. The man would walk into the kitchen and find the terse note on the kitchen counter: "Call me when it's off." The man would read the note over and over and his devastation would be real, his pain so overwhelming that he would need to lean back against the counter to keep from falling.

For a minute or two, the man would remain slumped in his kitchen, Björned and alone and feeling as though he would never again have the strength to straighten himself. Then, because delusion is sometimes the only realistic option, he would regain his composure and prepare a bottle of formula.

THREE

Choosing a Name
Everybody's Trying Not to Be Just Like Everybody

AT FIRST IT WAS ONLY THE CELEBRITIES. They named their babies Phinnaeus and Coco and we laughed. They named them Shiloh and Suri and we thought, *Oh boy, now they've really lost it.* And then, as we tend to do, we started copying them.

Of all the strange things about this particular moment in American parenting, our obsession with naming might be the strangest. In a 2007 feature on naming trends, *The Wall Street Journal* revealed that sociologists and name researchers are reporting unprecedented levels of angst among parents as they struggle to figure out what to call their babies. The article lacked any hard data to back up the claim, but if the sales of baby name books are an accurate indicator, then expecting parents in America are in the midst of a naming-induced frenzy. In 1962, the publication of a book of names was still novel enough to warrant a brief article in *The New York Times.* Now more than twenty baby name books are published in a typical year. And the books are only one outlet for our naming needs. Parents looking online can find hundreds of naming sites and "baby names" has become one of the top ten most common generic search terms according to one Internet research firm. Some especially name-challenged mothers and fathers are even turning to naming consultants for help.

Prior to Jennifer's pregnancy, I'd laughed about the weird baby names I sometimes heard in our neighborhood. But once it was our turn, I saw that naming is much harder than it seems. Jennifer and I struggled with names from the start. At first we referred to the embryo only as "It." We were trying to protect ourselves. The chance of a miscarriage was still relatively high and we feared that giving "It" a real name would make the loss that much harder if something went wrong.

The strategy worked so long as It was still an abstraction. When we left Jennifer's three-month ultrasound with a photo, It no longer felt right. It might not have had fingerprints or functioning eyelids, but It was still more than an it.

The new name we came up with, Siemens, wasn't particularly original; it appeared atop the ultrasound image. We knew Siemens was the company that made the ultrasound equipment, but it was only a temporary name and it was conveniently gender neutral.

Still, while preferable to "It," "Siemens" came with a problem of its own. Jennifer and I are both serial nickname givers and as we went through the countless variations of Siemens—Siemey, Siemster, Siemenbytheseashore, Siemiansky the Great, Siemen-TovAndMazelTov—it was inevitable that from time to time I would refer to our offspring as Semen, a name Jennifer didn't particularly care for.

"But the fetus sort of is semen when you think about it," I said.

"The fetus is not semen," Jennifer said.

Our conversation about postbirth names turned more serious after Jennifer's five-month ultrasound, when we learned that Siemens had a penis.

From that moment on, Jennifer became slightly name obsessed. She bought a book of fifty-five thousand baby names and in the evenings she would lie in bed and scan the pages as though studying for an exam. Every few minutes, she would look up from the book to yell out a new name and every few minutes I would come up with the flimsiest of reasons to reject them.

"What about Henry?"

"Sorry, I can't. It makes me think of this obnoxious kid I knew in junior high."

"Randy?"

"Randy Apple? Are you serious? People will think of rancid apples. It will make them sick."

There was a brief period when we thought we had it, when Jennifer looked up from her book and called out "Jack," as though it were a great revelation, as though it had not come from the book at all but from some deeper, more spiritual place.

"Jack Apple." I repeated it aloud several times. I liked the way the hard *c* at the end of "Jack" softened into the *A* of "Apple." I liked that the name was masculine and unpretentious.

"I think that's it," I said. We kissed, feeling the weight of fifty-five thousand names lifting from our backs.

Then Jennifer Googled "Jack Apple." The second result was for a slang dictionary. In the United Kingdom a "jack apple" was another term for "a dottering fool."

To LEARN MORE ABOUT NAMING and to get advice on our own search, I called Laura Wattenberg, a baby name consultant and the author of *The Baby Name Wizard.* Wattenberg's background is in psychological research and software design, and to help parents solve their naming dilemmas she spent years compiling her own enormous database of naming trends, using everything from the popularity of different names around the world, to birth announcements in Ivy League alumni magazines, to soap opera cast lists. She then used the information together with data on American names from the Social Security Administration to create a computer program that spots naming patterns. If you give Wattenberg's program, dubbed the "Name Matchmaker," one name you like, it will suggest others that you might also like, just as Amazon.com tells you which additional books you might enjoy after you make a purchase. So, for example, if you like the style and feel of "Dylan" but have decided that there are already too many Dylans in your neighborhood, Wattenberg's model suggests the following alternatives: "Logan," "Colin," "Reese," "Connor," "Gavin." If you like "Miranda," the program thinks you might also like "Sabrina," "Diana," "Ariel," "Gabriela," "Adriana." "I knew I was onto something when I told the Matchmaker the names of my two daughters, and the top boy's match it suggested was the very name my husband and I had picked out for a boy," Wattenberg writes in her book.

Wattenberg told me that she had become interested in naming in 2001 while living in New York. She was pregnant with her second child, and as she traveled around the city she was surprised by how often she would hear children's names that had been uncommon in her own generation. Everywhere Wattenberg turned there were little Hannahs and Olivias.

But the real surprise was not that names like "Olivia" and "Hannah" had become popular. It was what people told Wattenberg about why they'd chosen these names: They were looking for something unique. Parents thought they were distinguishing their kids with uncommon names, only to discover that everyone else was trying to distinguish their kids with the very same supposedly uncommon names.

By reviewing the Social Security Administration's records, Wattenberg confirmed what she'd already learned anecdotally: American parents were choosing somewhat less common names. The percentage of children with a name in the top ten or top one hundred most common names had dropped dramatically over the prior twenty years. "Uniqueness as a goal is absolutely the distinguishing characteristic of the past generation of names," Wattenberg told me. "I get hundreds of letters from parents who are choosing names for their children and almost all of them are looking for something unusual."

Wattenberg's data also confirmed her other suspicion: Most of the "unique" names weren't nearly as unique as the parents who chose them might have thought. "If you look at the top one thousand boy's names right now, the number of different variants rhyming with 'Aden' is just extraordinary," Wattenberg said. "There are a half dozen Adens, Bradens, Jaydens, Caydens, Haydens—each with every spelling you can imagine." In fact, in 2006 "Jayden" was the number one boy's name in New York City once all the different spellings—"Jayden," "Jaden," "Jaiden"—were added together.

The problem, Wattenberg explained, is that when you try to choose a name that stands out, you discover that what feels like your personal taste is often a social creation that you share with people of the same generation and similar backgrounds. "You might grow up with a name you think is so beautiful and so uncommon," Wattenberg said. "From the time you're five years old, you might think, 'Hannah' is my own secret name. Then by the time you're ready to have a baby, there are Hannahs everywhere." Wattenberg paused. "It's a little disconcerting, frankly."

I knew exactly what Wattenberg was talking about. Before we knew we were having a boy, Jennifer and I talked about girls' names and it seemed as though every name we liked just happened to be among the trendiest names of the moment: "Lily," "Amelia," "Sophie"—it was as though we were trapped in a cliché of our making. ("Lily," in particular, was so deeply woven into the naming zeitgeist that almost every friend who suggested a name would mention it.)

I wasn't even sure why it mattered if the name we chose was already extremely popular. It's not as though there is any obvious downside to having an extremely popular name—or, for that matter, any obvious upside to having a unique name. I still can't explain it, but perhaps more than any other parenting trend, our longing for unique names seems to speak to a larger shift in the American parental psyche. A few generations ago, American parents aspired for their children to fit in. Now we aspire for them to stand out.

Jennifer and I eventually realized that if we wanted a name that would actually be uncommon in our son's generation, the only options were to either choose a name from our own generation—Brian, Mark, etc.—or to go the celebrity route and choose something insane—Grillbor, Flimpini, etc. But names from our own generation inevitably felt stale to us and going with an insane celebrity name would make it seem like we were trying too hard—the worst naming sin of all. The dilemma reminded me of the paradox I'd once heard in a folk song by Jim Infantino: "Everybody's trying not to be just like everybody," Infantino sings, "and I don't want to be like that."

After talking with Wattenberg about naming trends for half an hour, I remembered that I also wanted personal advice. I shifted gears and asked Wattenberg if starting with the last name "Apple" raised any special considerations.

"Ideally a full name is almost like composing a little poem with rhyme and meter," Wattenberg told me, clarifying that it shouldn't actually rhyme so much as have a natural flow. "Apple," for example, wouldn't go well with a two-syllable first name that has a stress on the second syllable. "Renee Apple makes you stop cold," Wattenberg said. "I think you would want the stress on the first syllable."

Wattenberg said that it was also important to watch out for

alliteration when your last name is a common word. "You don't want to be named Wally Wall," she said.

"Apple," according to Wattenberg, was a fun last name and would therefore work best with a more conservative first name.

"Do you have any specific ideas for my son?" I asked.

Wattenberg thought for a moment. "Walter," she said.

"You think we should name our son 'Walter'?" For unknown reasons, the name made me think of someone with a perpetual nosebleed.

"No," Wattenberg said. "I would need to know more about you and what other names you like before making a real suggestion."

I was relieved, temporarily forgetting that Wattenberg did not, in fact, have the final say on our baby's name.

I WAS IMPRESSED by how much thought Wattenberg had put into the problem of naming, but then, the whole name discussion was predicated on a single question that I still didn't know the answer to: Does a person's name really matter?

Wattenberg, not surprisingly, thinks that names do matter. "The reason we all care so much and spend so much time focusing on names is because they signal things, and we want them to signal the things we value," she told me.

A number of different studies have concluded that names can affect the way an employer treats you. In one such study, economists at the National Bureau of Economic Research found that people who submitted résumés with common African American names like "Lakisha" or "Jamal" were less likely to get called in for interviews than people with identical résumés and non–African American names. But in *Freakonomics,* authors

Steven D. Levitt and Stephen J. Dubner explain how a mountain of data on Californians born since 1961 reveals that, while someone with a distinctly African American name is more likely to end up with a low-paying job, the name is not the cause of the problem, but rather a reflection of the real cause: growing up in a low-income community. Levitt, an economist at the University of Chicago, reached this conclusion by running a regression analysis that allowed him to look for the relationship between a woman's first name and her level of education and income. According to *Freakonomics,* if someone with a typically white name and a typically African American name grow up in the same neighborhood in families with similar financial backgrounds, there's a good chance they will end up with similar incomes and levels of education. Levitt's data doesn't rule out the possibility that employers are racist, but it does suggest that the life outcomes of people with typically African American names cannot be explained by the names themselves.

To drive home the point, Levitt and Dubner tell the story of two brothers, Loser and Winner Lane. Why the parents thought it would be a good idea to have a son named Loser remains a mystery, but the names did not turn out to be destiny. Winner has been in and out of jail for years. Loser is a sergeant in the New York Police Department.

Still, if Levitt and Dubner make a strong case that a name won't ruin someone's career, the Loser Lane example left me wondering if they might have missed the real story. The California data, after all, only suggests that a name will not affect a child's success. It says nothing about the broader question of whether a name can affect a person's happiness. Loser Lane might have grown up to be a big-shot cop, but that didn't mean he hadn't been harassed at school every day.

I emailed Dubner and asked him about names and happiness. He wasn't familiar with any studies on the subject,* but he did have an interesting solution to the naming dilemma: a "National Self-Naming Age," when we all have the option to opt out of our birth names.

I liked this idea, although there was still the problem of what the self-naming age should be. Had I chosen a name before age twenty, I would almost certainly now be named Hakeem Olajuwon Apple after my favorite basketball player.

WHEN MY RESEARCH ON NAMES WAS DONE, I reported my findings to Jennifer. We still didn't know what to call our son, but I decided that I didn't care as much and that I'd been overly worried about the impact of names on happiness. After all, I've never been bothered by the many variations I've heard on "Apple" over the years—"The Big Apple," "Sour Apple," "Apple A Day."† The only time I could recall being upset by a nickname was in second grade, when a precocious kid at my lunch table realized that with the addition of one small sound "Samuel" becomes "Sam-U-Smell." And if an innocuous name like "Samuel"—a name I've

---

* At the time I wasn't familiar with the research of Michael Sherrod and Matthew Rayback. In their 2008 book, *Bad Baby Names*, Sherrod and Rayback interviewed adults with unusual names—Candy Stohr, Cash Guy, Mary Christmas, River Jordan—and found that most of them were actually happy to have unusual names.

† The one time "Apple" became a problem was at my wedding. Jennifer's last name is "Fried," and though it's pronounced *freed*, people often read it as *fried*—as in "fried chicken." Our wedding hotel listed the event as the Fried-Apple wedding, and the hotel employees thought that it was just about the funniest thing they had ever heard. Every time a wedding guest checked in, the clerks would be hunched over in such hysterical laughter that I began to wonder if there might be an unusually short person behind the registration desk with a tickling feather.

never even gone by—could be turned against you, then the lesson seemed to be that there is no hope. In the end, we are all defenseless against the creative cruelty of children.

But a day or so after arriving at this great insight, I changed my mind and decided that I did still care about names. The turning point occurred when I recalled that but for a twist of fate—my father's father took the last name of his cousins when he came to America—my name today would be "Sam Slavatitsky."

I tried to think of myself as Sam Slavatitsky. For some reason, I was unable to do so without imagining myself shaking someone's hand and saying, "Hi, I'm Sam Slavatitsky." And as I said this over and over in my head, "Hi, I'm Sam Slavatitsky," "Hi, I'm Sam Slavatitsky," I realized that I was glad to be an Apple.

I'm not sure why I felt a preference for "Apple," and I fear that it might reflect some deep-seated anti-Slavic bigotry or perhaps an unconscious discomfort with my ethnic identity. But, then, it could also just be that I didn't want the word *tits* in my last name.

FOUR

Water Birth

The Baby in the Aquarium

On October 28, 1980, the first documented water birth in America took place in a rented fiberglass hot tub in La Jolla, California. After a two-hour labor, the baby, Jeremy Lighthouse, spent twenty minutes underwater, at which point his father fished him out of the hot tub and handed him to Binnie A. Dansby, a therapist and healer who assisted with the birth. Shortly before the birth, Dansby had dreamed of wrapping America's first water baby in a receiving blanket moistened with apricot kernel oil and, with baby Jeremy in her arms, she made that dream a reality. Dansby later described the birth as the most peaceful moment of her life to that point.

It is impossible to know how many American water births have taken place since that day. Proponents of water birth insist the trend is on the rise, and over nine thousand American hospitals are said to have protocols for water births, but most American water births occur at home and reports of the births often fail to distinguish between women who labor in water and women who deliver their babies in water. The practice is more common in England, where the majority of maternity wards have tubs for women to at least labor in.

Jennifer did not want to have her baby underwater or to teach her baby to swim shortly after birth—as other water baby enthusiasts are now doing. I was glad. Neither of us knew much about water birth or postnatal swimming, but newborns and water sounded like a risky combination and neither of us is a risk taker when it comes to questions of health.

On the contrary, although I am somewhat worse off than Jennifer, we are both hypochondriacs. It makes us a good team. We both appreciate the importance of playing the rationalist for the other. When Jennifer thought she had lupus, I shook my head in dismay and told her how ridiculous she was being, even though I knew that if it had been me and not her whose doctor had wanted to test for lupus, I would have been in a state of such wild panic that Jennifer would probably have had to call the keepers at the nearest zoo to borrow one of the sedating guns they keep on hand for the day someone forgets to the lock the Grizzly Wonder Land— and that would have been even before I found out what lupus was. And when I thought I had AIDS—a surprisingly regular occurrence for someone in a monogamous relationship who had already tested negative—Jennifer would return the favor and tell me to get a grip. Any show of concern from the person playing the role of reassurer was considered a betrayal of the highest order because the concern of another robs hypochondriacs of the only thing they have to hold on to: the awareness, somewhere deep inside, that they're completely nuts.

Jennifer and I share many but not all of the same fears. Jennifer is much more afraid of flying. I am much more afraid of rabies. I am also more afraid of drowning, which made the idea of mixing water and babies that much more frightening to me.

And yet of all the strange parenting trends of recent decades, the water babies movement was the one I was most curious about.

I'd been interested in water babies for years, ever since my dad told me that my mom had seriously considered teaching me how to swim as a newborn.

My mom died from complications of multiple sclerosis the day after my fourteenth birthday, but she was gone long before. Multiple sclerosis comes in two forms: relapsing-remitting and secondary-progressive. My mom had secondary-progressive MS, the type that takes hold and never lets go. Newer drugs can halt the progression of the disease, but at the time there was nothing to be done. She experienced her first symptoms of MS—dizziness and blurred vision—when I was one, and by the time I was five, her mind was gone. My only clear memories are of her body slumped and lifeless in a reclining chair.

The absence of my mother from my life has always made me hungry for clues to the person she was before she became sick and, perhaps inevitably, as I approached parenthood, I was thinking about my mom more than usual. Her interest in water birth intrigued me in part because it seemed so different from the picture of her I'd pieced together from the stories and memories of others. My sense was always that my mom was a lot like me: She liked folk music and she had an instinctive distrust of authority figures. She was shy and loved absurdist humor. One of my favorite stories about her comes from a friend of the family who recalled being in the car one day as my mom drove my sister and her classmates to kindergarten. Out of nowhere my mom turned to her friend. "There are a lot of boogers in this car right now," she said.

My mom's observation about boogers made perfect sense to me. It was exactly the sort of thing that I might say. And yet it seemed almost impossible that someone with half of my DNA could have considered dunking a baby in water.

○○○

JUDITH HALEK, a water birth doula—or birth coach—I found on-line, lived on New York's Upper West Side. She invited me to her apartment to talk about water birth, and one Sunday morning in the sixth month of Jennifer's pregnancy, I took the subway up from Brooklyn.

Halek welcomed me in with a warm smile. She had shoulder-length blond hair and wore dangling earrings with bright yellow stones. I followed her around the enormous metal wind chimes that blocked the hallway and into a living room crammed with candles and hanging plants.

I took a seat on the couch. Halek sat down in an antique arm-chair to my right. Across from us, light flickered through the green eyes of a cat candleholder.

In addition to helping women deliver babies and running a water birth resource website called Birth Balance, Halek was also a birth photographer and one wall of the room was covered with large framed photographs of mothers cuddling their newborns. I mentioned to Halek that I hadn't been able to access the photos on her website, and she explained that she had moved them into a password-protected gallery to ward off pedophiles in the Middle East.

"If someone from the Middle East emails me and says he wants to buy my photos, I don't care how much he offers, I won't sell them," Halek said, the tenderness in her voice slipping away.

This seemed unfair to me. "But what about the nonpedophiles in the Middle East who want birth photos?"

"I know who's weird and who's not," Halek said. "I've had peo-ple call me and say, 'I want to see births with women's vaginas and babies coming through.' And they're all men."

Halek looked me up and down. "You're having a baby. You're a writer. I felt okay with you."

I asked Halek about the origins of water birth, and she told me about Igor Tjarkovsky, the Russian boatbuilder and athletic coach who had invented the method. In 1962, Tjarkovsky's daughter, Veta, was born two months early. She weighed a little over two-and-a-half pounds, and her doctors told Tjarkovsky that she was unlikely to survive for very long. A distraught Tjarkovsky requested and received permission to take over Veta's care. Tjarkovsky didn't need a hospital for the treatment he had in mind. The remedy, he suspected, was as near as his own kitchen sink.

Tjarkovsky brought his tiny daughter home from the hospital, and placed her on her back in a small tub filled with 93–95 degree water. He kept the water level low and fed Veta with a dropper. The Soviet doctors, Tjarkovsky discovered, had given up on Veta too soon. All that Veta needed was a chance to heal in an environment with less gravitational force on the body. Without the burden of what Tjarkovsky calls "gravity's death blow," Veta began to thrive.

As his daughter grew bigger and stronger, Tjarkovsky added more water to her tub. Soon Veta was as healthy and plump as the next baby and Tjarkovsky moved her into a translucent tank with enough room for her to swim. Veta spent most of the next two years in this baby aquarium. To keep her company, Tjarkovsky put live fish and frogs into the tank and showed her pictures through the walls. To eat, Veta would dive down and retrieve a bottle from the bottom of the tank.

With Veta as living proof that he was right about the benefits of water for babies, it was an obvious next step for Tjarkovsky to test his theories on birthing. A newborn, he reasoned, would be especially sensitive to gravity after months of floating in the womb. And if a baby were born into water, the energy normally spent battling gravity could go to the brain, leaving the water babies physically and intellectually superior to their air-born peers. "Human development has been at a standstill for many thousands of years; has reached an impasse," Tjarkovsky is quoted as saying, in *Water Babies,* a book about his methods. "A life in the water opens up new possibilities."

Despite his complete lack of medical training, Tjarkovsky was able to find a number of women receptive to his ideas, and he began to deliver their babies in small pools. To prepare for their water births, Tjarkovsky instructed his patients to do push-ups and splits throughout their pregnancies and also to dunk their own heads underwater several times a day.

In the following years, often working in secret to avoid criminal charges, Tjarkovsky conducted a wide range of water experiments on himself (he spent a month in a shallow swimming pool, leaving only to go to the bathroom) as well as on premature babies and animals. He found that the life expectancy of a pig born in water was twice that of a pig born outside water and that water could also work wonders for kittens. Each experiment furthered Tjarkovsky's conviction that all animals, from cockroaches to humans, could enjoy the health benefits of water if only they could overcome their evolutionarily ingrained fears of sea monsters.

Halek left the room to take a call from someone interested in buying birth photos, then returned to her chair.

"How often did he change the water in Veta's tank?" I asked.

Halek didn't know. She assumed quite often. She told me that Tjarkovsky had stayed with her during a trip to New York in the eighties and had spent most of the time dubbing videotapes of cats giving birth in a bathtub.

In 1987, Halek herself assisted in the first home water birth in New York City. The baby was born in a copper butter urn in a Twenty-second Street loft. "We all ended up in the tub," Halek said. "The father was behind me and the mom was between my legs."

"And the newborn babies really don't take in any water as they come out?" I asked.

Halek shook her head. "The baby is going from one womb of water to another womb of water," she said. "It's still receiving oxygen from the placenta."

Tjarkovsky might have been the first to have the idea of giving birth in water, but it was the French obstetrician Michel Odent who popularized the method. Odent, who is something akin to a rock star in the natural birthing world, saw that the real beneficiary of the water was not the baby, but the mother, who could enjoy the relaxing benefits of a warm bath during her labor. In the 1970s, Odent placed specially designed birth pools in his maternity unit at Pithiviers Hospital and found that women who labored in the water were more likely to give birth without medical intervention. The women would always leave the pool for the deliveries, but one day in 1977 a woman gave birth before she had a chance to get out of the pool, and Odent then began to oversee underwater births as well.

"I call it an aquadural," Halek said of the relaxing effects of water. "I'm convinced the epidemic of epidurals and Cesareans would end if every single obstetrical room had a tub to at least labor in."

Halek asked how Jennifer and I were preparing for the birth, and I told her that we were signed up for a class at a hospital in Brooklyn.

"It will be Lamaze," Halek said, the disappointment visible on her face.

"Is that bad?"

"It's not bad or good. Lamaze has gotten better about teaching natural approaches beyond the breathing."

"You don't think the breathing works?" That a pregnant

woman was supposed to control her breathing during the delivery was about the only thing I knew about childbirth.

Halek shook her head. "Breathing is bullshit quite frankly. Once in nineteen years I've seen the breathing work for someone."

I liked Halek. Our conversation grew increasingly intimate. As I snacked on mixed nuts, Halek picked up a black baby doll, placed it between her legs, and demonstrated how a baby rotates through the birth canal.

I asked Halek if she had any kids of her own. "When I was younger I thought I was going to have twelve kids," she said. "But I'm fifty now. That's not going to happen in this lifetime."

I could hear the remorse in Halek's voice. I told her I'd recently read about a sixty-three-year-old woman who had just given birth.

"I know, honey. I don't want to do that," Halek said. "Mmmm. Mmmm. No thanks. I've had a cat for twenty-and-a-half years. She's my companion. If I met someone, and he was part of the relationship, adopting would be viable, but I'm not going to do it alone."

Perhaps because Halek was so honest with me, when she revealed that in addition to being a birth coach and photographer she was also a dream interpreter, I told her about my recurring nightmares.

For reasons that were never quite clear in the dreams, someone was usually hunting me with a machine gun. Often, that someone was a nondescript villain. Every now and then it was a uniformed Nazi. Once, mysteriously, it was Pearl, the affable housekeeper from the eighties sitcom *Diff'rent Strokes*.

Distressing as the dreams were at night, most of the time I would forget them within minutes of waking. And so for a long time I accepted my blood-soaked dreams as just one more weird tic I was helpless to change, like my unusually loud sneezes, or the way I cup my hands and bop awkwardly as soon as "Walk Like an Egyptian" comes on the radio.

But recently I'd had a dream that was harder to ignore: Security guards had caught me sneaking into the basketball courts at the Jewish Community Center in Houston. If strange—I don't recall ever being anxious about Houston's Jewish Community Center in my conscious life—the nightmare itself wasn't particularly unusual. The unusual part was that I talked in my sleep. As the guards wrestled me to the ground and cuffed me, I whimpered, "How dare you? How dare you?" aloud.

I described my Jewish Community Center nightmare to Halek and explained that I had grown up playing basketball at the JCC almost every day. I didn't believe Halek could find any real meaning in the dream, but I'd never met a dream interpreter, and I was curious to hear what she'd say.

Halek placed her hands on her knees, straightened her back, and closed her eyes. "I'm going to become you the dreamer," she said, lowering her voice. "I am feeling like my only sense of freedom and release is going to a place that is very familiar and very comfortable to me from childhood, like the basketball courts at the Jewish Community Center. At the basketball courts, I am moving my body and feeling like I can dance and express myself and release all the pent-up stress that's in my body."

Halek paused. I wanted to point out that I've never felt like dancing or expressing myself on a basketball court, but Halek's eyes were still closed, as though waiting for a signal to reach her. "And then I'm punishing myself. Because I'm everyone in the dream. I'm the police arresting myself, and I'm putting the handcuffs on myself and I'm screaming out, 'How dare you' to myself. I'm fighting myself and"—another pause—"and I need to take a look at what it is in my life that is stopping me from playing and enjoying and expressing myself."

Halek opened her eyes and smiled. I smiled back. I wasn't sure how to respond.

"Thank you," I said.

"No problem, honey," she said.

It's not easy to return to the role of journalist after the person you're interviewing has interpreted your dreams. After chatting for a few more minutes, I thanked Halek again, took one last handful of mixed nuts, and made my way home to look up the latest research on water births.

The most comprehensive water birth study to date found that the likelihood of a baby dying during a water birth is not substantially higher than the likelihood of a baby dying during a more conventional birth. But the authors of the 1999 British study have acknowledged that their research had a number of methodological flaws, including their inability to clearly distinguish between mothers who only labored in water and mothers who gave birth in water. For its part, the mainstream American medical community remains unconvinced of the safety of delivering in water, particularly because contaminated water could enter a baby's lungs in the unlikely, but possible, event that the placenta detaches before the baby is pulled out of the tub. In a 2003 issue of the journal *Pediatrics*, one doctor wrote that he considered having a baby underwater "a bad joke" and "idiotic." A year later another editorial in *Pediatrics* argued that water birth "fulfils no need for the infant, is of dubious benefit to the mother, is associated with significant, avoidable risks of morbidity and mortality, and currently is unable to pass the risk-benefit test."

○○○

NOTHING I HAD DISCOVERED had made me any less fearful of water birth, but learning about Tjarkovsky had left me curious about the water birth movement.

Not long after meeting Halek, I called Sacha, a Brooklyn-based water baby expert whose number Halek had given me.

Sacha said hello in a thick Russian accent. Then he said, "*Vait, vait,* something big *iz* flying." The phone went silent. "Okay, I've killed it," he said.

I told Sacha about my project and he offered to come to our apartment to talk to Jennifer and me about birth and his work with newborns. He seemed especially interested in speaking to Jennifer, and I tried to explain that I was calling on my own behalf and that Jennifer might not be interested in what he had to say.

"This *iz* good," Sacha said. "She will give me a good challenge."

Later that month, Sacha showed up at our door holding a small canvas bag. His bald head and goatee made me think of Lenin.

After shaking my hand, Sacha removed his flip-flops. I assumed he intended to remain barefoot, but Sacha then produced a second pair of flip-flops from his canvas bag and put them on.

"I must save my foot for tennis," he said.

Jennifer joined us in the living room, and I asked Sacha to tell us what exactly he did with babies. At this point I still had no idea beyond that he worked with newborns and was somehow involved in the water birth community.

"*Vait, vait,*" Sacha said. "First you can tell me what you are doing."

It was a hard question. I did my best to explain.

Sacha said that he had been collecting information on babies "like a sponge" and planned to write a book.

I tried to convince Sacha that I was not going to steal his ideas, but I could see the skepticism on his face when I again asked what exactly he did. "Okay, I will show you something," he said. Sacha went back to his canvas bag and produced several badly charred pieces of paper. "There was a fire ten years ago," he explained.

The charred paper Sacha handed me was in Italian. Next to the text I couldn't read was a photo of a man sitting on the ground with his feet on his thighs in a traditional yoga pose. The man's arm was outstretched and on his upturned palm, a baby stood on one leg.

"Is that you?" I asked.

"Me and my daughter," Sacha said.

I saw Sacha's full name under the photo and began to write it down.

Sacha reached over and took the paper back from me.

"I just want to write your name down," I said.

"This *iz* not important," he said.

I looked at Jennifer. I was beginning to wonder who this man was and whether it had been wise to invite him into my home.

"So you, um, work with babies?" I asked.

Sacha again went to his bag, this time producing a videotape.

"Okay, let's go to the videotape," he said, breaking into a loud, high-pitched laugh. The line was a reference to a popular New York sportscaster who says it before showing the highlights from the latest games.

The three of us walked back into the bedroom where we had a TV and VCR. Jennifer and I sat on the couch. Sacha chose to sit on the floor so that he could stop and start the VCR.

As he looked for the appropriate spot on the tape, I managed to get a few biographical details out of Sacha. He was fifty-five and had moved to the United States from Saint Petersburg (then Leningrad) seventeen years earlier. He had degrees in mechanical engineering and economics.

Sacha pressed play. The video showed him holding a small baby over a bathtub.

Sacha pressed pause. "This baby is seven days old," Sacha said, smiling at Jennifer. Then he pressed play again and the video resumed with Sacha dunking the baby in the water and pulling him back and forth from one end of the tub to the other.

I held my own breath as I watched, and when Sacha finally brought the baby up for air after several laps, I was relieved. Then Sacha dunked the baby back down for a few more laps.

On the other side of the tub, a woman stood and looked on approvingly.

"The mother," Sacha said to us. "The father films."

Sacha pushed stop and turned to Jennifer and me with a look of satisfaction, as though everything were now crystal clear.

Jennifer and I were silent.

"*Vait.* I will show you a better one," Sacha said. He began to fast-forward the tape.

I didn't think I could take much more, and I could see in Jennifer's eyes that she felt the same way.

"So babies can hold their breath?"

Sacha broke into another loud laugh. "Ohhhhhh boy," he said. "Ohhhhh boy."

I didn't see what was so funny.

"What do you read about this?" Sacha asked.

"Well, I talked to Judith Halek and she—"

Sacha cut me off. "I asked you what you read about this."

"Nothing," I said.

"Babies have many inborn reflexes," Sacha said.

Then he paused, looked down as though in pain, and snapped his fingers eight times.

"It's better if you don't write when I talk," he said.

I said okay and told him that I would only tape-record.

Sacha agreed and continued. He said that newborn babies reflexively hold their breath when submerged into water headfirst. "If you continue this kind of swimming," he said, "the inborn reflex becomes a learned reflex."

Sacha's first claim, I later learned, is true. Newborns do instinctively hold their breath when dunked headfirst, an evolutionary relic from a time when our ancestors plunged beneath the water for food. And while I found no evidence for the second claim, it seemed at least plausible that babies who are regularly dunked get the hang of it.

I asked Sacha how long it takes for a newborn to lose the instinct if there is no dunking. He said that it was best to start the training in the first month.

Sacha turned away from me and looked to Jennifer. "These questions aren't important," he said. "You are really my subject in this case."

"That's okay," Jennifer said. "I'm interested in the questions, too."

"Okay, okay, you will be my lawyer with all of his questions." Sacha broke into another laugh and then leaned forward and put his hand out to Jennifer for a high five.

I was glad that the tense mood was lightening. I asked Sacha why he thought it was important for babies to swim.

"You could write a whole book about this," he said.

I waited for him to go on, but he didn't.

"So the water helps the baby—"

Sacha stopped me. "You could write three hundred pages just on this," he said.

I agreed that I could. I probably should have given up, but I wanted to understand whatever it is that drives a man to a life of baby dunking.

"So it makes the babies stronger?" I asked.

"With swimming, the first year is wonderful for parents," Sacha said. "A baby out of water can barely do anything. Underwater it can move and swim."

Sacha turned back to Jennifer. "Do you plan to nurse your baby?" he asked.

Jennifer said that she did.

"That's number one," Sacha said. "That's even before swimming."

Jennifer nodded.

"I'll help you to maintain natural lactation," Sacha said. "In this field I have experience for thirty years."

I began to think about how I was going to make this up to Jennifer.

"Sometimes mothers I work with stopped nursing and then I helped them to continue," Sacha said. "I can give you stories and stories."

He looked at Jennifer. "Do you exercise your nipples?"

Jennifer shook her head.

"It's better to start earlier, but it's not too late," Sacha said. "You sit in a chair and start with a soft towel like this." Sacha lifted his arms and motioned as though pulling a towel from side to side across his chest. "You do this two or three times a week," he said. "Then when you feel it gets a little stronger, you can increase the hardness of the towel."

Jennifer looked at me. I tried to think of a way to get Sacha off the subject of her breasts.

"They used to do that with puppies," I said.

It was a dumb thing to say, but it was true. I'd just started reading about birth practices around the world and was disturbed to discover the long history of puppy-assisted lactation.

Jennifer and Sacha were now both staring at me as though I was the one who had just shown videos of babies getting dunked.

"Do you know Igor Tjarkovsky?" I asked Sacha.

"You could write a book about him," Sacha said.

I agreed that I could. "So you know him?"

Sacha said that they had been friends in Russia and that when Sacha's daughter was two years old, Tjarkovsky had dunked her in the Neva River.

I didn't know it at the time, but I later discovered that dunking babies in icy water has a long history. By 1584 the practice was already being described as "barbarous" in Scevole de Sainte-Marthe's *Paedotrophia,* or *The Art of Bringing Up Children,* one of the earliest and most influential parenting guides of all time. I also later discovered that cold water dunking had led to Tjarkovsky's downfall. In 1988 Tjarkovsky infuriated a group of British admirers when he showed them footage of himself dunking a newborn's head into a hole in a frozen lake, and his reputation never recovered—it probably didn't help when Tjarkovsky began to twist the limbs of the babies in attendance, in what he reportedly said was an effort to improve their postures.

Sacha said that he had more videos to show us but Jennifer had seen enough and resisted Sacha's pleas for her to stay.

I was now alone in my bedroom with a clearly agitated water baby enthusiast. It was obvious that Sacha had seen the visit as an opportunity to take Jennifer on as a new client and he had no interest in hanging out with me. I tried asking him more questions but he said he wasn't sure he wanted me to record any more and asked me to turn off my tape recorder, which I did.

We talked for several more minutes. After each question, Sacha closed his eyes and paused as though in terrible pain.

"This all feels a little unkosher to me," he finally said.

Then Sacha walked over to his bag, changed back into his first pair of flip-flops, and headed out into the Brooklyn night.

OOO

I'D LEARNED A LOT about water babies but found nothing that helped me understand my mom's interest in the subject.

I am fairly certain that my mom did not know about Tjarkovsky or his strange experiments, and it may be that her interest in postnatal swimming was as much a product of the moment—her college hippie days were only recently behind her—as of a serious commitment to the idea. But the fearlessness she showed in wanting to dunk her baby still seemed foreign to me, and it bothered me that I couldn't identify with her.

As I continued to wrestle with my frustration, I finally realized my obvious mistake. I wasn't looking for clues to who my mom was, but for confirmation of whom I wanted her to be. My mom was no doubt like me in some ways, but she was inevitably very different from me in other ways, and if I really wanted to understand her, I would have to stop pretending that I could re-create my mother in my own image. The dead are their own people as much as the living, and parents are more than the idealized figures their children create.

FIVE

Prenatal Education

The Genius in the Womb

ALL PARENTS WANT THEIR BABIES to be smart, and Americans are
no exception. If American parents are exceptional, it's only in
how badly we want intelligent offspring and how much we're willing to spend to achieve this goal. In one 2004 report, almost two-
thirds of parents said that educational toys were "very important"
to a child's intellectual development, and sales figures of electronic educational toys have risen dramatically since the 1990s.
Between 2003 and 2004 alone, the learning toy industry bal-
looned from $496 million to $694 million.

We are now so anxious to educate our babies that a growing
number of American parents are beginning the process even before the babies are born, with prenatal education devices. The
simplest device, the eighty-dollar Bellysonic, is a small MP3
player and speaker system worn over a pregnant belly in an "organic sherpa cotton" pouch. Parents are left to choose the fetal
curriculum for themselves. For a more comprehensive program,
parents can choose the Baby Bee Bright prenatal learning system,
a CD player worn around the waist that comes with "fetal speakers," educational CDs, and a microphone for speaking directly to
the baby. The most unusual device, the BabyPlus Prenatal Education System, forgoes music and instead teaches fetuses with

drumming sounds that can be played at sixteen different speeds. According to the company's literature, fetuses exposed to the BabyPlus's drumming sounds are born with an "intellectual, developmental, creative, and emotional advantage" over other children.

I first discovered the phenomenon of prenatal education before Jennifer and I decided to try to have a baby. I was working at an online magazine, and I noticed a pregnant colleague wearing a small oval-shaped device around her stomach on a belt—it looked like a plastic money pouch.

I assumed that something had gone wrong with my colleague's pregnancy and that the device was a monitor, but I later learned that she was wearing the BabyPlus.

I was skeptical as I examined my colleague's BabyPlus. It sounded suspiciously like the drumming button on a cheap toy keyboard, and it was hard to imagine how drumming noises could make a fetus smarter.

Still, I didn't spend much time thinking about the device, and I probably would never have thought about the BabyPlus again had Jennifer not been reading a book about development in the womb during her pregnancy. The book had large color images of embryos and fetuses, and looking at them during the first months made me nervous. It wasn't only that the embryos looked like an evil race of Martian tadpoles. It was also that I didn't want to become attached to our own Martian tadpole before we could be confident it would survive. Even after six weeks, some 8 percent of pregnancies end in miscarriage.

Jennifer understood my reluctance to look at the images. She too was anxious about losing the baby. It seemed as though every food item in the world had been linked to miscarriages or birth defects at some point or another. During the first months of Jennifer's pregnancy, sitting down for a meal felt like playing Russian roulette with our baby's life.

But for Jennifer, the embryo was not an idea that she could avoid thinking about. It was inside her and she wanted to know what was happening to her body. And so at night, in the last minutes before she collapsed from the exhaustion that accompanies the first trimester of a pregnancy, she would flip through the pages of the book of fetuses. In addition to the photos, the book was filled with fun fetal trivia and Jennifer would occasionally share the information with me as we lay in bed together.

"Did you know that the heart is already beating at five weeks?"

"No, I didn't know that."

"Did you know that a fetus can make a fist at ten weeks?"

"Nope, didn't know that, either."

It wasn't until the fifth month of her pregnancy, when Jennifer mentioned that a fetus develops hearing in the second trimester, that I took a real interest in one of the fun fetal facts.

"Really?" I said.

"That's what it says," Jennifer said.

I thought about this surprising news for a moment. Then, as though it were the only logical thing one could do in light of the information I had just learned, I leaned over Jennifer's belly and began to sing Bon Jovi's "Living on a Prayer." I was mostly joking, but as I made my way through the opening verses, something amazing and wonderful happened: Jennifer did not ask me to stop.

I am the world's worst singer and this fact, coupled with my compulsion to spontaneously break into song while hanging around our apartment, can make me a challenging person to spend a life with. I've long maintained that there is nothing I can do about the songs; they seem to come from somewhere inside of me, like musical hiccups. Every now and then, Jennifer, almost in spite of herself, would join me and the two of us would suddenly be standing in the kitchen lost in a duet of "Born in the USA" or "Sweet Home Alabama." If Jennifer seemed really into it, I might even get cocky and break out the air guitar. But most of the time I was lucky to make it through a full line of a song without Jennifer's imploring eyes requesting an end to her misery. And so I was amazed when I looked up from Jennifer's belly button after completing a full chorus of "Living on a Prayer" and saw nothing but tenderness in her eyes. The sweetness of directing the song to the fetus apparently outweighed the suffering caused by my voice.

From that day on, I serenaded our unborn child as often as possible. I went through the cast album of *Hair* and then on to Paul Simon and then on to the early works of LL Cool J. I had no idea if my songs were getting through, and considering my voice, it was probably a good thing if they weren't. But the more I sang, the more I wondered if I was being heard, and if maybe, just maybe, our baby was somehow benefiting from the early exposure to music.

That's when I remembered the BabyPlus.

THE BABYPLUS IS NOW THE INDUSTRY LEADER in the prenatal education sector, a status formally confirmed when Nicole Ritchie was spotted wearing one during her pregnancy. The device retails for $149 and is available at popular maternity stores, as well as on Amazon.com, where it's consistently a popular item—sales are growing between 15 and 25 percent each year—and where there are more than fifty raving reviews of the product.

The BabyPlus Company is run by Lisa Jarrett, and the product comes with an endorsement from her husband, a fertility doctor.

The Jarretts licensed the technology from its inventor, Brent Logan, a psychologist in Seattle. When I looked Logan up online, I was surprised to learn that his website says he had earned a master of fine arts degree from the University of Iowa's Writers Workshop, the most distinguished creative writing program in the country. Intrigued, I found Logan's email address and requested a telephone interview. Logan agreed to talk, but asked that I first watch *Brave New Babies,* a British documentary about his work, which he would mail me.

One night, in the sixth month of her pregnancy, Jennifer and I sat down to watch *Brave New Babies.* I had borrowed my colleague's BabyPlus, and I encouraged Jennifer to wear it as we watched. I didn't believe that it worked, but I didn't think it could hurt, and I was curious.

In the opening sequence of *Brave New Babies,* Logan, a tall hulking man, walks along a misty beach. His features are hidden by the fog, but his voice is clear: "After looking at this phenomenon of prenatal stimulation, I truly feel that a watershed moment in human history has arrived."

Jennifer turned to me. "Do you really want me to wear this thing?"

"Maybe just try it for a few minutes. You never know . . ."

Logan is one of several prenatal educators featured in *Brave New Babies.* The producers also interviewed Mikhail Lazarev, a Russian doctor who plays classical music to fetuses and who likens babies who are not exposed to prenatal stimulation to bad dough that will never rise. Rene Van de Carr, the pioneer of the field, is shown sitting in a classroom at his Prenatal University in Haywood, California, calling out "pat pat pat" and "rub rub rub" to a room full of pregnant women who diligently pat and rub their wombs.

With each increasingly weird scene, I looked over at Jennifer.

She looked more disturbed than amused, but it wasn't until Logan said that the BabyPlus was creating a new, more intelligent species that Jennifer yanked the belt off her waist. "I'm sorry," she said, "I can't wear this thing."

I called Logan in Seattle later that week. We chatted for a few minutes, and I mentioned that my wife was six months pregnant. Logan asked if we were using BabyPlus. I confessed that though we had a unit and had tried it briefly, we were not using it.

Logan let out a pained grunt.

"It's my wife," I said. "She's really not into these sorts of things."

It was lame to blame Jennifer, considering that I was equally skeptical of the device, but it was true that I had asked her to try it.

"God, I wish she'd stuck with it," Logan said. Another pained noise. "You should put her on the line and let me massage her verbally for a couple of hours."

I thanked Logan for the offer and asked him how he had come to invent the BabyPlus. He said that he had first learned to build machines as a child when he and his friends would assemble powerful five-thousand-pound potassium perchlorate rockets for sport. His interests turned to prenatal learning in 1982 when his late wife told him about an interview she had heard on the radio with Joseph and Jitsuko Susedik, an Ohio couple with four unusually brilliant daughters. The Susediks claimed that all four daughters could talk by three months and count to one hundred by the time they turned one. Joseph, a retired machinist who had never finished high school and who once claimed to have been abducted by aliens, didn't believe genetics had anything to do with his daughters' brilliance. He thought the difference between his children and other children was an educational program Jitsuko had devised that involved talking to children in the womb.

The family's story made national headlines when the eldest Susedik daughter began taking a premed course at Muskingum College at age ten.

Logan wasn't convinced that talking to a fetus could make it smart. He wondered how much of the Susediks' success was due to the postnatal, as opposed to the prenatal environment—presumably parents who would go to the trouble of teaching their children before they are born would continue with the curriculum after the birth.

But Logan thought it was at least possible that the Susediks were onto something. And he thought *something* was desperately needed. At the time Logan was a social worker for the state of Washington, dealing with criminals, from petty thieves to rapists and murderers. The dysfunction and suffering he witnessed on a daily basis haunted him. "I was beginning to feel that some things were very much out of kilter," Logan said. "Human behavior to me looked so miserable."

Logan had studied English before going into social work, and his initial fascination with prenatal learning led not to an invention but to a four-hundred-page futurist novel set in the Polynesian islands.

Despite the enthusiasm of a number of agents and editors, the manuscript never sold. But the writing wasn't in vain. Logan's research for the book laid the groundwork for the creation of the BabyPlus. He learned that Marian Diamond, a neuroscientist at the University of California at Los Angeles, had found that raising baby rats in stimulating environments could have lasting effects throughout the rats' lives. Logan also discovered that mammalian fetuses have millions of extra neurons, "a phenomenal glut of neurology," Logan called it, that die off if they are not used. And most significant of all to the BabyPlus, Logan learned that scientists had found that the beating of the mother's heart is the loudest noise inside the womb and that it comes through blaringly loud at 95 decibels.

"We had this very Disney-like picture of the womb as being this lovely retreat we like to go to in times of great stress," Logan said, the volume of his voice rising with his passion. "No! It's a howling chaos from which it would be a relief to be born."

Logan saw these studies of fetal life as pieces of a puzzle and in one bizarre and imaginative leap, he put them all together. If you wanted to stimulate a fetus and prevent some of the excess neurons from dying off—and thereby create smarter people who wouldn't behave so miserably—you had to speak to the fetus in the only language it knew: the one-two beat of its mother's heart.

Logan was speaking so quickly as he explained all of this that I found myself drifting off. But then, perhaps it would have been better if I had not regained my focus. When I did, Logan was talking in apocalyptic terms about overpopulation and nuclear disasters. And his message was clear. If we didn't do something dramatic, we were headed for total destruction. This was the great promise of BabyPlus. It could save the world by providing a "designer upgrade" that would create a new and better species that would be less prone to destroying itself.

I told Logan that I found his vocabulary a little frightening, that he sounded like a eugenicist.

Logan said that there was a key difference. He wasn't interested in one race or another. He wanted to enrich all babies.

"But a new species?"

"I mean, why not?" Logan said. "Evolution is the creation and the re-creation and the constant upgrading of a species. If a species' niche changes, like the dinosaurs, then they're out of luck, and if we decide that Palestine and Israel become nasty enough to trigger a nuclear world war, then we're out of luck."

"But—"

"The problem is not outside of us. It's in us."

I had been on the phone with Logan for more than two hours. It seemed time to wrap the discussion up, but Logan cut me off and made one last plea for Jennifer to use the BabyPlus. I told him that I would mention it again, but that it was a long shot.

Logan groaned. "What if you tell her that I can promise your baby a scholarship to Harvard if she does it?"

"I've got that on tape," I said with a nervous laugh. I was recording the interview.

"I'll even give it to you in writing and sign it," Logan said, then clarified that the offer was contingent on the success of his next two books.

"As I see it, for every child who is not prenatally stimulated, there's just another opportunity lost. The world does not need another American to be just an American."

Before we hung up, I asked Logan if he was working on any other inventions. He said that he was conducting interferometric experiments with lasers in an attempt to physically access the multiverse.

"Okay, thanks again," I said.

MY INTERVIEW WITH LOGAN did nothing to lessen my skepticism of the BabyPlus. The science behind the device sounded wildly speculative at best, and when I questioned Logan about the one small study he had done on the first fetuses to be subjected to the BabyPlus several decades earlier, the most he could say is that they had grown up to be more empathetic and better athletes. My skepticism only grew when I learned that all of the medical literature on the product's website was either written by Logan himself or published by the Association for Pre- & Perinatal

Psychology and Health, an unaccredited organization set up by prenatal psychology professionals.

Still, for all my doubts about prenatal education in general and the BabyPlus in particular, I believed that Logan believed in the product. And though I hated the idea that people were wasting their money on the BabyPlus, there was a part of me that couldn't help but identify with what I took to be Logan's willful delusion.

Amid the flood of scientific jargon, Logan had also spoken openly about his own life. He said that he had grown up in a repressive home and that his parents hadn't been interested in his inventions or writing. He said that his late first wife had had three miscarriages and that the foster daughter they had taken in after giving up on biological children had become a schizophrenic. And when I listened to the recording of the interview, I noticed how many times Logan had mentioned that the BabyPlus could make children not only more intelligent but also more empathetic. I wondered if this might be the real story behind his invention. Logan had had no luck with parents and children. Maybe the abstractions of the BabyPlus had emerged out of the concreteness of his suffering. Maybe Logan needed to believe in the BabyPlus to get out of bed every morning.

Or maybe I was reading Logan's life through the lens of my own experience. When Jennifer and I first began to talk about having a baby, I had myself tested for a long list of diseases that have been linked to the genes of Jews of Eastern European heritage. I was convinced that I had to be a carrier of at least one or another of these diseases, and when all the results came back negative I felt almost as shaken as I would have if one of them had turned up positive. My neurotic sense of self was so linked to illness that it was jarring to know that I carried not even one of these harbingers of Jewish doom.

But, then, there were still plenty of diseases to worry about that

I could not be tested for. In particular, I was concerned that I might carry a genetic predisposition to multiple sclerosis, the disease that ravaged my mother's mind and body in her late twenties and ended her life at thirty-nine. I remembered being told as a child that having a mother with MS didn't mean that I was more likely than anyone else to develop the disease, but that was twenty years earlier and I had never bothered to find out if any new studies had been done.

I looked online—a terrible mistake for a hypochondriac—and almost immediately found the news I dreaded: A typical man has a .1 percent chance of being diagnosed with multiple sclerosis. As the son of an MS patient, I have a 3 percent chance.

I looked at these numbers on my computer screen, .1 and 3, and then I looked at them again and again and again. I knew that I was probably at an even higher risk for developing many other diseases, and I was afraid of those diseases, too. My search for tumors has given me a cartographer's familiarity with the contours of my flesh. My fear of diabetes keeps me jogging long after my lungs and legs have given out.

But I was more afraid of MS than any other disease. When the numbers on my computer screen would not go away, I did the only thing I could: I searched for something, anything, that would make me feel better.

What I found was vitamin D. The theory that vitamin D might help prevent MS has been around since the seventies, but the research to support the theory only began to emerge in the last decade.

As I read the studies on vitamin D and MS, I didn't think about the studies my grandmother would regularly cite as she searched for a way to save my mom. I didn't think about the acupuncture or the bee sting treatment or the trip to Florida for hyperbaric oxygen treatments or the experimental surgery to remove the thymus gland from my mother's chest or even the countless times my grandmother told my sister and me that if we loved our mother enough, she would get better.

What I thought about was how quickly I could get my hands on vitamin D supplements. And when I took my first pill the next day, the nightmarish vision that had been playing and replaying in my head, the vision of my family's tragedy repeating itself with me in the role of my mother, faded away.

I believed that vitamin D could save me and, like any true believer, I hated to keep my truths to myself. When my research revealed that vitamin D might help prevent a wide range of diseases in addition to MS, I began to preach about my magic pills to anyone who would listen. I emailed my friends and relatives a long list of studies. When they ignored my email, I ordered a shipment of vitamin D and began handing out bottles.

Now I can see that my fervor was directly proportional to my fear, but I also can't entirely rid myself of a belief that widespread use of vitamin D supplements in childhood is one day going to wipe out MS.

Logan had his BabyPlus. I had vitamin D. What we shared, I thought, was the human yearning for simple solutions to complicated and frightening problems.

SIX

Lamaze and the Birth Class

The Stalinist Natural Birth Method

LAMAZE CLASSES AND ORGIES have a lot in common. They both in-
volve loud panting, stretching, and considerable doubt among the
participants as to whether the whole process can really work.

In the 1950s, the Lamaze method arrived in America via France
with the promise of a drug-free solution to the pain of childbirth.
The naturalistic approach and the inclusion of fathers struck
a nerve with young liberal couples in the sixties and seventies—
including my parents when my mother was pregnant with me—
and soon Lamaze classes were springing up in community centers
all over the country. Some classes have evolved from the early
days to include new trends in childbirth, like aroma therapy,
but the core elements of the original Lamaze program—general
childbirth education, as well as breathing, stretching, and massage techniques—are still taught today.

If the popularity of the method has diminished in the last few
decades, it's in part because much of the Lamaze approach has
been absorbed into the mainstream of birth education in America. And if something strange is going on with American parents
today, it can probably be traced back to Lamaze and the freedom it
gave a new generation of parents to challenge the established
medical authorities on birthing practices and babies.

I was introduced to the ideas of Lamaze at a birth education class during the sixth month of Jennifer's pregnancy. The class was not a Lamaze class, and neither Jennifer nor I had realized that we'd be learning Lamaze techniques when we sat down for our first session in a dingy radiology conference room at our neighborhood hospital.

Jennifer, in particular, was curious to learn about Lamaze. She had already decided that she was going to get an epidural, an anesthetic delivered directly into the spine that is now used by three-quarters of American women giving birth. But the promise of the epidural was only a moderate comfort. She knew she still might face plenty of pain before she got the epidural and perhaps also considerable pain at the time of the delivery, when the amount of medication is typically reduced. As Jennifer saw it, the more lines of defense she had against the pain the better, and if the Lamaze method, or any other natural birth method, might help, she wanted to learn about it.

During the first months of the pregnancy, I had a hard time grasping Jennifer's anxieties about the pain of childbirth. I knew that giving birth was tremendously difficult, and I felt bad that she would have to go through it. But the pain would be temporary. I was more worried about the long-term health risks to Jennifer and the baby. This is among the top ten worst things about being human. At times it's hard to empathize with even the entirely reasonable concerns of the people you love most.

As the months passed, and I had more time to reflect on my callousness, I tried to recall a time when I had been in the situation of knowing that in a matter of months I would experience almost unthinkable pain. I thought hard, but the best I could come up with was the panic-filled year that preceded my bar mitzvah. And yet, terrifying though that year was, the object of my fear—the public recitation of a handful of Jewish texts followed by a brief speech about Jacob wrestling with an angel—didn't quite measure up to the drama of childbirth.

The reality of what Jennifer was facing only began to sink in when I imagined myself being told that in a few months someone was going to punch me in the balls over and over and that the process might last several days. If I was in that situation, I thought, I too would want both drugs and the chance to prepare with whatever method was the Lamaze equivalent for someone about to be punched in the balls for hours on end.

Lamaze first came up at the second meeting of our birth education course when our instructor, Carol, announced that she was going to do a brief training session in Lamaze breathing.

I assumed that only the mothers would be participating in this training, and I wasn't thrilled when Carol said that she wanted *all* of us to take one deep breath and then three short panting breaths. As much as I appreciated the gesture of inclusiveness, I didn't particularly like the idea of panting with strangers.

But, then, I also did not want to disobey Carol. I'd had a hard time taking Carol seriously at our first class. After introducing herself and telling us a bit about the hospital, Carol had produced a doll and a foam pelvis and shown us how a baby twists and turns through the birth canal. When she'd finished the demonstration, Carol had put the doll down but kept the pelvis around her wrist like a bracelet. For the next hour I did my best to take in all the information but found that it is almost impossible to focus on what a person is saying when he or she is wearing a foam pelvis.

Now at our second class, the foam pelvis was gone, and I could see Carol in all of her intimidating glory. She was tall and her thick shoulders filled out her long white nurse's coat, a coat that only added to her no-nonsense demeanor. She was the type of nurse you didn't mess with no matter how large the needle she was carrying in your direction or how long it had been since she'd changed your bedpan.

And so when Carol told us to pant, I panted along with the others. It was even worse than I expected. There was nothing wet about the breaths and yet as the breathing grew louder and louder, I was overcome with a grotesque sense of moistness, as though I was bathing inside of someone else's mouth. If I'd had a bottle of Purell on me, I would have drunk it.

And the feeling wasn't even the worst part. The worst part was thinking about what would happen if someone walked by and heard us. Probably he or she would call the police. Probably whenever someone Googled me for the rest of my life the first thing to come up would be a story about how I had been arrested for lewd breathing in a hospital.

The huffing and puffing went on and on. I scanned the room for another set of eyes to join mine in silent acknowledgment of the wrongness of what was happening, but everyone else was focused on their breathing. I was alone in my immaturity, and as I sat and panted, a question arose in my mind, a question that probably occurs to most parents within twenty-four hours of their first introduction to Lamaze: If childbirth was as painful as everyone said, how was panting like a tired dog going to make the least bit of difference?

THE FIRST THING I LEARNED about Lamaze when I started my research was that the method was named after Fernand Lamaze, the French doctor who popularized the method. This wasn't particularly surprising. But almost everything else I read about the origins of the Lamaze method was.

Fernand Lamaze was an excitable man with a round, fleshy face. He had a lifelong passion for literature, and as a young doctor he would write poetry and recite Balzac and Flaubert from memory. In a biography of Lamaze by his granddaughter, he comes across as well intentioned, if deeply conflicted. His concern for the pain of childbirth was seemingly genuine, but he tended to be less concerned about the pain of the women in his own family when he regularly brought his mistress home for dinner.

Lamaze ran the maternity ward in Paris's Communist Party–affiliated Metal Workers hospital, and in 1951 he was invited to join a French delegation to an international medical conference in the Soviet Union. Lamaze was excited about the trip. Not long before, a Soviet doctor had attended a gynecological conference in Paris and claimed that his country had discovered a natural method of painless childbirth. Lamaze was intrigued but skeptical. He would have to see it with his own eyes to believe it.

The trip turned out to be a classic Soviet propaganda tour designed to show the world how the U.S.S.R. had revolutionized modern medicine. With each passing day of the trip, Lamaze was growing increasingly frustrated. He had come to see the natural birth method he had heard about in Paris, but every time he asked to witness such a birth, his hosts made excuses. Lamaze began to suspect that all the talk about painless birth was a hoax and forty-eight hours before he was scheduled to return to France, he threatened to denounce the Soviet doctors to the international press as frauds unless he was allowed to witness a woman giving birth with the new painless method. The Soviets gave in and brought Lamaze to a maternity ward, where he watched a woman in labor and then, according to his own account, began to weep with joy, as she delivered her baby with no sign of distress. "Pain may seem to be the inevitable ransom of childbirth, but it isn't any longer," Lamaze told the newspaper *Libération* upon his return to France. "I saw with my own eyes a woman give birth without pain. I witnessed it. I've been in obstetric practice for thirty years. I couldn't have been fooled. Painless childbirth's success, without any other treatment or the use of drugs, is almost unbelievable."

The Soviet childbirth method that Lamaze witnessed was then sometimes referred to as the Pavlov method and accounts of the method's origins often note that it was invented by the famous Russian physiologist Ivan Pavlov. But while it's possible to draw a line from Pavlov and his salivating dogs to Lamaze, the connection is tenuous at best. The man more closely linked to the origins of Lamaze—if still only indirectly—is the other titan of turn-of-the-century Soviet psychology, Vladimir Mikhailovich Bekhterev.

Bekhterev's genius was obvious from a young age. He entered medical school at sixteen and would go on to study experimental psychology, psychiatry, general physiology, and physiology of the brain, publishing more than eight hundred articles in his lifetime. His knowledge of the brain was so renowned that the apocryphal story was that a German scientist had once remarked that only two beings could fully understand the workings of the human brain—God and Herr Bekhterev.

At the end of the nineteenth century, Bekhterev was doing what every self-respecting neurophysiologist was doing at the time: cutting apart animals bit by bit to figure out how the brain and nervous system control the different parts of the body. Bekhterev would cut out the cerebral cortex of a cat and then prod the animal's body to see which, if any, of the reflexes still functioned. He would remove the cerebrum of a dog to discover if it could still bark—it could, if properly stimulated. For the pure physiologists of the era, figuring out the internal mechanics of an animal body was an end in itself. But for the more philosophically inclined nineteenth-century physiologist such as Bekhterev, the goal was much broader; the goal was to chase ideas about the mind or the soul out of science, to prove that humans are mechanical creatures, and that everything about us, including our thoughts, can be explained by physical laws.

For most scientists, exploring the boundary between the ethereal mind and the material brain would have been enough to satisfy their intellectual curiosities. But Bekhterev was rarely content to focus on a single line of research. In the 1880s he traveled to Europe to study with the great scientists of the day. In Leipzig he studied with Wilhelm Wundt, the founder of experimental psychology, whose emphasis on introspection Bekhterev would later reject, and in Paris he learned about the new medical uses of hypnosis in the clinic of the famous French neurologist Jean-Martin Charcot.

Like many of the scientists who passed through Charcot's clinic at Salpêtrière, including a young Sigmund Freud, Bekhterev was excited about the medical potential for hypnosis. Bekhterev focused his own research on alcoholism, spending years trying to cure drunks, but one of his many students, Konstantin Ivanovich Platonov, was more interested in the possible uses of hypnosis as an anesthetic in surgery.

A number of European scientists were also studying hypnosis as a method of pain relief at the time, but for the young Soviet republic, where pain relief medications were scarce, the interest was more urgent. Realizing that childbirth would be a convenient way to test his ideas about hypnosis and pain, in 1923 Platonov found a thirty-two-year-old medical student who agreed to let him hypnotize her during her labor. In preparation for the delivery, Platonov repeatedly put the woman in a trance and then told her that her pregnancy would be painless. When it came time for the woman to have her baby, Platonov was at her side and managed to put her into a drowsy state. According to his own account, the woman gave birth to a ten-pound baby and felt no pain.

A year later, Platonov and his student Ilia Zakharevich

Velvovski presented a paper to the Second Neuropsychiatric Congress in Leningrad on hypnosuggestive analgesia in surgery, gynecology, obstetrics, and stomatology. But if Platonov and Velvovski were expecting applause, they were disappointed. Bekhterev's enthusiasm for hypnosis notwithstanding, the Russian medical establishment didn't take the idea seriously and the paper generated little interest.

Platonov and Velvovski's work would likely have been lost to history but in the mid-1930s, a handful of historical circumstances came together to create a window of opportunity for hypnosis in childbirth.

More than a decade after World War I, the Soviets were still coming to terms with their losses: more than three million citizens dead, thirty-four times the number of dead Americans. The communist leadership concluded that for the country to realize its grand ambitions, the Soviet Union would have to be repopulated, and in 1935 the government introduced a year long "motherhood campaign" to encourage more births. The following year abortion was banned.

The Soviet longing to repopulate the country was reasonable enough, but the plan faced a significant hurdle. It was hard to run a motherhood campaign if women dreaded the pain of childbirth. And so in addition to expanding child-care services, the Soviets decided to tackle the problem of labor pain once and for all.

In a 1981 article in *Slavic Review*, Eastern European history professor John D. Bell recounted the next developments in the story. In a 1935 editorial in *Pravda*, the official paper of the Communist Party, a prominent obstetrician called on Soviet obstetrical science to fulfill its obligation to make childbirth painless, so that the mothers could go about bringing joy to the whole country. The People's Commissariat of Health created a Council on Painless Childbirth to address the issue, but in 1936 *Pravda* ran another editorial criticizing the commissariat for failing to make any progress on its promise to develop a comprehensive program of painless childbirth or even to hold a single meeting. The next year, the leading medical journal in the country called for a "crash program" to solve the pain dilemma.

The Soviets showed no particular interest in natural birth programs. The 1936 editorial specifically called for the production and distribution of new drugs. But medication wasn't a promising route for Soviet doctors and scientists at the time. The pain relief medications then available, both in the West and the Soviet Union, often proved dangerous to both mother and child, and the Soviets were struggling to distribute the few drugs they did have.

Convinced they had the solution to the Soviet childbirth problem, Platonov and Velvovski began to hypnotize women in groups. And they weren't alone in the effort. "Hypnotariums" began to spring up across Russia. In Leningrad one researcher attempted to hypnotize as many as one hundred pregnant women at once. A Moscow scientist was reported to have tried to hypnotize more than one thousand women in 1941.

Despite occasional claims of success, Platonov and Velvovski found that hypnosis didn't lend itself to mass implementation. It was time-consuming and worked best when there was an ongoing, one-on-one relationship between doctor and patient. And, even if the hypnotarium approach had worked, there was still the near impossible chore of convincing skeptical obstetricians across the Soviet Union to be retrained as hypnotists.

The Soviet experiment with natural birth might have ended in the 1930s if not for another demographic crisis. After World War II, the call again went out for more Soviet babies and, because pain relief drugs were still scarce, a new urgency arose in the search for a natural method of pain relief.

This time Velvovski came up with a new answer. Instead of

hypnotizing pregnant women, he proposed small classes at which mothers would learn both about the birth process and about what the doctors and nurses would be doing during the labor and delivery. From the classes the women would also learn that child-birth did not have to be painful. He recommended breathing exer-cises and massage so that the mother would remain alert and aware of what was happening to her and suggested that a nurse or midwife be present during the delivery to reassure and coach the mother.

Velvovski's new approach was essentially the Lamaze method as it exists today. Because he left no personal papers, no one knows exactly how Velvovski's thoughts progressed in the second half of the 1940s. It seems he reasoned that if it was too difficult to use hypnosis on a wide scale, then perhaps doctors could achieve a similar effect without putting women into trances. Maybe the message could be absorbed directly into the conscious mind through education? Maybe all that was necessary for a painless childbirth was to convince a woman that she did not have to experi-ence pain?

However he arrived at this new approach to painless childbirth based on education and breathing, Velvovski was anxious to test it, and in 1949 he received permission from Ukrainian medical authorities to open a maternity clinic in Kharkov to formally experiment with the new technique. Not surprisingly, the local obstetricians weren't thrilled to learn that a neurologist was op-erating an experimental maternity clinic in their midst. They lodged a complaint and Velvovski was called to Moscow to re-spond to the charge that he was misusing government funds.

Velvovski was savvy enough to know what happened to people who upset the Soviet authorities. And, as the government officials questioned him, Velvovski did what people in trouble have prob-ably been doing since the beginning of time: He faked a heart attack.* He was granted a three-month convalescent period and it was during these months that the founder of the Lamaze method came up with his most brilliant idea of all.

VELVOVSKI HAD GOOD REASON to be worried about his call to Moscow. Upsetting the wrong official was often equivalent to writing one's own death sentence in Stalin's Russia, and the 1930s and '40s were an especially dangerous time to be a Soviet scientist. Unwilling to accept the limits of Mendelian genetics on agriculture, the government simply abandoned an entire body of knowledge in favor of outdated Lamarckian ideas about the inheritance of acquired traits. Hundreds of scientists were rounded up and imprisoned for the offense of pointing out that these ideas were wrong.

In the late forties, the regime's focus moved from agriculture to physiology and psychology, but sound scientific evidence was just as irrelevant to the discussion. In 1949 the Soviets held a national celebration in honor of the centennial of Ivan Pavlov's birth. While most pre-Revolution scientists had been written out of the history books, Pavlov was a Nobel Prize winner and a source of national pride. And, more importantly, with enough twisting, Pavlov's experiments lent themselves to a vision of humanity that fit well with Stalin's dark mood at the time.

As most high school students learn at some point or another, Pavlov demonstrated that if a sound was made every time dogs were fed, eventually the sound alone would be enough to make the dogs salivate. Pavlov called the salivation in response to the sound alone a "conditional reflex"—often mistranslated as a "condi-

---

* After Velvovski's death, people who knew him said that he had faked the heart attack. Velvovski himself never acknowledged any deceit.

tioned reflex." But when Pavlov showed that a dog could be trained to associate the sound of a bell with feeding, the real significance was not that animal behavior could be modified with environmental stimuli. As historian David Joravsky had pointed out, people have always known that animal behavior can be shaped by regular patterns of reward and punishment. The real meaning of Pavlov's dogs was much larger; the real meaning was that the philosophers and scientists who believed that humans were mechanical and that the mind and the soul were obsolete notions now had a stronger argument. The mechanistic thinkers had spent the nineteenth century arguing that all of human behavior could be reduced to reflex reactions to the environment, no different than a leg jerking in response to a tap on the knee. But explaining the jerk of a leg was easy. The challenge for the mechanistic thinkers was to explain more complicated behavior, and conditional reflexes promised a solution: Just as the brains of Pavlov's dogs had linked the sound of a bell and food, human reflex reactions were linked, one upon the next, in long chains. As the creative logic at the time went, human inclination toward monogamy was a conditional response to the feeling of love, which was conditioned by the sexual reflex. A feeling of honor might be traced to admiration for swords, which could be linked to a child's attraction to bright objects.

On the surface this reflex-centered psychology looks similar to associationist theory, a classical idea about how people learn. But associationist theory argues that we learn by linking one idea to the next in our minds. The radical physiologists were trying to do away with the idea of the mind altogether. Thinking according to the reflex theory was only a delay, the background noise that filled the time during which the brain made connections between the various linked reflexes.

Though Pavlov sometimes made sweeping claims about the importance of his discoveries, he was a scientist's scientist and not generally inclined toward philosophical insight. He saw his experiments only as small building blocks out of which a new science might one day emerge. Bekhterev meanwhile had been doing his own research on conditional reflexes at the same time as Pavlov— he called them "associate reflexes" and was perpetually annoyed that Pavlov received all the credit—and Bekhterev was the more expansive thinker and daring scientist of the two. Pavlov could spend his life playing with dogs as far as Bekhterev was concerned. Bekhterev was going to go ahead and solve the great questions of Western thought. In the first decade of the twentieth century, Bekhterev dreamed up reflexology, a far-reaching theory that explained how all of human social life could be traced to brain reflexes. (Although he is rarely credited for it, Bekhterev had essentially laid out the behaviorist theory that would soon take over American psychology and dominated the field for half a century.)

Pavlov and Bekhterev regularly took public swipes at each other over who had the superior approach. His own occasional rhetorical flourishes notwithstanding, Pavlov thought Bekhterev was recklessly applying his discovery before the basic research had been completed. And because the physiologists never managed to find the neural pathways they were looking for nor established the chain of conditional reflexes the theory relied upon, Bekhterev's reflexology never became the dominant school of thought in the Soviet Union. As the famous psychologist L. S. Vygotskii put it in 1931, "A person is not at all a sack of skin filled with reflexes, and the brain is not a hotel for a series of conditioned reflexes accidentally dropping in." In fact, Bekhterev himself never seemed entirely comfortable with the idea that mental life was nothing but reflexes and sometimes escaped the problem by using the term *reflex* as only a metaphor.

If Bekhterev wasn't able to convince everyone of the merits of reflexology, he did have a strong following in the first decades of the century. But reflexology began to fall out of fashion when Bekhterev died in 1927, and after it was officially condemned by the Stalinist regime in the 1930s it became dangerous to even espouse Bekhterev's ideas. (Although it remains unproven, it was widely rumored that Stalin had had Bekhterev poisoned, possibly because Bekhterev had diagnosed him with paranoia.)

Soviet scientists, then, must have been entirely baffled when the regime, as part of its 1949 centenary celebration of Pavlov's birth, called on them to create a new science that would explain everything with conditional reflexes. To anyone who remembered the twenties, the new approach, later dubbed "neo-Pavlovianism," sounded suspiciously similar to Bekhterev's reflexology. Pavlov would presumably have been horrified by the turn of events.

In his 1951 essay "Contemporary Psychology in the Soviet Union," Harvard Russian scholar Ivan D. London expressed his own dismay. "Thus, the wheel has gone its full circle. Bekhterev's reflexology, done in by public denouncement at the end of the third decade, now returns as 'correct Pavlovian theory,' " London wrote. "Bekhterev, Pavlov's enemy, now becomes victor in principle."

Scholars are still trying to understand how exactly an outmoded and oversimplified view of human nature was suddenly thrust upon Russian science a decade after it had vanished from the scientific landscape. It's hard to believe that the bizarre turn of events could be explained only by the Soviet regime's anxiousness to bask in Pavlov's famous name. Historian Robert Tucker has argued that Stalin's embrace of so-called neo-Pavlovianism was about something much darker. "To the outsider who studies the materials of the neo-Pavlovian movement, nothing is more striking than its insistent endeavor to empty man of all inner spring of action, to visualize human nature as motivationally inert," Tucker writes. "Man is 'hollow.' He has no wishes, instincts, emotions, drives, or impulses, no reservoir of energies of his own. No motive is allowed to intervene between the stimulus emulating from the environment and the person's reflex response."

It's not hard to see why a hollowed-out man might have appealed to Stalin at the height of his paranoia. If mental life was nothing more than a reflexive response to an environment, then mental life could also be molded, the personality of man shaped according to a tyrant's fantasies. Or, as Tucker puts it, "Man had to be understood as a being whose character and conduct are controlled at every step by the conditioning process, whose every psychic step is a reflex."

Whatever the explanation for the neo-Pavlovian movement, in June 1950, a special joint session of the Soviets' Academy of Sciences and Academy of Medical Sciences met to address the issue of how to bring Pavlov back into the forefront of Soviet science. In his opening remarks, the vice president of the Academy of Medical Sciences declared that Pavlov "must be the foundation of the whole edifice of medicine," and leading scientists of the day were made to apologize for failing to embrace Pavlovian thought sooner. The session ended with the establishment of a watchdog commission to make sure that scientists didn't sway from the official line.

It was in the midst of this upside-down moment in Soviet history that Velvovski emerged, as if on cue, from the recovery of his fake heart attack. It turned out that Velvovski had been busy during his months of recovery. He now had a new set of neo-Pavlovian ideas and could explain the pain of childbirth through conditional reflexes. The theory was wrapped in the neo-Pavlovian jargon about cortical dominance—despite plenty of evidence to the contrary in his own lifetime, Pavlov believed that all learned behavior relied upon connections made in the cerebral cortex. The explanation amounted to this: Childbirth was painful because when women heard stories about painful births, their brains were conditioned to associate messages from the uterus during labor as pain stimuli. Velvovski's birth education program, in turn, would decondition women's brains so that they did not misinterpret these naturally nonpainful messages from the uterus.

Velvovski was an obscure scientist at the time but another well-known Leningrad obstetrician who had also experimented with hypnosis and labor in the 1920s persuaded the Ministry of Health to quickly set up a pilot program to test Velvovski's new Pavlovian birthing method. At the end of 1950, Velvovski published the results of the pilot program, claiming that in 82.7 percent of the cases he had "eliminated" or "nearly eliminated" the pain of childbirth and that drugs had been unnecessary in 95.9 percent of the births. Several months later at a follow-up conference on the method in Leningrad, the president of the Academy of Medical Sciences described Velvovski's program as "one of the most brilliant examples of the practical adoption of the principles of the great Pavlovian teaching in medical practice."

Even in those highly politicized times, several attendees of the conference found the nerve to speak up. One obstetrician who called Velvovski's success rate into question pointed out that it was hard to believe that the pain could be wiped out, considering that childbirth requires stretching tissue full of sensitive nerve endings by thirty-five centimeters.

But common sense was no match for fear or ideology, and on February 13, 1951, the Soviet Ministry of Health issued Order No. 142 making Velvovski's birthing method, newly dubbed psycho-prophylaxis, the official birth method of the Soviet Union.

A plan was quickly set in motion to train physicians across the country in it.

The government-endorsed psycho-prophylaxis method called for all pregnant women to attend six group training sessions exactly fifty-six days before their due dates and noted that a woman should have constant support throughout her delivery from a coach who would massage her, guide her breathing, and offer assurances. According to Bell, the plan also called for the instructor to "emphasize that Pavlovian science and a benevolent Soviet government had freed women from the curse of labor pain."

It was at this dark moment in Soviet history that Lamaze arrived on the scene and wept for joy at a laboring woman's bedside. Upon returning to Paris, Lamaze set about preaching the greatness of the Soviet birth method with an evangelical fervor. He immediately retrained the entire staff at his hospital in the Pavlov natural birth method, campaigned for it to become national French policy, and wrote a book filled with scientific claims about the cerebral cortex that had been proven false fifty years earlier.*

Lamaze was a great cheerleader and his enthusiasm briefly spread across France. In 1954, French national radio played the breathy sounds of a Lamaze delivery, which led to a bestselling Lamaze album. But Lamaze's critics were suspicious from the

---

* Lamaze became particularly fixated on a 1912 study done by M. N. Erofeeva, a scientist in Pavlov's lab who had apparently shown that a dog could be conditioned to salivate in response to an electric shock if it coincided with the serving of food. But regardless of the merits of the study, it made little sense for Lamaze to focus on it. The central claim of the so-called Pavlov method was that childbirth was not painful to begin with, and so the dog study would be analogous only if Lamaze also believed that a dog's initial pain response to an electric shock had also been conditioned. The most logical conclusion to draw from the Erofeeva study would have been to accept that childbirth is naturally painful but could perhaps be deconditioned by giving women, say, ice cream every time they experienced pain—the Ben and Jerry's Natural Birth Method.

start, and he was twice called before a French medical board and accused of false advertising. When, in 1957, Lamaze's own hospital turned against him, it was more than he could take. A day after a contentious meeting about the hospital's plans to dismiss his closest colleagues and limit his activities, Lamaze had a heart attack and died.

The excitement about the Lamaze method quickly fizzled out in France, but the method had already been imported to America, where its early champions, conscious of the Cold War mentality, were careful to call it the "Lamaze" rather than the "Pavlov" method.

The Soviets, meanwhile, grew frustrated with the method when it failed to live up to its grandiose promise of painless birth for all women. Stalin died in 1956 and the zeal for neo-Pavlovian thinking quickly came to an end. A *Washington Post* article in 1976 on the state of the psycho-prophylactic birth in the Soviet Union reported that, while the method was still nominally official policy, it had been more or less abandoned. "To tell us that birth can be pleasant without injection against pain is a joke no one believes," said one mother.

The article, nevertheless, ends on an uplifting note. At the time the Soviet Academy of Medical Sciences was in the midst of testing a new device, the electronarkon-1, which would solve the problem of childbirth pain once and for all by shocking a laboring mother with electrodes attached to her head with four rubber rings.

After learning about the Stalinist roots of Lamaze, I couldn't help but be skeptical of the method, but just because it had emerged out of ideological nonsense didn't necessarily mean the method didn't work. After all, the Lamaze method couldn't have spread across America if not for the many satisfied customers who were eager to pass it along.

In the 1980s, Ronald Melzack, a psychologist and highly regarded pain expert at McGill University whose pain-measuring model has been widely adopted in the scientific community, turned his attention to the pain of childbearing and found that Lamaze-style pre-birth training does have a statistically significant impact on pain reduction. But the impact turned out to be small. Most women still experienced considerable pain even when Melzack took the pain reductions into account. Melzack determined that, on average, natural childbirth hurts considerably more than chronic back and cancer pains and that, at its most intense, the pain feels almost as bad as having a finger cut off.

I wasn't surprised to read Melzack's finding. But something else Melzack had written about childbirth and pain troubled me more. In a May 1993 issue of the medical journal *Pain*, Melzack discussed a new body of research that put a twist on his own findings. While some women were benefiting from natural birth classes, others were planning for natural births and then experiencing intense guilt when they ended up needing an epidural. One study found that women who didn't achieve the natural births they had planned for were more likely to become depressed and have suicidal thoughts.

The problem with many of the natural birth classes, Melzack concluded, is that the students aren't psychologically prepared for the very real possibility that they might end up needing medical intervention. And at the root of this problem is a failure to recognize a broader truth: People are different. The classes convey the message that one method can work for everyone, but people experience pain differently. Melzack's research had found that on average natural childbirth caused intense pain, but he also found considerable variation in the degree to which women suffered. Some women found the pain of giving birth overwhelming, but 10 percent of them reported only mild pain. Women who tended to have painful menstrual cramps also tended to have painful contractions. Older women tended to have less pain than younger women and overweight mothers suffered more than slimmer mothers.

I don't doubt that Lamaze himself was entirely sincere in his desire to help women or that many women have benefited from the method. But in spreading the gospel that natural childbirth can be a painless process, Lamaze also no doubt left countless women feeling like failures when, unable to achieve the natural pain-free births he promised, they requested pain relief drugs.

And the more I thought about the plight of a woman who is made to feel guilty for choosing pain relief in childbirth, the more annoyed I became. One night while reading some of the ridiculously unbelievable claims in Lamaze's book, *Painless Childbirth,* I again thought about my male reference point for the pain of childbirth. It occurred to me that what Velvovski and Lamaze really needed was a good punch in the balls. Then, as they were holding their respective groins in agony, they needed to be told that the pain they were feeling was only a product of misplaced fears that had arisen from stories they had heard about other men getting punched in the balls.

That would have shown them, I thought. I felt oddly triumphant for a moment, as though I had gone back in time and personally delivered the blows.

Then I remembered that in the photo I had seen of him, Lamaze looked like a pretty hefty guy, and it occurred to me that if I were to go back in time to punch him in the balls, it might not go so well for me.

I returned to my reading.

SEVEN

Labor Coaches

Dads, Doulas, and Semi-Pornographic Birth Videos

AMERICAN FATHERS USED TO KNOW what to do when their wives
went into labor. Before the twentieth century, most American
women gave birth at home, and fathers often played an important
role. In colonial times, the father's first job was often to literally
get on his horse and hurry to the home of the nearest midwife.
And even when horses were no longer part of the process, fathers
remained involved in their wives' labors. As the midwife tended
to the mother, the father would boil water, clean the linens, and
care for the other children.

The more passive role of the American father only came about
with the rise of the hospital birth. Banned from delivery rooms,
fathers could do little more than pace around the hospital in a
state of panic. (To keep the pacing to a minimum, some hospitals
opened special "stork clubs," where fathers could instead watch
TV and smoke in a state of panic.)

I first realized just how far things have swung back in the direction of father participation when Carol, the instructor of our
birth class, showed us labor videos.

The videos looked at least twenty years old and were so ridiculous at moments that I wondered if Carol's real purpose in

showing them was to provide comic relief from the seriousness of the rest of the curriculum.

In one of my favorite moments, a laboring woman in her hospital bed turns to her husband and says she feels nauseous.

"It must be that cheesesteak you ate," the husband responds without a trace of humor.

Even more memorable was the footage of the mother with the perfectly coiffed blond hair reclining on her bed between her husband's spread legs and shouting "My baby's coming, my baby's coming!" in a voice so high and breathy that it was hard not to feel like I was watching hard-core porn in a roomful of expecting parents.

Carol had mentioned that some women like to bring pictures from home to focus on as they labor, and in another scene a woman is wincing in agony as her husband waves a photo of a cat in her face. Later this same woman is shown sitting in the shower as her husband sprays her belly with the detachable shower head and sings "She'll be coming 'round the mountain."

Amusing as the videos were, I probably should not have been laughing. I can only imagine how much more ridiculous I would look if anyone had a video of me in action during the second birth class Jennifer and I attended.

We made the decision to sign up for the second class after losing confidence in the first. There were plenty of good reasons to be concerned about our first birth class—Carol's failure to show up for one of the sessions comes to mind—but the tipping point was the discussion of fontanels, the soft spots on a baby's skull that allow the infant head to compress and squeeze through the birth canal.

As Carol pointed out the location of the fontanels on the head of a doll, one of the fathers in the class, a man who had previously mentioned that he already had a four-year-old daughter, raised his hand.

"Don't the babies breathe out of those things?" he asked.

"No, I think you're confused," Carol said.

"Nah, I'm pretty sure they do," the man said.

Carol, to her credit, showed no sign of being taken aback by the craziness of the question. "You must be thinking about something else. A baby can't breathe through the top of its head."

The man nodded, but I could see in his eyes that he was unconvinced, that for the rest of his life he would be telling people that babies breathe out of their heads and that even some birth education instructors don't know about it.

The man's question had no real impact on Jennifer or me, but the oddness of the moment added to our growing sense that we were not in an especially stellar academic environment, and when a friend recommended a birth class in Manhattan, we decided to give it a try.

The new class was at a birth education center and the atmosphere was a big improvement upon the dreary radiology conference room at the hospital. Framed photos of happy toddlers lined the classroom's bright yellow walls, and mats and pillows had been placed along the edges of the carpeted floor. Best of all, there were snacks in the lobby. I probably consumed two dollars' worth of apples and crackers but the presence of the snacks made the class feel like it was worth all the money in the world.

Ellen, the instructor of the second class, was an energetic actress-turned-masseuse-turned-doula with curly brown hair and a passion for father-assisted labor positions.

At our first four-hour session, I practiced placing a pillow behind Jennifer's back as she reclined in a chair. Then Jennifer turned around, and I practiced placing a pillow between

Jennifer's chest and the back of the chair. When it was clear that the partners, as Ellen called us (perhaps in deference to the lesbian couple in the class), had mastered pillow placement, we were instructed to squat against a wall while each mother leaned against her respective partner's legs.

Squatting against a wall isn't particularly easy even when a pregnant woman isn't putting all of her weight on your legs, and I was still recovering from the position when Ellen, seated at the front of the room on a large exercise ball, called for the partners to get down on all fours so that the mothers could stand over us and lean down with their hands on our backs. (Why the mothers could not have leaned on, say, the empty chairs they had just been sitting on was never made clear.)

And these were just the labor positions. We hadn't yet made it to the massage portion of the curriculum. After a brief break, Ellen had the partners sit on the floor at the feet of the mothers. First we massaged their legs and then, when the maternal calves were good and loose, we moved on to full-body massages, delivered, according to Ellen's instruction, in downward, two-handed "we're not worthy" strokes. By the end of the class, I would hardly have been surprised if Ellen had announced that some women in labor find it relaxing to taser their partners with each contraction.

Jennifer was amused by my forced submissiveness and after another break spent stuffing cheese and crackers into my face, I was laughing along with her. But as we rode the subway home, I also couldn't help but wonder how we had arrived at this point. How exactly had we gone from fathers only one generation ago being banned from the delivery room to fathers turning themselves into human coffee tables in the delivery room?

○○○

As soon as I looked into the history of fathers in the delivery room, I came across the Bradley method of natural childbirth. The Bradley method uses many of the same breathing and relaxation exercises as Lamaze but differs in its emphasis on coaching and its more rigorous ideological commitment to natural births—coaches are trained to steer mothers away from drugs even when they cry out for them in fits of pain.

The method takes its name from Robert Bradley, a folksy, outspoken obstetrician who was known affectionately as "Dr. Bob" and less affectionately as "Barnyard Bradley" for his habit of comparing women's births to the animal births he had witnessed while growing up on a farm in Kansas. Bradley's journey into the world of father-assisted labors began when his wife urged him to read a book on childbirth by the British obstetrician and natural childbirth pioneer Dr. Grantly Dick-Read. At the time, Bradley was training in obstetrics at the Mayo Foundation in Minnesota. It was the late 1940s and most mothers in American hospitals were giving birth with pain relief medication, often medication so powerful that the mothers were not even awake during their deliveries. Bradley, though still skeptical, was curious enough about natural childbirth to want to study the phenomenon, and he located ninety nurses at the University of Minnesota graduate school who agreed to let him deliver their babies without drugs.

Bradley's epiphany about fathers in the delivery room came just after nurse #36 gave birth. In a speech at the University of Southern California in 1965, Bradley recalled that nurse #36 had been an attractive woman—"one of the most statuesquely, physically built specimens" of the ninety. After nurse #36 had her baby, Bradley removed his gloves and went over to the beautiful new mother to shake her hand. His approach was formal, as always, but nurse #36, still exuberant from her delivery, grabbed Bradley for a kiss. The kiss itself would not likely have been a memorable event, but Bradley's feet, as it happened, were wet with what he referred to as "the salt water that comes with babies" and as nurse #36 planted her lips on his, Bradley fell on top of the physically built specimen—a slapstick moment that left the residents and interns who had observed the birth in hysterics.

The story might have ended with that hearty laughter, but as Bradley left the delivery room, he came across nurse #36's "young, handsome lover and husband" in the waiting room. Bradley recalled the encounter vividly in his speech.

> This young husband was in that waiting room, his pupils dilated with fright to begin with, "Did my wife pull through all right?" And here I was, as the doctor, with her lipstick on my lips, with laughter and gaiety in the minds of everyone—we had forgotten all about the man who had started the whole business. I was so shocked and obstetrically so ashamed of myself, literally, that she would feel so much gratitude towards me. . . . [S]he was so grateful that I had coached that the thought occurred to me . . . why doesn't she fall more in love with her husband instead of her obstetrician?

Wanting to immediately right the wrong of nurse #36's misplaced love, Bradley marched downstairs to the hospital administrator's office and requested that the policy be changed to allow husbands to join their wives as they labored.

The hospital gave Bradley permission to conduct a study on the effects of men in the delivery room and as soon as the husbands joined their wives, Bradley noticed something: The mothers acted differently. They were more relaxed. A husband could sit in a room and do nothing and it still made a difference. But if Bradley moved a husband's chair out of his wife's sight, the effect would disappear and she would begin to panic.

At some point in his study, it occurred to Bradley that, as long as the husbands were hanging around in the delivery rooms, he might as well put them to work. Bradley assigned the fathers the job of rubbing their wives' backs, adjusting their pillows and feeding them ice. When he discovered that a mother responded much better to a father's call to relax than to the same request from a doctor, he instructed the fathers to put their hands on the mothers' abdomens to help with breathing and to whisper sweet nothings into their ears. "I discovered by actual experimentation that there is nothing as effective as the familiar voice of the husband whispering in his wife's ear the same love line of gobbledygook he whispered in her ear in the moonlight that started this whole business in the first place," Bradley said. "Nothing is more interesting to hear; I am continually amazed at the variety of patter."

Bradley later expanded the role of the father from labor coach to coach of the entire pregnancy. Husbands were even instructed to oversee their wives' diets so that they could be sure that they only ate from a list of permitted foods. "You would be amazed how the men see to it that their wives maintain their figure," Bradley noted.

In 1962 Bradley published a review of four thousand father-coached births. Ninety percent of them were unmedicated and Bradley saw the review as conclusive evidence that fathers were the key to successful, natural deliveries. In the following decades his crusade for *more* fathers in the delivery room led to the development of a full-fledged natural birth program with instructors around the country.

Bradley wasn't single-handedly responsible for the opening of delivery rooms to fathers. The feminist movement and the rise of other natural birth methods, particularly Lamaze, were also key factors in the gradual liberalization of American maternity wards. But Bradley played an important role and there is little question that his efforts paid off.

And yet, as dramatic as the change in the father's role has been over the decades, in recent years there has also been a quiet but unmistakable father backlash. Michel Odent, one of the most influential figures in the natural birth movement, now believes that women are better off without the father around. Odent cites anecdotal evidence that the presence of a father slows down a labor—exactly the opposite of what Bradley had found. "They [women] are convinced that they cannot give birth without the participation of the baby's father," Odent wrote in 2000. "But on the day of the birth, they say something different with their body language."

The best evidence for the father backlash is the rise of the doula, a woman who supports other women in childbirth but does not deliver babies herself—the word comes from the Greek word for "woman servant." In 2005 an estimated 120,000 to 200,000 births were attended by doulas, and the trend is gaining strength.

The rise of the modern doula can be traced to two American pediatricians, John Kennell and Marshall Klaus. Kennell and Klaus were studying maternal bonding in Guatemala in 1975, when, like Bradley, they arrived at their discovery almost by accident. As the story is recounted in the author and journalist Tina Cassidy's *Birth: The Surprising History of How We Are Born,* Kennell and Klaus were at a Guatemalan obstetric facility to investigate whether mothers who received emotional support during and after the birth of a child would form stronger bonds with their babies. The Guatemalan women were laboring in a room without any medical attendants, and, not wanting to barge in, Kennell and Klaus sent their female assistant into the room to obtain consent signatures for the study. It might not have seemed like the best time to ask someone to sign a consent form, but the Guatemalan women were happy to see the young assistant with her clipboard. The assistant stayed in the room and spoke with the women and apparently her presence alone led to a birthing frenzy. Three of the women delivered right there in the room before they could be brought to the delivery area. Three others had milk spurting out of their breasts.

Just as Bradley had found that the mere presence of fathers in a room helped women in labor, Kennell and Klaus would go on to publish a series of studies indicating that the presence of another woman in the delivery room could make a birth easier and reduce the need for medical intervention.

While there isn't a huge body of research to support the ideas of Bradley or Kennell and Klaus, there is an evolutionary theory that might explain both why human companionship *helps* a mother in labor and why giving birth alone is so rare in recorded history. Unlike our primate cousins, human babies are born facing away from their mothers, making it much more difficult for a woman to deliver her own baby. With this fact in mind, biological anthropologist Wenda Trevathan has theorized that the anxiety women feel about giving birth could be a biological adaptation, since women who failed to seek help during labor wouldn't have been very likely to have had babies who survived.

For her part, Jennifer did not want a doula. She said that while she could see the appeal, she feared bringing someone into the process who might have her own naturalist agenda that Jennifer didn't share.

I was pleased with Jennifer's decision. I felt bad about how little I could do during the labor and delivery and I didn't want to outsource my limited role to a stranger. But I could also see the broader case for replacing fathers with women who know what

they are doing. Our birth class instructor had said that it was crucial for the father to keep eye contact with the mother during the
advanced stages of labor, but I wasn't convinced that constant eye
contact with me was such a great strategy for a happy birth. In fact,
I could hardly think of anything more annoying for a woman wal-
lowing in pain than having to also deal with my worried gaze
locked on hers.

If anything, I thought, fathers should show up at the hospital
with their own respective dad doulas. While Jennifer's doula encouraged her along, I could sit off to the side with an experienced
father who would massage my shoulders and feed me trail mix, as
some female doulas are known to do for their clients. Perhaps dad
doulas could even bring along bottles of whiskey, and, if things
got tough, the dad and his doula could start taking shots together.

The more I pondered the dad doula, the more convinced I became that it was a genuinely good—if extremely gay—idea. Still, I
decided not to mention it to Jennifer at the time.*

---

* Upon further reflection, I'm no longer so sure that sharing a bottle of whiskey
with a dad doula is a good idea. While it may help to soothe the father's nerves, it
could lead to disaster if the doula dad turned out to be an angry drunk and began
trashing the delivery room.

EIGHT

Hypnotized Births

The Mother in the Trance

THE FIRST HYPNOTIZED BIRTH IN AMERICA is believed to have taken place in New Hampshire in the summer of 1837. According to an 1845 report by a well-known Parisian magnetizer, as hypnotists were then called, a Dr. Cutter of Nashua was called to attend the birth of a Mrs. Fern, a woman he had never met. Mrs. Fern had been in labor for forty-eight hours and had not slept for three nights. Dr. Cutter arrived on the scene and managed to put Mrs. Fern into a hypnotic trance in less than a minute. The midwives in attendance were astonished to discover that even while under Dr. Cutter's spell, Mrs. Fern's contractions continued "with perfect regularity." Even Dr. Cutter acknowledged his surprise.

It took another 160 years, but hypnotized birthing has finally caught on in America. There are now at least three separate schools of thought on how best to hypnotize a woman in labor. Two of the schools are engaged in an ongoing legal battle for the rights to the term *HypnoBirthing.* Choosing to remain above the fray, the third school calls itself Hypnobabies.

Marie "Mickey" Mongan is the biggest name in hypnotic birthing. Since opening her HypnoBirthing Institute in New Hampshire in 1989, she has traveled the country to train more than two thousand practitioners in "The Mongan Method." Most

of her students are doulas and midwives but Mongan also sometimes trains doctors and nurses.

I was surprised when one night, during the seventh month of
Jennifer's pregnancy, I found Mongan's book on our bed. It didn't
seem like the sort of thing Jennifer would be into. I brought the
book into the living room and held it up like a piece of evidence,
as though I had just uncovered Jennifer's secret porn stash.

"So you're into HypnoBirthing?"

"I'm just curious," Jennifer said. "It could help with the pain
before the epidural."

I started to express my doubt, then realized that I had no idea
what I was talking about. While I had read about the use of hypnosis in childbirth in the Soviet Union, I hadn't bothered to look up
any contemporary research on the subject.

I put Mongan's book down and took out my computer. A 2004
meta-analysis of the latest research on hypnosis in childbirth
found that hypnosis does appear to reduce the need for drugs, although the paper in the *British Journal of Anaesthesia* concluded
only that "there was a need for well-designed trials to confirm the
effects of hypnosis in childbirth." It wasn't a ringing endorsement, but it was more evidence than I expected to find.

I began to read Mongan's book in bed that night. As she tells
the story, Mongan's path to hypnosis began when she herself became pregnant for the first time in 1954. She was twenty-one and
her theological convictions had left her questioning the com-
monly held notion that childbirth was always painful. "I could not
believe," she writes, "that a God who had created the body with
such perfection could have designed a system of procreation that
was flawed."

Mongan's search for confirmation of her belief that having a
baby did not have to be a grueling experience led her to a copy of
Childbirth Without Fear by Dr. Grantly Dick-Read. The natural

birth movement is often traced to Lamaze but, though he only became famous after Lamaze arrived on the scene and popularized natural birth, Dick-Read came up with a birth program very similar to the Lamaze method a number of years before Lamaze first traveled to the Soviet Union. After reading Dick-Read's book, Mongan threw out all of the books she'd read about painful labors. She had found the safe, natural, and pain-free birthing method she had been looking for.

Dick-Read's interest in natural birth arose from a chance encounter. One rainy night in 1913, he was called to attend the labor of a woman in a squalid building near the railway arches in London's East End slums. Dick-Read stumbled up a dark staircase into a small room lit only by a candle stuck in the top of a beer bottle. The window was broken and rain was pouring into the room. In the light of the candle, Dick-Read saw his patient lying on a broken bed covered with sacks.

The birthing anesthetic of choice at the time was chloroform, and Dick-Read took his mask out of his bag. But to Dr. Dick-Read's great surprise, the woman did not want to be chloroformed. He put his mask away and stood by as the woman gave birth with no sign of distress.

It was the first time in Dick-Read's career that a laboring woman had turned down his chloroform mask, and it presented him with a puzzle: How could it be that some women could give birth with almost no discomfort while others screamed in agony?

Dr. Dick-Read was a man of medicine and he saw the pain of birth as a scientific question. But he was also a Christian, and despite the church's endorsement of painful labors—when James Young Simpson became the first doctor to anesthetize a birthing mother in 1847, the church rebuked him for robbing God of "the deep, earnest cries" of women in labor—Dick-Read also saw the intense pain of childbirth as a theological problem. If God was love, as he believed, and the birth of a child grew out of the great love between man and woman, how could this love culminate in such horrible agony?

In *Childbirth Without Fear,* Dick-Read sometimes sounds like a romantic poet:

> What manner of thing is this love that leads its most natural and perfect children to the green pastures of all that is beautiful in life and urges them on by a series of ever-increasing delights until their ultimate goal is in sight, then suddenly, and without mercy, chastises and terrifies them before hurling them unconscious, injured and resentful into the new world of motherhood? I strongly suggest there is only one answer—this is not the course of the Power of Love. This is not the purposeful design of creation. Somewhere, for some reason, an interloper has crept in, and must be eradicated.

Fortunately for Dick-Read and for the natural childbirth movement he helped to inspire, the woman lying in the sacks had given him an important clue for how to eradicate the suffering of childbirth. Before leaving her room, Dick-Read asked the woman why she hadn't wanted to be chloroformed.

"It didn't hurt," the woman said. "It wasn't meant to, was it, doctor?"

"For weeks and months afterward," Dick-Read wrote, "as I sat with women in labor, women who appeared to be in the terror and agony of childbirth, that sentence came drumming back into my ears . . . until finally, even through my orthodox and conservative mind, I began to see light."

The woman in the sacks hadn't felt pain, Dick-Read came to

think, because she hadn't expected to feel it. Childbirth wasn't a painful process, it was the fear of childbirth that caused the pain.

Over time, Dick-Read came to believe that women feared birth because they had grown up in societies where it was seen as a frightening rather than a joyful process. In *Childbirth Without Fear*, Dick-Read spends a lengthy chapter lamenting the depiction of birth in popular culture, even criticizing novelists for failing to write more positive accounts.

Dick-Read's proposed solution to the dilemma—breathing exercises, education, and a more welcoming and relaxing hospital environment to counter women's misplaced fears about birth— would turn out to be strikingly similar to a program being developed independently by Soviet scientists at the same time. And, perhaps because the British medical community didn't take Dick-Read's ideas seriously when he first published them in 1933, Dick-Read would later repackage the concept in scientific terminology much as the Soviets did. In the 1953 revision to *Childbirth Without Fear* (first published in 1944), Dick-Read put forth what he called the "Fear-Tension-Pain Syndrome of Childbirth." According to the theory, fear causes muscles to tense up as the body readies itself for a fight-or-flight response, and this tensing causes blood to flow away from the uterus. Without a sufficient blood supply, the uterus doesn't get enough oxygen and can't function properly. The poorly functioning uterus is the source of labor pains.

For Mongan, the leap from Dick-Read to hypnosis wasn't very far. Dick-Read himself had considered describing his method as hypnosis but feared the word might create the misleading impression that women were not in control of the process. Mongan added classic hypnotizing techniques, such as having women visualize objects and repeat mantras—to deepen the relaxation and prevent the onset of the Fear-Tension-Pain Syndrome.

As my research continued, I saw that Dick-Read was far from a saint. He subscribed to the nineteenth-century notion that working-class women and native African women felt less pain in childbirth because they were less civilized and so less influenced by modern misconceptions about childbirth. And despite making the Fear-Tension-Pain Syndrome the centerpiece of his theory, Dick-Read showed little interest in proving his famous theory with clinical data—a particularly strange omission since the core idea, that fear makes it harder to labor, is entirely plausible (adrenaline has been shown to stop contractions, which may be why many women report that their labors slow down when they arrive at the hospital). Perhaps even stranger, Dick-Read never seemed to have given any thought to the best explanation for why the poor woman in the sacks experienced less pain than most women: Not all people experience pain in the same way.

And yet the more I read about the history of Western birthing practices, the more I also started to see that to only criticize the natural birth movement for its failures is to overlook an important part of the movement's larger story.

The hospital birth is a relatively recent phenomenon from a historical perspective. Throughout most of recorded history, women have given birth in their homes. American lying-in facilities began to open in the early nineteenth century to treat homeless and poverty-stricken women who were grateful to have even a bed and a warm room. The wards were filthy and sometimes overrun by rats, and the unsanitary conditions increased the likelihood that mothers would die from infection. The biggest threat was puerperal, or childbed fever, a bacterial infection that killed two to three of every one thousand women in childbirth in the eighteenth and nineteenth centuries. And the bacteria continued to kill women well after germ theory was understood. In the 1920s the infections still accounted for 40 percent of maternal deaths in American hospitals. One 1933 report published by the New York Academy of Medicine found that women who gave birth at home were better off and that two-thirds of the hospital deaths were preventable and due to unhygienic practices.

The infections only came under control with the arrival of antibiotics in the 1940s, and by 1955, 99 percent of American women were giving birth in hospitals. But just because the worst was over didn't mean hospital births were a happy experience for most mothers. In the 1950s, at the time Dick-Read's book became a bestseller in America, delivery rooms often looked more like S&M chambers than hospitals. It was still common practice to strap women's legs to stirrups and bind their wrists to beds with leather cuffs. Once strapped down, women were sometimes left alone for hours, unable even to see their husbands.

This wasn't only misogyny on the part of hospital administrators and doctors. Many of the draconian measures had been made in the aftermath of studies such as the 1933 New York Academy of Medicine's report that unhygienic practices were killing women. Doctors had finally come to understand that germs were the leading cause of maternal death and they took the battle against those germs to a fanatical extreme: The less a woman in labor moved, the less likely she would be to contaminate herself.

But there is also little doubt that misogyny played a role or that few people were particularly worried about the emotional state of the mother as she lay bound in her germ-free chamber. Among the most frightening and common practices of twentieth-century obstetrics was "twilight sleep." In a twilight sleep delivery, a woman was given a combination of morphine and scopolamine, a drug that caused amnesia. Once a woman was out, the obstetrician would remove the fetus by whatever means he could come up with, even if it meant yanking it out with forceps—Robert Bradley, founder of the Bradley method, referred to it as "knock-em-out, drag-em-out obstetrics." Incredible though it now seems, twilight sleep was championed by the early feminists who noticed that doctors and scientists of the era had put great effort into finding surgical anesthetics without giving much thought to the pain of childbirth. But the practice continued long after the truth of what was happening to many women during twilight sleep births was well known. In her history of birth, Tina Cassidy writes of women in twilight births being forced to wear helmets, straitjackets, and wrist cuffs so that they would not be injured as they thrashed about.

It was against this backdrop that Dick-Read published *Childbirth Without Fear,* and if the book was short on science, it made up for it with empathy.

Dick-Read spends several pages describing the plight of a laboring woman in a 1940s maternity ward and then imagines a disoriented woman walking into her delivery room for the first time:

> She does not fail to notice the glass-fronted cupboard in which hangs a large collection of instruments; she has heard of instruments but had no idea that they looked like that. On the table by her bed are bowls, dressings and towels; at the head of the bed, or somewhere nearby, are stands with cylinders of gas. Then she climbs upon a high bed, harder and more uncomfortable than any she has ever known; she probably feels the chill of the mackintosh sheet with only one thin covering over it. She lies in whatever position she is told.

I wonder if the average man can even imagine the thoughts that would go through his mind if he were subjected to a similar experience?

There were plenty of awful things for Dick-Read to notice about the experience of women in hospitals. But Dick-Read also noticed the sheets. It's no wonder then that *Childbirth Without Fear* resonated with so many women. When his wife first read the unfinished manuscript, she told Dick-Read it was the book women had been waiting for for centuries.

And so to the many pregnant women who embraced Dick-Read in the 1950s, it probably didn't matter that his Fear-Tension-Pain Syndrome was never proven, or that he seemed strangely uninterested in finding empirical evidence for it. What mattered was that a doctor was finally taking the indignities of laboring women in hospitals seriously.

If Dick-Read and many of the other natural birth pioneers often got their science wrong, just as often they got the larger human story exactly right.

A FEW WEEKS AFTER I first discovered Mongan's book on Hypno-Birthing, Jennifer and I went into Manhattan together to meet with Suzanne Fremon, a retired concert pianist who had studied with Mongan and found a second career in hypnotizing pregnant women.

Fremon welcomed Jennifer and me into her apartment and led us into a musty, book-filled living room with a grand piano in the corner. She was tall and thin with wavy gray hair. Her light blue T-shirt said "Hypnodoula" across the chest.

Jennifer and I sat down on a worn red couch next to a Turkish coffee table. We chatted for a few minutes, and then I asked Fremon if she really believed it was possible to enter a hypnotic trance while giving birth.

"We slip in and out of trance states all the time," she said. "There's a part of the brain that's below the conscious level, below the cerebral cortex. It's the part of the brain that you access when you're just looking out of the window, and you tune out."

Fremon went on. "Athletes call this trance state being in the zone and musicians talk about the alpha state. All we do with pregnant women is cumulatively develop the techniques to enter these trances."

Fremon spoke in the soft, reassuring voice you'd expect of a hypnotist. I could tell she had given this answer before.

"The truth is that the body knows what to do during labor," Fremon said. "All we need to do is get out of its way."

Fremon asked Jennifer and me to follow her into a spare bedroom where she kept a TV and VCR, and then showed us footage of hypnodoulas walking over hot coals at a hypnodoula retreat.

After a minute or two, the video switched to the scene of a HypnoBirth that appeared to be taking place in a hospital. The decidedly relaxed-looking mother was lying in bed with a wet towel wrapped around her head. Off camera, a woman chanted in a quiet voice: "Mother and baby working together. Mind and body working together . . ."

"That's Marie Mongan," Fremon said. "She's giving the affirmations."

Mongan's book recommends that pregnant women read or listen to affirmations every day during the last months of pregnancy and includes a list of sample phrases:

I am relaxed and happy that my baby is coming to me.
My cervix opens outward and allows my baby to ease down.

My baby's birth will be easy because I am so relaxed.
The tissues in my birth path are pink and healthy.
As my baby is born, my blood vessels close to the appropriate
  degree.

"I can't believe how calm the mother looks," Jennifer said.

"You hear about pain pain pain," Fremon said. "In nature, pain is a sign that something is wrong—a broken bone, an appendix, a sore tooth. In childbirth, there's no reason for it to be painful except fear and tension."

I noticed the slightest tightening in the laboring woman's face. "Is she having contractions?" I asked.

"Yes," Fremon said. "But it's important what words you use. We do not refer to contractions. We call them surges or waves."

Mongan's book includes a list of similar translations. "Pushing" in HypnoBirth is "Birth Breathing." A "Due Date" is a "Birthing Time." "Complications" are "Special Circumstances." The translations are more than wordplay. Mongan believes that words have a physiological impact on people and that negative words and thoughts come back to negatively impact the bodies of the people who think and speak them. This is why affirmations are so important. A successful HypnoBirth relies upon positive words and thoughts. As evidence for the power of words, Mongan notes that healthy people rarely speak of becoming ill, whereas unhealthy people tend to talk about sickness.

When the baby's gooey head began to emerge out of the still relaxed-looking mother, Jennifer and I both instinctively turned away.

"It's messy, but it's not painful," Fremon said. "It feels like a very large bowel movement because that's where the pressure is."

I looked at Fremon. She seemed to see the skepticism in my eyes.

"It feels wonderful," she said.

We sat and watched as the baby was born with no sign of exerting on the part of the mother, and then Fremon turned the TV off.

"Couldn't it just be called 'relaxation birth'?" I asked.

"Well, you can't really copyright that," Fremon said. "But when you say HypnoBirthing people don't think you're nuts anymore. They used to. Up until maybe three years ago, you had to either not mention it or explain it very carefully because people thought hypnosis and voodoo were kind of the same thing."

"How about 'meditative birthing'?"

"That would have been even creepier," Fremon said. "It is hypnosis and you might as well say so."

I let it go. We followed Fremon back into the living room. She handed Jennifer a pin that said "Shhh! Only Good Birth Stories," and offered to give us a hypnosis demonstration. She said that it was late in Jennifer's pregnancy to begin the training, but that if Jennifer practiced a lot she could still enjoy some of the benefits of HypnoBirthing.

At a more advanced stage in the training, Mongan recommends specific visualizations. The pregnant mother is asked to picture the opening of the perineum as "the gentle unfolding of the petals of the rose." The muscles that thin and open the cervix are visualized as "blue satin ribbons." Jennifer and I would be starting with something simpler.

"Imagine heavy, sand-filled buckets attached to our left wrists," Fremon said.

I stood in silence and thought about a sand-filled bucket on my left wrist.

"Imagine a helium balloon on your right wrist," she said.

After ten seconds, Fremon told us to open our eyes. "Now look," she said. "Is there a bucket on that arm or a balloon on the other arm?"

I shook my head. "But you could feel something, couldn't you?"

I nodded. I don't know if my arm felt anything like how it would feel if I'd been holding an actual sand-filled bucket, but I did notice an unpleasant tenseness in my muscles.

"The point is that the body can follow what the mind tells it," Fremon said.

For our next exercise, Fremon said that we'd be taking a trip. "Close your eyes and imagine yourself in a very special place," she said. "It can be somewhere you've been, where you feel comfortable, relaxed, and safe, or somewhere you'd like to go."

I closed my eyes and thought of Bermuda. I have never been to Bermuda and have no real sense of what it looks like but it is apparently the place I most identify with relaxation. I saw myself alone by the ocean. The white sand of the beach was littered with coconuts and every one of them had a tiny umbrella sticking out of it.

It was a nice vision, and I would like to have stayed on that beach for a while. But my brain had its own agenda, and within a few seconds I had moved on to my other association with Bermuda: plane crashes; another few seconds and the coconuts had been replaced by Amelia Earhart's rotting bones.

I changed course and pictured a hilly Alpine expanse. In no time Julie Andrews was spinning and singing on the hills, and I enjoyed her angelic voice for a moment. Then I recalled that *The Sound of Music* had given countless Americans a false picture of Austria's role in Hitler's crimes.

"I'm going to count from one to five and then I want you to come on back," Fremon said.

I opened my eyes. Fremon was smiling. "You can take these little trips anytime you want," she said.

NINE

Labor

Evolution and the Problem of Childbirth

As if the entire process is not nerve-racking enough, the end of a pregnancy comes with its own built-in practical jokes, also known as Braxton Hicks contractions. Braxton Hicks, or false, contractions feel just like real contractions, only they don't signify the onset of labor.

The first time Jennifer had a Braxton Hicks contraction, a few weeks before her due date, I was ready to rush to the hospital. This isn't what the pregnancy experts tell you to do. Even when the contractions really are the start of labor, there is still usually a long period, often days, between the first wave of pain and the birth. Dr. Spock recommends waiting until the contractions continue for over an hour and are less than five minutes apart.

I was aware of all of this expert advice, but I was no fool. I had seen enough half-hour sitcoms in the 1980s to know how it really works: A pregnant woman feels a pain and then puts her hand on her belly with a look of consternation. After a brief dramatic pause, she says, "I think I'm having my baby." The man in the room with her—it is always a man—looks as though he has just swallowed a golf-ball-sized portion of horseradish, and within twenty-two minutes the woman gives birth, usually, but not always, in a stuck elevator.

Knowing what I knew about the sitcom births, we probably would have been camped out in the hospital for the entire third trimester if I had been calling the shots. Even getting to the hospital three months early struck me as vaguely risky. In a perfect world, I thought, there would be hospital-hotels that couples would move into on the day they learned they were expecting. In addition to the standard amenities, the hospital-hotels would offer free ultrasounds until 9 P.M. every night of the week and twenty-four-hour all-you-can-eat buffets with enough weird ingredients to satisfy every possible pregnancy craving. In place of porn, there would be on-demand birth videos and every morning the cleaning staff would leave enormous prenatal vitamins on the pillows. In the gym, women with unusually fit pelvic regions would lead intensive Kegel workouts and chairs would be set up around the room for those mothers who preferred only to watch and make kegel jokes. Once a week shuttle buses would take the would-be parents to baby superstores and upon their return, a team of crisis counselors and financial advisors would be waiting in the lobby. On the day a woman went into labor, she or the father would push a button on the phone—the same as one might for clean towels—and doctors and nurses would be there within two minutes or your entire birth would be free.*

But the world is not perfect, and, fortunately for everyone involved, I was not calling the shots. Jennifer recognized the Braxton Hicks contractions for what they were and after a while even I stopped worrying about them. There are only so many times you can freak out before your nervous system says the hell with it and begins to ignore you, and I had reached my limit.

---

* Although it's not integral to the idea, ideally the obstetricians would stay on floors above the guests and slide down firemen's poles to the women in labor—the act of sliding, as with firemen, is as much about the theatrics of urgency as about saving time.

In fact, impossible though it now seems, I became too calm. The Braxton Hicks contractions had lulled me into such a stupor that when Jennifer told me she thought she was in labor late one June night, I hardly paid attention. It was still six days before her due date, and I was sure it was yet another false alarm.

By noon the next day, Jennifer was increasingly convinced that she was in early labor, and I understood that the baby would be coming sooner rather than later. But I only fully grasped what was happening that evening when I walked into our bedroom and found Jennifer sprawled across our bed writing down times on a small piece of yellow paper.

"What's going on?" I asked.

"I'm writing down the contraction times," Jennifer said.

"But don't you only do that when it's, like, officially started?"

"Haven't you heard me collapsing onto the bed in pain every fifteen minutes?"

"I, um . . . no," I said.

I had only been about twenty feet away, and yet I had somehow failed to notice my wife repeatedly experiencing the worst pain of her life.

It was not an auspicious start to fatherhood, and, anxious to do better, I snatched the yellow piece of paper from Jennifer and told her that I would take over the recording of the contractions. For the next hour, I shadowed Jennifer around our apartment, pen and paper in hand, like her authorized pregnancy biographer. Boswell never paid such attention to Johnson. By comparison the paparazzi were ignoring Britney Spears.

Jennifer, seemingly in the grips of the nesting instinct that leads birds and women alike to prepare their homes for newborns, was furiously scrubbing the kitchen. When a contraction came on, she would drop her sponge and race to our bed, and I would race after her, feeling miserable that I could do so little to help.

The only good thing about the contractions was how quickly Jennifer would recover from them. One minute she would be face down on our bed, bitch-slapping the mattress with an open palm, and the next she would be back in the kitchen scraping gook out of the cracks of our tiled counters. It was like watching a professional house cleaner with a severe personality disorder.

At some point Jennifer told me to stop following her around with my pen and paper and to start helping her get the apartment ready for the baby. I told her I would, but, much as I wanted to help, there was little left to do. In the previous week I had worked hard to make sure that everything would be in order when Jennifer went into labor. I had assembled both our new oak wood changing table—a process that had somehow left me flat on my back with the changing table resting on my face—and also our new deluxe co-sleeper—a process that had somehow left me flat on my back with the co-sleeper resting on my face. I had removed all unidentifiable items from our refrigerator and cleared our pantry of everything that had been expired for more than a year.

I had even packed for the hospital. I am almost constitutionally incapable of filling a suitcase more than fifteen minutes before I have to leave on a trip, but for this special occasion I had abandoned even this most cherished of idiotic habits and filled two backpacks with everything that Jennifer and I might need: clothes, a video camera, granola bars, bottled water, flip-flops, a birth plan with instructions for the nurses to not give our baby formula, a radio, a still camera, batteries, and my laptop. Those items I hadn't managed to fit into the backpacks—a robe, a regular pillow, a breastfeeding pillow, DVDs to watch on my laptop, including *The Sorrow and the Pity,* a four-hour documentary on the

French Nazis that happened to be the only unwatched DVD in our collection—had been stuffed into a large white garbage bag.

Even the baby's name, "Isaac," was ready. The name comes from the Hebrew for "laughter," and we'd both liked it from the start. Because "Isaac" is my father's middle name, we'd initially ruled it out in deference to the Jewish superstition against naming a child after a living relative. But after giving it some thought, I made my own emergency rabbinic ruling and declared that the superstition didn't apply to middle names. Besides, we'd already disregarded the superstition against buying things for the baby before the birth. If anything, I reasoned, the two infractions would cancel each other out and we'd be back on firm theological footing.

By 1:30 A.M., our apartment was cleaner than it had ever been in the four years we'd lived there, and Jennifer's contractions were still around seven minutes apart. I'd remained mostly calm up to that point, but with each passing hour, I was growing more anxious to get to the hospital.

It didn't help that at some point during those few hours—I believe it was shortly after I'd finished using our brand-new diaper disposal system to bang out a stuck joint in the co-sleeper—I'd had a disturbing thought: The law of the sitcom birth is not only that the entire labor must take place within twenty-two minutes with the assistance of a man who looks as though he has just swallowed a golf-ball-sized serving of horseradish. The law also dictates that the least competent character on the show—Skippy on *Family Ties,* Balki Bartokomous on *Perfect Strangers*—always ends up delivering the baby.

The thought of Skippy delivering a baby is disturbing in its own right, but that wasn't what troubled me at that particular moment. The troubling part was that, with no bumbling neighbor to fill the void, I was without question the least competent character in the sitcom of our lives. If the sitcoms offered even the murkiest reflection of the world as it is, then I was going to end up delivering our baby—quite possibly in a stuck elevator.

Of all the different births playing on my mind's big-screen TV, the harrowing elevator delivery overseen by Vinnie Delpino, the sexually frustrated sidekick on *Doogie Howser, M.D.*, bothered me most. I can only guess at why, of all the countless things I might have thought about on the verge of fatherhood, my mind had settled on a dramatic comedy about a mild-mannered teenage doctor that hadn't been on the air for over a decade. Part of the explanation may be that my thoughts at a given moment have only a tenuous connection to what is actually happening around me at that moment. But I think I was also drawn to the heightened irony of Delpino's dilemma. His best friend was a teenage doctor-genius. Delpino's role in life was to be the anti-Howser, the goofball foil to Doogie's astonishing precociousness. Doogie was the one who should have been stuck in that elevator with that pregnant woman and everyone knew it. And even if part of me knew that real labors could not be anything like sitcom labors, it seemed at least possible that the eighties shows got this one larger truth right: In life, as in television, the ironic twist is always a looming threat—the cat sometimes bites the dog; the anti-Howser is sometimes forced to play the Howser.

At around two in the morning, with Jennifer's contractions still six to seven minutes apart, I stopped doing whatever I was doing and turned to Jennifer.

"I think we should just go to the hospital," I said.

"Yeah, you're right," Jennifer said. "Let me just finish sweeping the kitchen."

I'D DONE ENOUGH READING to have at least a vague idea of what was beginning to happen inside Jennifer's body. And what I'd come to appreciate is wonderful news for ten-year-old boys everywhere. It turns out that we are all Houdinis—or, at least, everyone who was born vaginally is a Houdini.* To make it out of a woman's body and into the world a baby has to go through an ordeal so cumbersome that I'm almost surprised natural selection didn't find a way to encase the uterus in a chained box, complete with padlocks for babies to pick on the way out.

Labor begins with contractions, a tightening and relaxing of the muscles of the uterus. Some women describe contractions as intense cramps. Others find them more like a radiating ache that moves through the lower back and abdomen. The contractions gradually push the baby down to the cervix, a cylindrical muscle at the base of the uterus that slowly opens, or dilates, as labor progresses. The cervix needs to be fully dilated to ten centimeters for a baby's head to make it all the way through, and even once the cervix is fully dilated, the most complicated part of the process is yet to begin. The opening of a woman's pelvis is widest from side to side, but at about the midpoint of the pelvis, the passage narrows and becomes deeper from front to back. To make it through, the ideally positioned fetus will begin the passage facing the mother's side and then rotate anywhere from 45 to 90 degrees—imagine trying to get out of a cave with an opening so small that you have to wiggle your head and face through and that, once you manage this incredible feat, you still have to figure out how to get your shoulders out.

Depending on your perspective, the real culprit in the difficulty of human childbirth is either walking or intelligence. Upright walking requires a small fixed pelvis and human intel-

---

* C-section babies shouldn't feel left out. In their ability to move from inside to outside the womb in a blink of an eye, C-section babies are at least Copperfields. And admittedly, while being a Houdini is much much better than being a Copperfield, being a Copperfield is not nothing.

ligence requires a head that is far too large to have any business making its way through a small pelvis. Women's bodies did what they could to keep up with our ever-expanding heads over the last few million years, and the lower part of the pelvis widened bit by bit over the millennia. But there is only so far you can push a pelvis if you want to walk on two feet, and so a series of additional biological tricks evolved to make human birth possible. The joints of the pelvis loosen during pregnancy to make the passage slightly larger and the bones of the fetal skull are left unfused so that our heads can squeeze through the birth canal—this is why some babies enter the world looking like new additions to the Conehead family.

Still, strange though it is that human pelvises can expand and baby heads can be squeezed, natural selection found another, even more radical, solution to the problem of big brains and small pelvises: We are all born prematurely. In the last few decades a number of biological anthropologists have pointed out that human babies are essentially fetuses for the first year of life. We have to be born at forty weeks or else our heads would be too big to make it through the birth canal, but our brains are still in a fairly early stage of development relative to most mammalian newborns, even relative to the newborns of chimpanzees, our closest cousins. Most mammals are born precocial, meaning that almost immediately after birth they are somewhat independent. A new sheep, thanks to its mostly-formed brain, can stand up and walk around from the moment it lands on the earth. Human newborns, by contrast, are altricial, meaning that they are physically helpless and entirely dependent on their parents for food and protection as their brains continue to grow at a rapid, fetuslike pace throughout much of the first year of life.

It took decades for anthropologists to accept the idea that babies are really fetuses, with immature brains, because it makes little sense from a Darwinian perspective that our babies would develop so differently from chimp babies. The answer to the mystery appears to be that human newborns are only secondarily altricial. Strange though it is to imagine a baby emerging from the womb and crawling around, at one point in early hominid history, when our brains were much smaller, our newborns were developmentally much more like one-year-olds than newborns today. The helpless altricial stage came only later, when the constraints of childbirth made a full gestation period incompatible with the size of our heads. In his 1997 book *Ever Since Darwin,* the late evolutionary scientist Stephen Jay Gould argues that if women gave birth when they "should," they would be pregnant for a year and a half.

But if the trade-off between walking and big brains explains why birth can be so difficult and why it's hard to care for newborns, it doesn't explain a broader evolutionary puzzle: How could natural selection, a process that revolves around successful reproduction, have given us such dangerous births? Prior to modern medicine, childbirth was the leading cause of death among young women and babies, and even today some five hundred thousand women around the world die in childbirth every year, most of them in third-world countries. As Darwinian scholars explain it, the seeming contradiction only disappears when you remember that from natural selection's perspective, it doesn't matter if a mother's method of reproducing, or more specifically, of making copies of her genes, is difficult. What matters is whether the mother does a better job of making copies of her genes than her competitors in a given environment. And the question of whether a mother's genes will survive the Darwinian dogfight can only be answered by looking at a number of generations.

Take the case of two prehistoric mothers. One mother gives birth to lots of small-headed babies with gorilla-like ease and another suffers and dies while delivering a single surviving big-head baby. In the next generation, there will be more copies of the genes of the mother of the small-headed babies, but if those small-headed babies don't have the intellectual equipment to survive and reproduce themselves, their mother's genes will die out. Meanwhile, if the large-headed baby of the dead mother survives and has a child, by the third generation the genes of the dead mother will continue to circulate in the population.

Put another way, human births are difficult because nature doesn't care about us. Natural selection is a blind process guided by gene replication rather than concern for our suffering. This is what the romantics and religious natural birth pioneers like Dick-Read failed to understand or refused to accept. In most cases natural selection only relied on physical pain to keep us from doing stupid things, like sticking our hands in fires. But in some instances, pain is a by-product of other selective pressures—as teething babies might point out if they could talk.

It could be worse. In some insect species, mothers always die after laying their eggs. And some mammals have more difficult births than humans. The ratio between the size of the infant head and the size of the mother's birth canal in tarsier monkeys makes human birth seem like a blast. And even tarsier monkey births can seem easy compared to what female spotted hyenas go through. Spotted hyenas give birth through an elongated organ that looks almost identical to an engorged hyena penis. Some 65 to 70 percent of firstborn spotted hyenas die trying to get out of that engorged penis, and 18 percent of the birthing mothers die during their deliveries.

I DIDN'T KNOW quite what to expect when Jennifer and I stepped out of the cab we took to the hospital in Manhattan and then walked through the maternity ward's swinging metal doors. If I'd had to guess, I probably would have said that our experience wouldn't be so different from that of someone with a serious injury entering the emergency room: A team of nurses would whisk Jennifer away on a gurney and I would chase after them knocking over the surprising number of metal carts in my path. As I ran I would be shouting "Everything is going to be okay" over and over until finally, one of the nurses would let go of the gurney, grab me by the shoulders, and say, "Sir, I'm going to need you to calm down now," at which point, depending on the state of my panic, I would either apologize profusely or shout "That's my wife and my baby, damn you" and take off after the gurney again.

What actually happened when we arrived at the maternity ward reminded me less of walking into an emergency room than of walking into an Olive Garden with a bad hostess. The woman behind the admitting desk was talking to a nurse, and, though she glanced in our direction, she seemed entirely unconcerned that a pregnant woman who looked like she was about to die was standing three feet away from her.

"I'll be with you in a minute," the woman said, returning to her conversation. At the time I was angry, but later I realized that the woman probably sees fifteen women in Jennifer's state every night. Probably outside of the CIA's interrogation units, there are no Americans as immune to the suffering of their fellow citizens as the people who admit women into hospital maternity wards.

After what felt like an hour but was probably five minutes, a Caribbean nurse with dyed red hair emerged from a door behind the admitting desk and led us into a tiny room. The nurse asked Jennifer to lie down on an examination table and then attached a monitoring device to her belly that made the baby's heartbeat audible.

"You're doing so good," I said, putting my hand on Jennifer's arm.

Jennifer flinched. She looked not only uncomfortable but also disgusted, as though I'd dipped my hand in a vat of horse urine just before reaching out to her.

"Please don't touch me right now," she said.

The nurse said that a doctor would arrive soon and left us alone.

This was the moment I'd been looking forward to, the moment when we'd be safely in the hands of the professionals who would take over the process and give us our baby. But now that the moment was upon us, I felt more scared and sad than relieved.

"I just want the doctor to come," Jennifer said.

"She'll be here really soon," I said.

I saw a small roach on the floor and tried to quietly step on it before Jennifer spotted it. "You're doing so good," I said.

For the next minute or two, we were silent, the whooshing, thumping sounds of our baby's heart the only noise in the room. I stared at Jennifer and the wires running from her body, and couldn't escape the feeling that Jennifer was sick and that I was visiting her in the hospital.

"You're doing so good," I said again, fighting back tears.

A young doctor with short curly hair arrived, examined Jennifer, and announced that her cervix was only three centimeters dilated. "I think it would be best if you came back in a few hours or when the contractions start to really pick up," she said.

Start to pick up? It was like telling someone who's just finished a marathon to get ready for the real race.

"So there's no way I can just get an epidural now?" Jennifer asked, the disbelief audible in her voice.

"If I admitted you and you got an epidural now it could slow down the process," the doctor said.

Although we didn't know it at the time, it isn't necessarily true that epidurals slow down labors. A study from the 1990s did find that epidurals given near the halfway point (five centimeters of dilation) increase the likelihood of a C-section, and for this reason, the American College of Obstetricians and Gynecologists still recommends that "when feasible," first-time mothers should only be given an epidural when the cervix is at least four or five centimeters dilated. But a 2005 study in *The New England Journal of Medicine* found no difference in the C-section rate among women who received epidurals when only several centimeters dilated and those who received them later. And there's another reason that hospitals may not want to admit women early in labor. Insurance companies have long resisted paying for long hospital stays for pregnant women. The problem became so bad in the early nineties that many hospitals began forcing women who delivered vaginally to leave within twelve to twenty-four hours—women who had C-sections were allowed to stay for forty-eight hours. "When someone says 'push' in a delivery room these days, you don't know if it's to get the baby out of the womb or the mother out of the hospital," one New Jersey state senator remarked in 1995.

"So, you really want us to leave?" I asked the doctor. It was the middle of the night, and we were not about to take another forty-five-minute cab ride back to Brooklyn.

"I think that would probably make the most sense at this point," the doctor said.

It didn't make the most sense to me. If Jennifer had been suffering from any overwhelming pain other than the pain of childbirth, she would almost certainly have been admitted without question. In retrospect I realized that I should have put up a fight. There is a precedent for fathers making a stand in the maternity ward. A California college student once chained himself to his wife's hospital bed when he was told he couldn't stay for the delivery. But Jennifer and I were both too tired and confused to argue with a doctor. And so I gathered our belongings and Jennifer and I headed out into the unknown, a modern-day Adam and Eve exiled from the garden of epidurals.

It was three in the morning. Not particularly wanting to wander the streets of an unfamiliar New York City neighborhood, we did the only thing we could: We set up shop in the dim and abandoned hospital lobby. Jennifer spread out on a couch in a small lounge area, and I removed a pillow from our garbage bag and put it under her head.

"We look like we're homeless," Jennifer said.

It was the first sign of life I'd seen from Jennifer in the last hour, and it made me feel much better. "We're going to be the first couple to get to the hospital hours early and still not make it to the delivery room," I said.

I was joking but a few minutes later, giving birth in the lobby was beginning to look like an increasingly realistic possibility. The cervical examination, as is known to happen, seemed to have sped up Jennifer's labor. Almost as soon as Jennifer put her head on the pillow, she was back up on her knees, leaning over the back of the couch and pounding the wall.

"You're doing great," I said.

Jennifer got up from the couch and began walking around and around the lobby's oval information desk, pausing and pounding on the counter every few minutes as another contraction swept through her. At some point she decided that it would help her if I counted aloud during the contractions and so I followed her and counted. Later it occurred to me that the scene of the two of us walking laps in that dark hospital lobby wasn't a sitcom scene at all but rather the final act of an existential comedy—*Waiting for Bebe?*—about a pregnancy that never ends. The mother would circle that information desk forever and the father would count to infinity but they would never get any closer to the immortality that is parenthood's false promise.

After an hour, Jennifer's contractions were three minutes apart and I wasn't sure if the hospital's furniture could hold out much longer.

"I don't care what they say," Jennifer said. "I'm going back upstairs and I'm having this baby."

Jennifer thinks I'm crazy and completely denies it, but I am almost certain that I noticed the slightest hint of an African American intonation when she said this last sentence. (The intonation, often exaggerated by comedians, is generally used in statements that begin with a drawn-out "girlfriend.") I didn't say anything at the time, but as I gathered our belongings, it momentarily occurred to me that while the use of this voice might at first appear to be an offensive racial stereotype, the fact that nonblack women regularly adopt a distinctly black mannerism to convey their determination might also be seen as a wonderful triumph for black feminism, a small but significant testament to the growing influence of the black woman in American society.

At another time I almost certainly would have stayed with the thought longer. I probably would have continued to flesh out the argument in my head and then imagined myself publishing an editorial on the subject and becoming a celebrated figure in black feminist circles. Probably within five minutes I would already have been envisioning my NAACP Award acceptance speech: *Girlfriends, we did it!* . . .

But at that particular moment there was no time to imagine myself as the champion of black feminism. A small person had been hanging out inside Jennifer for more than nine months. It was time to get him out of there.

PART TWO

...AFTER

TEN

Delivery

The Rise of the C-Section

OBSTETRICS HAS ALWAYS INVOLVED GUESSWORK. The first-century A.D. Roman author Pliny the Elder recommended that a woman in the midst of a difficult labor drink goose semen mixed with water. If that didn't work, she might also try a glass of "the liquids that flow from a weasel's uterus through its genitals." It was strange advice, and it is hard to imagine that Pliny the Elder had solid evidence for the benefits of goose semen or weasel liquids. But for most of the next two thousand years, the field of obstetrics didn't become much more scientific. In a 1911 report of the American Gynecological Society on recent advances in obstetrics, one OB marveled at how far the profession had come. "Twenty-five years ago it would have been difficult to find a doctor who had not many times had his hand and arm as far as the elbow in the uterus," he noted, in reference to the mistaken belief that a placenta needed to be yanked out almost immediately after a birth.

By the time Jennifer walked into the hospital delivery room doubled over in pain, she probably would have been willing to down a shot of weasel liquids if it would have moved things along. It was four-thirty in the morning, and Jennifer had already experienced much of the agony she had hoped to avoid.

"Try and rest," I told Jennifer as she climbed onto the reclining bed in the middle of the room.

"I just want to know when I can get the epidural," Jennifer said.

It took another hour for the anesthesiologist to arrive but when he finally did, the drugs worked almost immediately, and Jennifer was free from pain for the first time in twelve hours. This was the point at which I'd planned to break out my laptop and *The Sorrow and the Pity,* but we were both far too exhausted and overwhelmed to watch a Holocaust documentary. And, besides, from the moment I sat down, I was already fixated on another screen.

Just to the left of Jennifer was a computer monitor with three different colored lines running across it. I knew that one line was tracking the contractions and that the others were monitoring the respective heart rates of Jennifer and the baby, but I didn't know which line was which, or what exactly the up-and-down movement of the lines indicated. I was watching the lines like a policeman watches a peaceful crowd: I just wanted to be sure that everything kept moving along as it should.

For the first half hour, one of the lines, presumably the contraction line, would sometimes bounce up and down, while the other lines moved along in steady up-and-down peaks like a mountain range. Jennifer was resting with her eyes closed and as my eyes followed the lines across the screen, I began to fade in and out of a trancelike sleep, perhaps inadvertently becoming the world's first HypnoFather.

But at around five-thirty in the morning, I noticed that something had changed. One of the previously steady lines was rocketing up and then falling at sharp angles. I didn't know what the change meant, but I knew that it couldn't be good.

I hurried out of the room to get help. A nurse stood in front of the neighboring doorway. "I think something's wrong," I said.

"What is it?"

"One of the lines is going crazy."

The nurse followed me back to the monitor, looked at it for about ten seconds, and then muttered the five words, other than "you are going to die," that you least want to hear from a medical professional looking at your vital information. "No, that can't be right," she said.

Jennifer opened her eyes, surprised to find the two of us standing by her side. "What's going on?" she asked.

"It looks like your heart rate is much too slow," the nurse said, "but that can't be right."

The nurse looked at the monitor for another moment, and then she must have pushed a button or run out into the hall. I don't remember. The next thing I recall is a half-dozen doctors rushing into the room.

In his book *Better: A Surgeon's Notes on Performance,* the surgeon and medical writer Atul Gawande lists just a few of the ways deliveries often jeopardized the lives of mothers and babies before modern medicine. The mother can hemorrhage; the placenta can tear or become stuck; the uterus sometimes ruptures or fails to contract after a delivery; once a mother's water breaks, bacteria can enter the uterus and cause infections, a problem that, prior to antibiotics, caused countless women to die in hospitals as doctors spread germs from one mother to the next.

And then there is the most common problem of all: Fetuses become stuck on the way out. Sometimes a fetus is just too big to make it through the birth canal—an increasingly common problem as improved diets have given rise to bigger fetuses. Other times the problem is not the size but the position of the fetus in the uterus. "The baby might arrive at the birth canal sideways, with nothing but an arm sticking out," Gawande writes. "It could be a breech, coming butt first and getting stuck with its legs up on its chest. It could be a footling breech, coming feet first, but then getting wedged at the chest with the arms above the head. It could come out head first but get stuck because the head is turned the wrong way."

Much of the history of obstetrics is the story of the different techniques midwives and physicians have developed over the centuries to deliver these stuck babies, and up until a few hundred years ago, most of the techniques left either the mother or the baby dead. If there was no way to deliver a fetus, a mother's best hope was for a surgeon to kill it with crotchets and blunt hooks and then to remove the body piece by piece.

In the middle of the sixteenth century, Ambroise Paré, a famous French army surgeon, made an important advance in obstetrics. Paré realized that he could save some fetuses in the wrong position by reaching into the womb and rotating them until he could grab hold of their feet—which were easier to grip than the head. A miniature foot in each hand, Paré would pull hard and hope for the best. If the head became stuck, a second labor attendant would press down on the woman's abdomen. The technique, known as the podalic version, had been practiced in antiquity but had fallen out of use.

The end of the sixteenth century brought another important discovery. Surgeons had used tools to kill and remove fetuses for centuries, but until Peter Chamberlen, a French Huguenot refugee in England, invented obstetrical forceps, no one had realized that tools could also be used to save fetuses. Chamberlen's forceps looked like scissors with large spoons in place of the blades, and by allowing him to clamp the head of stuck fetuses and pull them out, they promised to instantly revolutionize childbirth and save countless lives. But Chamberlen, like most sixteenth-century Europeans, wasn't particularly altruistic. Realizing that his invention gave him an advantage over other mid-wives and surgeons of the era, he decided to keep his forceps a family secret. The decision paid off. The next generation of Chamberlen men followed Peter into obstetrics and became the personal midwives of the British royal family.

To keep their secret safe, the Chamberlens carried their forceps around in a locked trunk and insisted that no one witness the deliveries. Because it was customary at the time for male mid-wives to tie sheets around their necks—the sheets prevented them from looking at a woman's genitals, but also forced them to work by feel alone—not even the birthing mothers saw the device.* Still, just to be on the safe side, the Chamberlens are believed to have also blindfolded some mothers.

How the secret of the Chamberlen forceps leaked remains a source of scholarly dispute but by the middle of the eighteenth century, the device was well known, and over the course of the next two hundred years forceps became a standard tool in West-ern obstetrics. A history of forceps published in 1929 describes over 550 varieties.

Then at the end of the twentieth century, everything changed. Doctors continued to use forceps in some instances but most of the time they were turning to the latest way of managing a difficult labor: cutting a hole in a woman's abdomen and pulling the fetus out.

The Cesarean section, or C-section, dates back to at least an-cient Rome. But until the twentieth century, C-sections were per-formed almost exclusively in cases where a mother was dead or dying and the operation was the only hope of saving the baby. The

---

* The concern for the laboring mother's modesty was so great that some male midwives would dress as women. In other instances, male surgeons called upon to assist with a delivery would sneak in and out of the room, sometimes even crawling to avoid being detected.

first woman reported to have survived a C-section, if the story is to be believed (it was recorded more than eighty years after the birth took place), was Elizabeth Alespachin of Siegershausen, Switzerland. Alespachin's labor had stalled and none of the thirteen different midwives who had been called were able to help her. In desperation, the midwives turned to professional bladder stone extractors, but the lithotomists, as they are called, turned out to be as useless as the midwives.

Alespachin's prognosis looked bleak. And had she been married to a baker or a lawyer, she almost certainly would have died. But Elizabeth Alespachin was lucky. She was married to a man who knew a thing or two about female reproduction. Alespachin's husband, Jacob Nufer, spayed pigs for a living, and seeing that time was running out, Nufer gathered his tools. He told the thirteen midwives that if they did not have the nerve to watch what was about to happen they should leave. Eleven of them walked out the door. The two who remained held Alespachin still as Nufer raised his knife and made an incision exactly as he did on his pigs. Elizabeth survived and the child lived to be seventy-seven.

If the story is true, then Nufer must have been a better surgeon than his contemporaries. In the following centuries, few doctors managed to save mothers with C-sections. In 1865, 85 percent of women who received a C-section in Great Britain died during or shortly after the operation.

It was only advances in twentieth-century medicine that made C-sections a viable option for obstruction of labor, and in the second half of the century they became increasingly common. In the 1960s, C-sections accounted for fewer than 5 percent of American deliveries, while forceps were used in more than 40 percent of births. By 1983, one in five American births were C-sections. Today the number is close to one in three and the use of forceps has declined dramatically.

It's not hard to understand why many women and even some doctors are uncomfortable with the growing C-section rate in most American hospitals. It takes much longer for a woman to recover from a C-section than a vaginal delivery, and like any major surgery, C-sections come with a risk of complications and medical mistakes. A British study in 2007 found that the odds of having a hysterectomy after a second birth were twice as great—if still relatively small—if one of the deliveries was a C-section.

The case against C-sections also makes sense in historical context. In the last decades of the twentieth century, American maternity wards were slowly waking up to the gross mistreatment of laboring women in hospitals. Fathers were being welcomed into delivery rooms and the practice of strapping women to their beds and drugging them into oblivion had become a thing of the past. And then, just when it seemed hospitals were moving toward a mother-focused view of childbirth, more and more women found themselves being rushed into operating rooms for surgical deliveries they didn't expect or want. "For some of us who really care about birth, it can completely crush you," one woman told *The New York Times* in a 2004 article on C-sections. "I wanted to birth my baby," the woman continued. "You have that taken away if you're lying in a room full of strangers and they cut your baby out of your abdomen."

In 1982, Esther Booth Zorn, a mother in Syracuse, New York, founded the International Cesarean Awareness Network (ICAN) to draw attention to America's rising C-section rate. In its statement of beliefs, ICAN claims that with the right support and education, "90 to 95 percent of women can deliver vaginally, joyfully, as nature intended." "If Cesareans were normal, we'd all be born with zippers," Zorn once said.

Much of ICAN's work is now focused on the VBAC, a vaginal birth after a mother has already given birth to a previous child by

Cesarean. Many hospitals have refused to perform VBACs since a 2001 study showed a greater risk of a ruptured uterus during a VBAC delivery. ICAN has responded that the study was flawed and sometimes holds rallies in front of hospitals that refuse to perform them.

But even ICAN recognizes that some C-sections are medically necessary. The real question is why so many unnecessary C-sections are being performed. ICAN and other activists argue that doctors turn to C-sections because they're more convenient, and profitable, and because doctors are afraid of being sued if they don't perform the surgery and something goes wrong.

There's almost certainly some truth to these claims. In fact, some hospital administrators readily admit that the fear of lawsuits is a factor in their VBAC policies. But in his book, Gawande makes a compelling case that the single biggest reason for the rise of C-sections has nothing to do with money. The real explanation, Gawande explains, is forceps, or, more specifically, the problems with forceps.

For all the benefits forceps provided to obstetricians, the invention did not turn out to be a reliable answer for twentieth-century urban hospitals seeking a way to safely deliver thousands of babies a year. The great limitation of forceps—and of all the manual maneuvers OBs developed over the centuries, such as the podalic version—is that they are only useful in the right hands. Becoming skilled with forceps takes years of practice and requires both a sensitive touch and extensive knowledge of when and how to use the many different models. And there is little room for error. An OB who doesn't have the feel for forceps and uses too much force risks not only injuring the mother but also fracturing the baby's skull and causing a fatal brain hemorrhage.

By contrast, performing a C-section is generally a straightforward procedure for a competent OB and requires no special skill. And so the move from forceps to C-sections can also be understood as an effort to bring standardized care to obstetrics. "Putting so many mothers through surgery is hardly cause for celebration," Gawande writes. "But our deep-seated desire to limit risk to babies is the biggest force behind its prevalence; it is the price exacted by the reliability we aspire to."

The related controversy over electronic fetal monitoring (EFM) reveals just how much confusion remains at the center of modern obstetrics. When continuous electronic monitoring came into widespread use in the 1970s, many experts thought it would revolutionize childbirth by giving doctors immediate feedback when a fetus was in distress.

But the story turned out differently. In fact, critics of hospital deliveries often point to continuous monitoring as the biggest problem. The monitoring requires women to remain on or near their hospital beds, and the lack of mobility can seem eerily reminiscent of the various constraints hospitals used on women in labor in decades past. It would be one thing if babies were better off with EFM, but study after study has found that EFM has no benefits over intermittent monitoring of the fetus. The only thing EFM clearly does successfully is increase the number of false alarms, and the false alarms lead to C-sections, sometimes with serious side effects. According to the World Health Organization, half of the C-sections currently performed in the United States are unnecessary.

The solution seems obvious: Abandon EFM and replace it with intermittent fetal monitoring. And some anti-C-section activists argue that this has not yet happened only because of the legal and financial obstacles. But while it's now widely accepted that EFM has not lived up to its initial promise, many doctors still believe that the monitoring is of some benefit and may prevent injury to the fetus in a small percentage of births. And if these doctors are right, then the debate may well come down to an unanswerable question: How many unhappy birth experiences and unnecessary C-sections are worth one fewer case of a baby born with brain damage? As with most debates about parenting and babies, the only certainty in the EFM debate is that it's almost impossible to be certain.

THE SCARE WITH JENNIFER'S HEARTBEAT lasted only another minute. Her heart monitor wasn't properly attached and once it was adjusted, the line on the monitor returned to a more steady up-and-down pattern. The doctors who rushed into the room, I later discovered, were residents—we were at a teaching hospital where apparently it's not uncommon for residents to rush around in groups terrifying patients.

Over the next hours, Jennifer moved into the second stage of labor. In the second stage, the cervix is fully dilated and the baby's head has passed through the opening of the pelvis. A woman can now begin to push to move the process along, and other people in the delivery room can now begin to shout at her to push.

I knew that I would not be good at shouting "push." I am not the shouting type. I am the "talk so quietly that people can't hear a word I'm saying" type. I was so unsuited to the cheerleading role that it later occurred to me that the concept could make for a good recurring segment on *Saturday Night Live:* Sam, the Unusually Quiet Labor Coach. And, besides, it seemed mean to shout when Jennifer was already working as hard as she could. It's difficult to think of an analogous situation, but if I were, say, extremely constipated and doing my best, the last thing I'd want is for Jennifer to be shouting at me to try harder.

Jennifer's obstetrician, Dr. Williams, a thin, bald man who had arrived on the scene at some point during the morning, wasn't much louder than I was, and had Jennifer been relying only on the two of us for motivation, we might still be in the delivery room today. But Jennifer wasn't relying only on us. There was also Kim, the nurse assigned to Jennifer's labor. Kim was a heavyset Caribbean woman and she had mastered the perfect shout, at once forceful and kind. "Come on, Jennifer, you can do it!" Kim yelled over and over in her Caribbean accent. "That's it, Jennifer, you are doing such great work!"

Kim was right. Jennifer was doing great. I barely had the energy left to stand next to the bed and yet from somewhere within, Jennifer was finding the strength to push as hard as she could. When I first heard of "push presents," the gifts—usually expensive jewelry—that some wealthy New York husbands give their wives after a delivery, I thought the whole idea was absurd and somehow even degrading to women. But after watching Jennifer struggle on that hospital bed, I thought that she really did deserve a formal recognition of her accomplishment. Later I imagined how nice it would be if, immediately after a birth, a hospital administrator handed every new mother a large trophy (the Birth Cup?). It seemed like a great idea until I remembered that mothers do get a baby after the birth, which is sort of like a big trophy, only you're not allowed to hold it over your head or pour champagne all over it.

By noon Jennifer had been pushing for over an hour, and we still didn't have a baby. Instead we got another scare, this time exactly the type of scare for which I was very glad we were in a hospital. During one of his periodic checkups, Dr. Williams announced that there was meconium in Jennifer's amniotic fluid. Meconium is a baby's first bowel movement. It's common for it to come out during labor and while it's not usually life threatening, if the baby inhales the meconium it can lead to dangerous respiratory problems.

The next time Dr. Williams left the room, I followed him into the hall.

"Excuse me, doctor," I said.

He looked surprised to see me.

"I just feel you should know that Jennifer and I talked about difficult births beforehand," I said. "We have no objection to a C-section if you think it's the safest approach at this point."

Dr. Williams nodded. I immediately recognized the look in his eyes, a look that every hypochondriac comes to know in time. It's the face doctors make when they realize for the first time that they're dealing with a complete loon. They continue to nod along as you describe your mysterious symptoms but you can see in their eyes that they are now elsewhere, that what they're really thinking about is whether to recommend a psychiatrist or to write the Xanax prescription themselves.

"Okay," Dr. Williams said. "I will take that into consideration."

I returned to Jennifer's side. Another hour came and went. Earlier in the morning, both Kim and Dr. Williams had predicted that the baby would be born before noon. Now it was 2 P.M. and I was growing increasingly nervous.

And then a sign of hope. After more than two hours of pushing, more than two hours of sweating and huffing and puffing and fist clenching, and "Sam, stop waving the oxygen mask in my face, I don't need it"-ing, the top of the baby's head began to appear and disappear again. I knew this not because I was looking but because I heard Dr. Williams tell Kim that the head coming in and out of sight reminded him of the arcade game in which players smash plastic moles with large foam hammers.

Kim laughed. "You're right."

I was not amused. Our son's arrival was the biggest moment of our lives, and I had not planned for the moment to include a discussion of his resemblance to a mechanical lawn pest. For a moment my exhausted body swelled with anger and indignation. Then I glanced over my shoulder and had to admit that it really did look a lot like Whac-A-Mole.

We are all Houdinis and we are all mechanical lawn pests.

At approximately two-thirty, Dr. Williams brought over a large bright light and aimed it between Jennifer's legs. Later, Jennifer said that the shining light at a moment when she was already nearly delirious felt like a hallucinatory experience, to which I responded, "The world is a stage, and the lights are on from the very first act," to which Jennifer responded with an exaggerated gagging gesture. Later still, I realized that it was a good thing I had not gone into obstetrics because I would almost certainly be unable to resist saying "it's showtime" every time I turned on that light.

By two-thirty in the afternoon, I knew we were close to the end. Kim's calls were growing increasingly passionate, and when I turned to look at her, I saw the excitement on her face. Her eyes were big and I think she may even have been jumping up and down. And then, in an instant, Kim's gleeful smile turned into a grimace. She looked as though she had just seen something she did not want to see.

I thought something horrible had happened, but before I had the chance to panic, Isaac Apple splashed into the world on a wave of his own feces.

BECAUSE OF THE MECONIUM RISK, Isaac was immediately taken to an adjacent room, where a pediatrician suctioned his nose and throat. Dr. Williams said everything was going to be okay, and I believed him—less because of his words than because I could see the calm in his eyes.

I wasn't expecting Isaac to look very good upon first sight. A few months earlier, Jennifer and I had taken a one-session class on newborn care. For some reason, I had imagined that most of the class would be spent diapering a plastic baby doll. Instead, our teacher, Diane, spent much of the two hours going over all of the unpleasant things a parent can expect to find on a new baby. She mentioned that babies are born cross-eyed and that their heads are often cone-shaped from their journey through the birth canal. She said that newborns can have a bluish-purplish tint due to an immature circulatory system and that they arrive covered in a "lotiony" goo known as vernix. "It's good for the skin," Diane said. "Some delivery nurses like to scoop it up and use it as hand moisturizer."

This was all gross enough—I didn't want anyone moisturizing with our new baby—and there was more. Diane said that a perfectly healthy newborn might have Mongolian spots (benign blue-gray or brown splotches on the skin), or milia (small white-head pimples), or a cephalahematoma (a fluid-filled lump on the side of the head), or bruising from forceps, or general newborn rashes ("monitor closely if it's oozing"), or swollen breasts, or swollen genitals, or crusty skin. By the end of the class, I was ready to vomit.

I am sure that Diane was right about the general grossness on newborns, but when a nurse finally brought Isaac over to Jennifer and me, I saw neither Mongolian spots nor fluid-filled lumps nor any other blemishes. Isaac was wrapped in a white blanket and already donning his first hat, a pink and blue striped number that had been pulled down to his ears. His cheeks sagged over the edges of his face and his upper lip had the same lovely upward arc as Jennifer's. It may have been because his eyes were closed, or because, like all babies, he bore a striking resemblance to Yoda, but I thought that Isaac looked not only handsome but also wise.

As Jennifer held Isaac against her chest, I stood by her side in silence. I rarely feel what I am supposed to feel. I didn't cry enough at my mom's funeral and I wasn't ecstatic enough when I found out Jennifer was pregnant. It's less a problem of emoting than of timing. My happiness or sadness arrives too early or too late. In the moment the pressure to feel makes feeling impossible. And yet as I gazed at Jennifer holding Isaac for the first time, it felt as profound and good as I thought it should.

THINKING ABOUT THE FIRST WEEK of Isaac's life is a bit like trying to recall my own early childhood. I have plenty of memories but they come back to me as a patchwork of loosely connected moments rather than as a coherent narrative.

I remember that as I took Isaac into my arms he stuck out his lower lip and that I was surprised that humans are born with the ability to pout.

I remember that after Jennifer and I had each held Isaac for a few minutes a nurse came to take Isaac away for a bath, and that my need to protect Isaac was already so powerful that I followed the nurse to the other side of the hospital until she took Isaac behind a closed door, and that the room the nurse had disappeared into had a window and that a few minutes later the nurse and Isaac reappeared in front of the window, only now Isaac was a different color, bright red, like no color I had ever seen on a human skin, and that in the midst of my panic, the nurse took out a comb and began to straighten the smattering of hairs on Isaac's scalp, and that I thought, My baby is the color of a tomato, and she's worried about his hair.

I remember that Isaac cried a lot in our hospital room during his first night and that the breastfeeding was not going well and that at one point Jennifer said "I give up," handed Isaac to me, and then wrapped a turquoise and lime green Boppy breastfeeding pillow around her face so that it looked like a pair of enormous futuristic sunglasses.

I remember that my in-laws rushed into Jennifer's hospital room with a helium balloon and that as they turned to Jennifer and Isaac the balloon hit me in the face and that I thought, This balloon in the face is a metaphor for my new second-rate status in the family, and that I later thought, Jesus, I really need to stop with the metaphors; sometimes a balloon in the face is just a balloon in the face.

I remember that on the second night another mother and baby moved into our double room and that she and her husband and relatives were astonishingly loud and that they talked more on their cellphones than to one another and that at one point I heard mother and father, talking to other people on their respective cellphones, speak the exact same sentence at the exact same time, a full sentence, word for word in perfect synchrony, and that later that night they sang the ABCs to their impossibly quiet newborn daughter in an impossibly sweet chorus, and that instead of being moved by this great show of parental affection I wanted to pull back the drape that separated our side of the room from theirs and say, "Give me a freakin' break, people," and that I then thought of Nell Carter, star of the eighties sitcom *Give Me a Break*, and felt sad that she was dead.

I remember that the next day the nurses wheeled Isaac away in the rolling Plexiglas box that was his temporary home at the hospital and that when he was wheeled back into our room, the cart had a small card in it that said "I can hear," and that I wondered if they have "I cannot hear" cards for the babies who do not pass the hearing test, and that when I walked by the same window through which I had seen Isaac briefly turn tomato red, I saw another father looking in dismay at his own tomato baby and that I said, "Don't worry, they get less red after a few minutes."

I remember that I undressed to go to sleep on the edge of Jennifer's bed and that a nurse later came into the room and told me that it would be best if I kept my pants on in the hospital.

I remember that I wondered if I had already bonded with our baby and that I wasn't sure, and that even though I didn't know what exactly a bond was supposed to feel like, I felt terrible about not feeling one and then briefly felt better when Jennifer admitted that she also didn't know if she had bonded, and that Jennifer and I then wondered if our failure to bond instantly meant that we would turn out to be the most monstrous, unfeeling parents of all time.

I remember that the nurses kept giving Jennifer various pads and cool packs that were supposed to help her heal and that Jennifer, unsure of which items to use or how exactly to use them, kept shoving the pads and packs into her underwear until it looked as though she was wearing a small garbage bag.

I remember that at some point a nurse whom none of us had seen before came to take some of Jennifer's blood and that Jennifer thought there was something strange about her and that when we asked the other nurses about it no one had any knowledge or record of this blood taking and that Jennifer was convinced that something sinister had happened and that I told her she was being ridiculous and that there was absolutely nothing to worry about, and that even as I spoke these words I was thinking that if I had been the one pricked by the mystery nurse I would already be hours into an intensive antiviral treatment in the hopes of staving off HIV.

I remember that at some point a nurse offered to take Isaac into the nursery so that Jennifer and I could get some sleep and that I shook my head no and thought, Fat chance, lady; our birth instructor warned us you would try to interrupt our bonding and give Isaac formula, and that I spent much of the next day regretting our decision to keep Isaac with us.

I remember that we took a cab home from the hospital, and that when we got into the apartment, I sat down on the couch with Isaac and thought, Okay, now what?

I remember that I brought Jennifer an astonishing number of glasses of water and that I regretted not having documented this water bringing as I would almost certainly now hold the Guinness record for the greatest number of waters brought to a person in a single week.

I remember that every one of Isaac's diapers leaked and that I spent a great deal of time pondering whether the little flaps near the leg holes on the diaper are supposed to be tucked in or not and that no one seemed to know and that I was washing onesies and burp cloths so often that it began to seem as though life was an interruption of doing laundry rather than the other way around.

I remember that one day I removed a diaper and discovered that Isaac had taken his first postbirth crap, and that I called out, "It's a number two," and that Jennifer and her parents hurried over to the changing table, and that we couldn't have been more excited if we had all been forty-niners, and I'd just announced that the diaper was full of solid gold nuggets.

I remember that one afternoon I carried a seemingly hungry Isaac from the living room into the bedroom where Jennifer was resting and that I laughed and said, "I think you know who is ready for another round of you know what," and that Jennifer couldn't have looked more distressed if I had been carrying a rabies-infected rodent toward her.

And I remember that on the seventh day of Isaac's life, I thought, This is already so overwhelming and confusing, and difficult, and tomorrow we have to cut his penis.

ELEVEN

Circumcision

In Search of My Foreskin

AMERICANS ARE A PENIS-CUTTING PEOPLE. While the American circumcision rate has declined somewhat in recent decades from 80 percent to closer to 60 percent, we still greatly outcircumcise Europe, where the rate is less than one percent.

Considering that the vast majority of Americans are Christians and that Christianity has a long history of rejecting the ritual and using it as anti-Semitic fodder, the rise of circumcision in America was highly unlikely. But two thousand years of anticircumcision sentiment turned out to be no match for Lewis A. Sayre, a nineteenth-century New York City orthopedic surgeon who did more than any other single figure to turn circumcision into a mainstream medical practice in America.

Sayre wasn't just any orthopedic surgeon. He was the leading orthopedic surgeon in the country and a famed doctor at Bellevue Hospital. During the Civil War he had served as the resident physician of New York City, an office similar to the surgeon general, where he fought for compulsory smallpox vaccinations and sanitary reforms.

As David L. Gollaher recounts the story in a 1994 issue of the *Journal of Social History,* Sayre's adventures in circumcision began on February 9, 1870, when he received a note about a young boy who was paralyzed from the waist down. "The little fellow has a pair of legs that you would walk miles to see," another doctor wrote to Sayre.

Sayre made the trip to see the boy, and the legs turned out to be as intriguing as the letter had claimed. The boy's knees were locked at 45-degree angles, but Sayre could find no sign of disease or nervous disorder. Sayre decided to treat the boy by shocking his paralyzed muscles with a galvanic battery.

It was at this point that the boy's nurse spoke out and forever changed the fate of the American penis. "Oh, doctor! Be very careful—don't touch his pee-pee," the nurse warned as a sponge was placed on the boy's thigh. "It's very sore." The nurse told Sayre that the boy's penis was so sensitive that even contact with his bedsheets could cause a painful erection. Sayre put down his battery and examined the boy's genitals. "The glans," Sayre later wrote, "was . . . tightly imprisoned in the contracted foreskin, and in its efforts to escape, the meatus urinarius had become puffed out and red."

The sight of the puffy meatus urinarius was Sayre's Sherlock Holmes moment. The next day Sayre brought the boy to Bellevue, gave him chloroform, and clipped off a small piece of his foreskin with scissors. When the foreskin still wouldn't retract, Sayre used his fingernails to tear the remaining flesh away from the glans. The results were miraculous. Sayre claimed that the boy began to improve within the first day. Within two weeks he could walk again.

Today a sore "pee-pee" wouldn't likely be considered a potential cause of paralysis, but in the nineteenth century, no two human ailments could be entirely separated. The exciting discoveries that a new generation of physiologists were making about the mechanics of the nervous system had made it possible to incorporate older ideas about vital energies flowing through the body into the more scientific language of nerves and reflexes. A small irritation in the foot wasn't only a problem for the foot. The irritation might travel through the nervous system and manifest itself in the kidneys or the lungs or the brain. And if the problem did make it to the brain, it might cause mental illness.

The theory known as "reflex neurosis" turned out to be a useful tool for solving medical mysteries of the era. If no obvious explanation could be found for a physical or mental problem, the assumption was that the problem had arisen elsewhere in the body. Rudolf Virchow, the famous German scientist who pioneered the field of cell biology, thought that even cancer could be explained by irritation in the cells giving rise to new malignant cells.

In the context of nineteenth-century medicine, then, it didn't take a great leap for Sayre to suspect that the boy's sore pee-pee might be responsible for the problem in his legs. The boy's astonishing recovery turned Sayre into a circumcision evangelist, and as the vice president of the newly formed American Medical Association, he was in an excellent position to proselytize. Sayre claimed that circumcision could cure everything from spinal curvature to epilepsy to hernias to insanity, and he began to cut just about every penis he could get his hands on. He even began making trips to the Manhattan State Hospital Idiot Asylum, where he would go on circumcising sprees.

As word of Sayre's success spread, other doctors were anxious to try out the new method, and the list of ailments circumcision could supposedly fix continued to grow. One doctor claimed circumcision could even cure crossed eyes. Sayre was so thrilled that he began to circumcise women as well, hoping that clitoridectomies might be the answer to hysteria. Other doctors followed his lead and began hacking away at the entire female reproductive system so that at the end of the nineteenth century, it wasn't uncommon for American doctors to remove the healthy ovaries from women who suffered from mental illnesses or undiagnosable physical maladies.

The turn to hysteria and the female genitals was a natural move for nineteenth-century doctors interested in the health benefits of circumcision. Hysteria comes from *hysteria,* the Greek word for the uterus. The ancient Greeks thought women became hysterical when the uterus, not receiving enough male attention, began to wander around the body like a restless animal. The wandering led not only to mental illness but also to strange symptoms all over the body, which the Greeks treated with pelvic massage and ovarian pressure among other remedies.

By the seventeenth century, some doctors had already become convinced that hysteria was a nervous disorder that could affect both men and women, but the link to the female reproductive system never disappeared and the medical literature of the eighteenth and nineteenth centuries is full of discussions of the phenomenon. In 1788 a prominent Scottish medical expert diagnosed a special form of hysteria, *hysteria libidinosa,* that he linked to nymphomania. Another doctor classified hysteria as the "genital neuroses of women." In 1816, the French physician J.-B. Louyer-Villermay theorized that all nervous and mental illnesses in women could be traced to a plexus of nerves emanating from the uterus.

And so the circumcision obsession that took hold in America and to a lesser extent in England in the late nineteenth century might be best understood as the extension of classical beliefs about women's genitals to men's genitals. But, then, plenty of other factors also contributed to the circumcision trend. The new understanding of germ theory led many doctors to see the secretions of the foreskin as unhygienic, and in the Victorian era, ideas about physical hygiene mixed easily with ideas about moral hygiene. Because it was believed foreskins made the penis more sensitive, circumcision was also thought to work nicely as a cure for masturbation and wet dreams.

The circumcision mania probably reached its apex in 1891 with Peter Charles Remondino's *History of Circumcision from the Earliest Times to the Present: Moral and Physical Reasons for Its Performance, with a History of Eunuchism, Hermaphrodism, etc., and of the Different Operations Practiced upon the Prepuce.* Remondino, a San Diego doctor and vice president of the California State Medical Society, met Sayre in the early 1880s and Sayre apparently made a strong impression. Remondino spent much of the next decade researching his book, which was widely read by doctors and the general public, and which approaches the subject of foreskin removal with a passion almost certainly unequaled in American letters. In Chapter XVIII, "The Prepuce as an Outlaw, and Its Effects on the Glans," Remondino lays out his evolutionary rationale for the existence of the foreskin, in typically insane prose:

> Times were, however, when—man living in a wild state, and when in imitation of some of our near relatives with tails and hairy bodies; when he still found locomotion on all-fours handier than on his two feet; when in pursuit of either the juicy grasshopper or other small game, or of the female of his own species to gratify his lust, or in the frantic rush to escape the clutches, fangs, or claws of a pursuing enemy, he was obliged to fly and leap over thorny briars and bramble-bushes or hornets' nests, or plunge through swamps alive with blood-sucking insects and leeches. . . . In those days, but for the protecting double fold of the preputial envelope that protected it from the thorns and cutting grasses, the coarse bark of trees, or the stings and bites of insects, the glans penis of primitive man would have often looked like the head of the proverbially duel-disfigured German university student, or

the Bacchus-worshiping nose of a jolly British Boniface. So
that in those days, unless primitive man was intended to have
an organ that resembled a battle-scarred Roman legionary, a
prepuce was an absolute necessity.

With Remondino's literary flair adding to the excitement in the
air, the circumcision trend continued to grow.* At first the sur-
geries had been reserved for the sick, but the more doctors
looked at the penises of small boys, the more common the problem of the unretractable foreskin appeared to be—the doctors apparently didn't realize that a normal foreskin often only becomes
fully retractable at around age ten.

By 1910, more than a third of American baby boys were being
circumcised. By 1940, it was almost two thirds.

ooo

* To prove his point that circumcision leads to robust health, Remondino
needed to prove that the Jews are a physically superior people, a tough case to
make even for the proudest members of the tribe. And yet Remondino explores
the topic at great length, citing statistics that Jews live longer and are less likely
to suffer from a wide array of diseases. He even makes a noble effort to explain
the failure of most Jews to excel at sports, arguing that anti-Semitism drove Jews
into seclusion so that they couldn't train for athletic events. After making this
observation, Remondino moves seamlessly into the most impassioned defense
of the Jew since Shylock:

> Although seeking neither converts nor political power and influence, he [the
> Jew] has been hunted down, massacred, and chased about as a dangerous beast.
> As the children of the great Rabbi Moses Mendelssohn asked of their father: "Is
> it a disgrace to be a Jew? Why do people throw stones at us and call us names?"
> It may well be asked, why? These actions have forced them into the social and
> retired habits for which they are noted; although it cannot be said that it is from
> a lack of spirit, as one of the Rothschilds is well known to have been present at
> the battle of Waterloo, where from a spot in the vicinity of the British, right-
> centre, he observed the events of the battle.

I CAN APPRECIATE the case against circumcision. I believe that newborns experience pain, and the idea of subjecting someone to an elective surgery without his consent makes me morally queasy. But as a Jew, I felt I had to circumcise my son. I have plenty of quarrels with Judaism but it is one thing to quarrel and another to reject, and choosing not to circumcise Isaac would have felt like a rejection of my people and my family. Regardless of the ritual's origins or how unbelievably weird it is when you stop and think about it, one fact is indisputable: Circumcision has been a central tenet of Jewish life for several thousand years. And considering that I wanted Isaac to grow up knowing that he was Jewish and learning about Jewish religion and culture, I thought that leaving his foreskin alone was more likely to cause lasting psychological pain than removing it.

Jennifer, to my great relief, felt the same way, and so on the eighth day of Isaac's life, I was busy preparing for the ceremony. By eleven that morning, thirty minutes before our start time, I had almost everything I thought we needed for a successful event: white fish salad, bagels, regular and low-fat cream cheese, orange juice, coffee, and topical anesthetic for Isaac's penis.

The only thing I did not have was a wife. Despite being in favor of circumcising Isaac, Jennifer had decided that the entire event was too much to bear and had taken refuge in a neighbor's apartment.

I was disappointed that Jennifer wasn't going to attend the ceremony and was delighted when she walked back into the apartment ten minutes before we were to begin. It looked like everything was going to be okay, that we would share this frightening but important moment together as a family. Then Jennifer walked into our bedroom and witnessed the mohel dangling Isaac's testicles above his head.

It turned out that what Jennifer saw was a small oval-shaped sponge that, after having been dipped in a mixture of red wine and sugar water, looked astonishingly similar to our newborn son's genitals. Indeed, had thousands of people entered a contest to create a model of Isaac's scrotum, I sincerely doubt that even one would have come up with a more perfect replica.

In any case, Jennifer had seen enough. She turned around and left the apartment.

I understood. If I was more ready than Jennifer for what was about to happen it wasn't because I have a stronger constitution. I am not entirely certain what it means to have a strong constitution but I am certain that I do not have one. I was ready for the circumcision only because I'd been preparing for the moment for a long time. Several years earlier, I had even considered writing an entire book on the subject.

Unlike most people writing about circumcision, I wasn't especially interested in the medical debates surrounding the procedure. It was the strangeness of the ritual that captivated me. Plenty of the Jewish rituals sometimes feel odd in the context of my otherwise modern life, but no other ritual seemed as archaic or mysterious as circumcision. I planned to learn about the origins of the ritual and about how circumcision had found its way into so many diverse religious cultures. But while I was most interested in the history, my plan was to extend the discussion to my own feelings about circumcision—my working title was "In Search of My Foreskin"—and, in the process, explore my own Jewish identity. And if I was going to write a personal book about circumcision, I thought that the scene of my own cutting might be a logical place to start.

I asked my relatives what they recalled about my circumcision, but to my frustration, the single clear recollection came from my grandmother, who remembered that my great-grandfather, Rachmiel, had led a celebratory conga line.

I was amazed to learn that the removal of my foreskin had generated so much enthusiasm. But I was looking for a more complete picture of my eighth day, and if my relatives couldn't remember the event, there was still one person who might: my mohel.

A mohel, or Jewish ritual circumciser, is sometimes but not always a rabbi. My mohel was an orthodontist. I learned this from my father, who said that he had been friendly with my mohel at our synagogue in Houston, where I grew up. My father recalled that my mohel had worn a cowboy hat and boots whenever he did a circumcision and that he had circumcised the sons of so many East Coast transplants that he became known as the Yankee Clipper.

It took only a quick Google search to find my mohel's phone number, but making the call wasn't as easy. I wasn't sure how to explain what I wanted without sounding like a lunatic.

I picked up the phone, put the phone down, paced around the apartment, and picked up the phone again. Then, I dialed my mohel's number.

My mohel said hello with a slight Texas twang, and I introduced myself as someone he had circumcised a long time ago. My mohel seemed entirely, astonishingly, unfazed by my announcement. "Great to hear from you," he said. It was almost as though he had been waiting for my call for the last thirty years.

"So I guess you're wondering why I've called you," I said.

"No," my mohel said. "You can call me anytime you want."

The response put me at ease. My mohel and I chatted about a few people we knew in common from Houston and then, even before I had begun to ask him about the scene of my circumcision, he invited me to visit him at his home in Howard, Colorado, where he was spending his retirement with his second wife.

Four months later, I was standing in the passenger pickup lane of the Colorado Springs airport, where my mohel and I had arranged to meet. I didn't know what my mohel looked like and for several minutes I peered through the windows of the idling cars, wondering if one of the drivers might have circumcised me. Then a Ford Explorer pulled up with a handwritten sign bearing my name taped to the window.

Inside the car, the Yankee Clipper waved excitedly. I opened the car door and shook his hand. He wore a gray polo shirt almost identical to my own, a black baseball cap, and a money pack around his waist.

We began the two-hour drive to my mohel's home in Howard, a small mountain town 150 miles south of Denver. My mohel did most of the talking. He was the type of guy who had acquired a lot of interesting information in his life, and he was not afraid to share it. He told me stories about his army years and about doing circumcisions in Beaumont, Texas. He had a full white mustache and boyish, darting eyes that came to life as he spoke.

I noticed a cut-up cereal box on the floor of the car. "Postcards," my mohel said, picking up on my interest. He explained that he rarely uses regular paper. Next to the postcards was a small pile of envelopes made from newspapers. Later, I learned that he mails about twenty of these homemade letters a week, not including his three or four daily sweepstakes entries.

After a few minutes, we stopped for lunch at an empty restaurant. We both ordered black bean soup and small organic salads. Between spoonfuls of soup, I inquired about my circumcision.

Had there been anything unique about the event? My mohel couldn't remember but didn't think so. Did he remember my family's conga line? No. Anything special about the food, perhaps? No. "Unless there was some sort of medical problem it's hard for me to remember much," he said.

I wasn't ready to give up. I had read that the foreskin is typically buried after a Jewish circumcision, and before my trip I'd wondered if my mohel might be able to recall what he had done with them after the ceremonies. Had he thrown them out? Tossed them into a Dumpster behind a Taco Bell like so many enchilada wrappers? Or was there a secret foreskin cemetery somewhere in Houston, perhaps in a public park, where every day the good people of Texas unknowingly picnicked atop the flesh of a thousand Jewish penises? I wanted to think that there was such a cemetery, but I wasn't sure what I would do if I found the spot. If, like some anticircumcision activists, I had been convinced that the removal of my foreskin had caused profound physical and mental anguish, then the journey to the grave would naturally lend itself to drama. I could fall to my knees *Platoon*-style, pound the earth, and weep for my lost lubrication. But, having no mixed feelings about my circumcision, the journey would inevitably be anticlimactic.

Still, my foreskin had been a part of me, and I wondered where it had ended up.

"So what did you do with all the foreskins?" I asked.

My mohel shrugged. "I would just drop them anywhere and stomp them into the dirt," he said.

"Oh," I said.

Within a half hour, I was out of questions. "Sorry I can't be of more help," my mohel said.

I told him I understood, and I did. It was ridiculous to have thought that he might remember me among the thousands of babies he had circumcised.

Our salads arrived and our conversation drifted to the historical origins of circumcision. An hour came and went. When my mohel and I exhausted everything we could think to say about foreskins, our conversation somehow shifted to the history of gazpacho soup in America, a subject my mohel seemed to know a lot about.

At the end of lunch, I still had twenty-three hours left in Colorado. I got back into the Explorer and we rode into the pale brown mountains.

At one point during the drive, my mohel turned to me. It seemed something important was coming. "Did I mention that I circumcised the sons of Michael Dell?" he asked, referring to the computer mogul from Houston.

When we arrived at my mohel's two-story ranch-style home, I met his wife and then retreated to the guest bedroom to take a nap. An hour later, my mohel tapped softly on the bedroom door. He said that he had something he wanted to show me and led me upstairs to a closet at the back of his office.

I took a deep breath. I didn't know what it would be, but I knew that something inside that closet was going to make the trip worth the trouble.

My mohel looked at me and smiled. "Do you want some financial advice that will change your life forever?" he asked, opening the closet door to reveal a row of shelves lined with dozens of binders. I hid my disappointment and said that I did, and for the next hour we pored over his investment portfolio. "Dividend reinvestment is the key," my mohel said as we reviewed handwritten records of his holdings in the Coca-Cola Company over the last decade. "You can start with almost nothing." He urged me to buy a subscription to an investment strategies newsletter called *The Money Paper*.

We still had a few hours before dinner. My mohel produced two floppy white sun hats. He put one on his bald crown and gave me the other. Then he grabbed a ski pole, his walking stick, and we hiked around his nine acres. The mountain air was hot and dry. My mohel wore a tube of ChapStick on a string around his neck and he applied it liberally.

The next morning, I tried to jog his memory one more time. I had come too far to give up so easily. I took out a baby photo I had brought with me.

"Anything?"

"Nope."

My mohel's wife and I had oatmeal for breakfast. The Clipper ate his own concoction of grains, beans, and buckwheat groats. It looked like cat vomit.

As I packed my bags, my mohel gave me his extra copy of Menachem Begin's biography and some blank circumcision certificates he used to fill out after he completed a ceremony. Then he and his wife drove me to Canon City, where I would catch a cab to take me the rest of the way to the airport.

We waited for the cab at a picnic table in a small park, and when it arrived I was surprised by how sad I felt to be leaving.

"I feel like the boys I circumcised are part of my family," my mohel said.

"I'm really glad I came here," I said. Then I hugged my mohel and his wife and stepped into the cab.

VISITING MY MOHEL wasn't the entirety of my preparation for Isaac's circumcision. In the last month of Jennifer's pregnancy, I had also taken a more practical approach, and decided to interview local mohels. After all, if you're going to cut someone's penis without his permission, the least you can do is make sure that the cutter is a true professional.

The first mohel I called was an Israeli rabbi who spoke English with a thick accent. When I told him that I was in the process of interviewing mohels, he invited me to watch him circumcise another baby. I wasn't sure what to do. I thought it could only help to see him in action, yet I felt strange about crashing a circumcision. In the end, I decided to attend the ceremony at the Jewish Community Center, but to remain as inconspicuous as possible. I realized my mistake when the baby was brought into the room and all the invited guests turned to the door to find me lurking nervously.

Not wanting to be arrested for lurking nervously at a circumcision, I stepped out of the room and waited in the hallway. After the ceremony, the mohel and his assistant, Melanie, joined me downstairs in the café.

The mohel ordered two Cokes. I did not want a Coke but the mohel would not hear of it. I asked him about his background. I was searching for signs that the mohel might be unfit for duty. The mohel said that he had trained at a hospital in Israel where he and the other mohels in training would do a circumcision every forty-five minutes, as many as thirteen in a day. When I expressed my surprise, the mohel grew serious. "My father taught me always to tell the truth in the face," he said. "Not behind the back, not under the back, but in the face."

Thirteen circumcisions in a day was impressive, and it was only the beginning. "I will show you something," the mohel said, getting up from his chair and opening his bag. He returned with a small book and pointed to a signature on the title page. "Jerry Seinfeld," he said.

I leaned over and looked at the signature. I was so impressed that it took me a second to wonder why the mohel had chosen this moment to show off his Seinfeld autograph.

"I circumcised Jerry's son," he explained. And there was more. Pride now visible on his face, the mohel pointed to another signature on the same page. "Judge Judy. I did her grandson."

It was obvious I was dealing with a world-class circumciser, but I didn't want to settle on the first mohel I met.

The next mohel I called is known as the eMohel. He has become something of a mohel celebrity since a *New Yorker* article in 1999 described his life of nonstop circumcising. As of 1999, he had done some nine thousand circumcisions over the previous twenty-two years. The first time I called the eMohel he said "mazel tov" before hanging up, then remembered that I had not yet become a father. "Sorry," he said. "Habit." When I called back later to set up an interview, he again said "mazel tov" before hanging up. I didn't doubt that the eMohel knew his stuff, but this struck me as a bad sign. I did not want a mohel who was circumcising on autopilot. I decided to skip the meeting and keep looking.

A website for parents led me to a female mohel, Emily Blake, and I arranged a dinner interview. Blake was middle-aged and wore her long brown hair parted in the middle. I'd never imagined using a female mohel but I had no objection to it. We both ordered the grilled salmon and then I asked Blake to tell me about her background. She said that she had taken an interest in circumcision while training as an obstetrician-gynecologist. The OB residents were given the job of doing the circumcisions in the hospital. Blake didn't mind circumcision duty but she recalled that most of the other residents hated it. One day a gay black friend told Blake that he thought black men, at least black men of his generation, had worse circumcisions than white men of the same generation. Blake then noticed that at her own hospital, whites were having private doctors circumcise their sons while disgruntled residents were circumcising the poor, mostly African American, patients in the hospital's clinic. From that point on, Blake did as many of the clinic circumcisions as she could.

"I decided it was a really important social responsibility issue to do the circumcision for the clinic babies," Blake told me. "Circumcision is something babies live with for the rest of their lives."

I was impressed. This was the type of devotion I had been looking for in a mohel.

And I was also surprised. Despite my search for the perfect mohel, I didn't really think there could be that much difference in the final product.

"So they can really turn out differently?" I asked.

"People can do a more careful or less careful job," Blake said. "They can do it at an angle, or make it unsymmetrical, or leave dog ears."

"Dog ears?"

"There are a couple of different clamps you can use," Blake said. "One of the clamps takes the three-dimensional cylindrical structure of the foreskin and squeezes it out into the two-dimensional clamp." She continued: "If you cut across here and pull it out too wide you can end up with little places on the side where there's a bit of tissue left. Dog ears."

Blake said that while the most common clamps are the Mogan and the Gomco, she preferred the Gomco. "It actually maintains the foreskin in a three-dimensional structure and gives you a lot more flexibility in terms of what you're able to see and cut," Blake said. "The Gomco is safer and aesthetically nice. I haven't used a Mogan in a long time."

Our salmon arrived.

"Do you mind eating while you discuss circumcision?" Blake asked.

"Not at all," I said.

"Me either," Blake said. "Do you want to see the Gomco?"

I nodded. Blake turned to her bag and took out a small metal instrument with a hole at one end—it looked like it could be a fancy corkscrew. She then produced a cherry lollipop and demonstrated how the penis goes through the device.

I liked that she wasn't afraid to brandish her Gomco in public. I also liked that she said that her multipronged strategy—Infants' Tylenol, sugar water, and a topical anesthetic—was so successful at eliminating pain that 80 percent of babies she circumcised slept through the procedure.

My comfort level growing, I asked Blake whether she thought

circumcision made sex less pleasurable. Based on my own experience, I've never thought of diminished pleasure as a serious concern for the circumcised male—how much better could it really feel?—but anticircumcision activists often claim that sex without a foreskin is not the same.

"I have had a lot of men come up to me and share their stories when they hear that I'm a mohel," Blake said. "Everybody who has been circumcised later in life has said that they enjoy sex more afterward, but it's a biased population, since these are clearly men who had wanted to be circumcised." Blake shrugged. "I don't think you can get a fair judgment of it. Everyone's got his own emotions underlying the procedure, and you can't do a good double-blind study because you can't go in both directions. You can only go from uncircumcised to circumcised."

The waiter arrived to refill our waters.

"I think the real bottom line is that the glans of the penis is less sensitive without the foreskin, but what most of these men have said to me is that they enjoy sex more because it lasts longer."

"But aren't there people who have been circumcised as adults who say that the sex is much worse afterward?" I asked.

"People talk about and talk about it," Blake said, "but you try to find the person who can really speak to it and there's nobody there. I'm sure there have to be some really unhappy men who were circumcised at a later age. I just haven't met them."*

---

* After talking with Blake, I found a 2005 paper in *Urologia Internationalis* that surveyed eighty-four men who had been circumcised as adults. Eighteen percent thought that penile sensation was made worse by the procedure while 38 percent thought it improved penile sensation. The rest found no difference. In the name of thoroughness, I also called a man who had restored his foreskin with a multi-year process of stretching the remaining skin on his penis forward and taping it over the glans. He said that his postrestoration sex was better and that his new foreskin felt like a pair of warm lips on his penis.

Our conversation wandered on. When Blake said that performing circumcisions was her calling in life, I put down my fork and asked her to circumcise my son.

She said that she would and I felt a great sense of relief as I finished my salmon.

SOME THREE MONTHS AFTER THAT DINNER, Blake was in our apartment holding a sponge that looked like an infant's scrotum over Isaac's face and Jennifer was back at our neighbor's apartment. The purpose of the sponge was to drip sugar water into Isaac's mouth in the hopes of relaxing him while the mohel did her pre-circumcision examination. I didn't particularly want to be present for the examination, but Blake had placed Isaac on his changing table, and because the standing lamp next to the changing table only worked when held at a slight angle, I had to remain by Blake's side to tilt the lamp. The changing table was near the back of the room, and, feeling too anxious to watch the proceedings, I turned to the corner.

Isaac, understandably enough, did not want a stranger examining his genitals, and he made his displeasure known. It is never easy to hear your baby scream, but minutes before the circumcision it was more than I could handle, and tears began to stream down my cheeks.

A few minutes later, my father walked into the room and found me crying in the corner. Seeing that there was nothing to be said or done, he took my hand and stood facing the corner with me. Then he too began to tear up. That Isaac's circumcision was causing three generations of Apple men to weep might seem like an argument against the ritual, but at that moment, my father's hand warm in mine, I felt more strongly than ever that it was the right thing to do.

The circumcision itself went as smoothly as the cutting of a penis can go. Isaac only cried for about fifteen seconds. He seemed much more upset by the preparation.

Her work done, Blake handed Isaac over to me, at which point my relatives joined hands and began jogging in circles—a practice the Jewish people refer to as dancing.

The completion of a circumcision ceremony is the time when most parents and relatives breathe a sigh of relief and wolf down some whitefish—usually, but not always, in that order. But I had something other than whitefish on my mind. Not wanting Isaac to suffer his father's hapless fate of not knowing the location of his foreskin, I asked Blake to bring the foreskin into the garden, where I buried it in a small bed of rosemary and thyme. In the name of caution, I then asked my cousin Norman to mark the co-ordinates on his GPS.

With that I thought my multiyear circumcision saga had finally come to an end. But there was a final act. Several days after the circumcision, I laughingly told our neighbor, Bill, with whom we shared our garden, where I had buried Isaac's foreskin. I was expecting a hearty chuckle but Bill absorbed the news without so much as a smirk. I felt terrible. It never occurred to me that perhaps I should have asked him whether he would mind if I buried a foreskin in the garden. After all, he did all the gardening. Who was I to have buried a foreskin in his rosemary and thyme? Would I have liked it if someone had put a foreskin in something I cared about, say inside my brand-new computer bag?

I thought that it might be best if I moved the foreskin and began to think about another appropriate place. I went into the garden and looked down at the spot, already disappearing beneath the sagging weeds. Then I thought, I cannot become the first person in the world to dig up and rebury a foreskin. It was all just too crazy, and I hated to ask Norman to schlep his GPS to Brooklyn again.

I NEVER WROTE THE BOOK on circumcision, in part because of a lack of enthusiasm from my publisher—my promise to include original short fiction about circumcision probably didn't help the pitch—and in part because I wasn't sure I wanted to spend three to four years thinking about the cutting of penises. But my journey to see my mohel did force me to think more about circumcision, and the more I thought, the more my thoughts returned to the initial question that had captured my imagination. How could such a counterintuitive idea possibly have arisen in so many different cultures around the world, from the Merina of Madagascar, where the foreskin is not only removed but also eaten (typically by a relative who takes it down with a small piece of banana) to the Aborigines of Australia, who cut all the way down the underside of the penis into the urethra.

The universality of the ritual suggests that rather than being a cultural quirk that spread from one group to the next, circumcision is about something deeper. Some universal aspect of the human psyche or of the ancient human experience time and again drove men to cut their penises.

When I raised this question over lunch, my mohel, like many scholars before him, suggested that in all these different cultures circumcision probably began as a medical practice. At some point, men figured out that they were less likely to get infections if they removed their foreskins and the medical discoveries blended into ritual life. This theory may be true, but, intriguingly, the ancient Egyptians practiced circumcision but never mentioned it in their medical texts.

Plenty of thinkers have taken a stab at a unified theory of circumcision. Freud, predictably, saw circumcision as the symbolic response of fathers who felt threatened by the sexuality of their growing boys. Bruno Bettelheim, a psychotherapist who became famous for his insights on fairy tales and myths, thought circumcision emerged from men's longing to share the characteristics of women. Unable to go all the way through with castration, men settled on circumcision. Others have pointed out that circumcision is usually an initiation rite and argued that different cultures arrive at it because it's the most powerful way for a man to demonstrate his submission to a group.

My best entirely speculative and vaguely scientific guess is that people all over the world arrived at circumcision independently because all humans share an evolutionarily ingrained revulsion to things that look unhealthy or impure, such as oozing wounds or pus. Perhaps before modern hygiene, the secretions of the foreskin looked unattractive and unhealthy even when they posed no health risk. Although it's not exactly solid evidence, the first people known to practice the ritual were the purity- and secretion-obsessed ancient Egyptians.

My best entirely speculative and entirely unscientific theory is that circumcision is the logical extension of a universal longing to demonstrate devotion to a god or higher power. I arrived at the idea after reading that comparative anthropologists have found that the ritual almost always tends to be associated with a sacrifice in return for a future reward. If circumcision is really about sacrifice, I thought, it made perfect sense that different cultures would have turned to the penis. The impulse to sacrifice is born of fear and desperation and when you are frightened and desperate, you will do anything for help, anything to prove to your god or gods that you are serious about your promise. And in a patriarchal society, at least, the cutting of the penis would have been the most extreme statement possible without wiping out the entire population. It's possible to go further than circumcision. Some biblical scholars have argued that Israelite circumcision might have arisen as a substitute for child sacrifice, a not uncommon practice in ancient Canaan. But any society that went to that extreme of child sacrifice or castration would have died out.

The evidence I have for this theory is my own obsessive-compulsive childhood. Like a lot of children, I developed my own secret ritual life. Before falling asleep at night I would recite long lists of people I wanted God to protect and if I stumbled on a word or made a mistake in the order of the names, I would start over and over and over. I kissed every mezuzah on every doorpost and sometimes even kissed imaginary mezuzahs on doorposts that had not been adorned with the small Jewish prayer boxes.

Usually the rituals were enough to get me through the uncertainties of daily life, but now and then, in a moment of true panic, I would also make spontaneous pleas to God for help. "Please, God," I would say in my head. "Let my father return home safely from Blockbuster Video." "Please, God," I would say. "Let this lumpy thing I feel on my head not be a tumor."

I was never selfish. I understood that God was busy and that the least I could do was to offer something in return for His efforts. "Please, God," I would say. "Cut off my arms if you have to." "Please, God," I would say. "Take my legs, if you have to, just please let my father come home."

And sometimes I went even further. Sometimes, when I was really terrified, I would offer the Lord my penis as well.

TWELVE

Crying
The Tears of the !Kung San

CRYING DRIVES PARENTS CRAZY. Everyone knows this, but, just to
be sure, several scientists confirmed it in the 1980s by snapping
two-day-old babies on the soles of their feet with rubber bands.
When, as expected, the babies screamed, the scientists were
ready and waiting with their tape recorders. Later the scientists
played the cries to twenty-eight mothers and confirmed the obvious: Mothers are more distressed by higher-pitched cries and
feel a greater urgency to respond to them.

Twenty-eight mothers is a small sample size, but the U.S.
patent office contains plenty of additional evidence for the impact of infant crying on parents. After discovering that driving his
baby around in the car was the only thing that would stop her crying fits, one Columbus, Ohio, father invented a crib that somehow re-creates the experience of traveling at fifty-five miles an
hour. A financial analyst in Boca Raton, Florida, who found himself losing control when his son screamed, invented a globe-
shaped "baby cry muffler" that fits over an infant's mouth. (The
patent notes that the globe can also be used as a rattle, though not
at the same time it's being used as a muffler.) Taking the opposite
approach, a frustrated father in Spain spent several years listening to babies cry and then used the data he gathered to invent the

Why Cry, a handheld electronic device that claims to translate cries into one of five messages: hungry, sleepy, bored, annoyed, or stressed.

At first Jennifer and I weren't especially concerned with Isaac's crying. We were more focused on Jennifer's crying. Like an estimated 70 percent of mothers, Jennifer came down with a case of "the baby blues" in the weeks after Isaac was born. For some women "the baby blues" come and go in a matter of days. But for 10 to 20 percent of women, the crying turns into full-blown postpartum depression.

While the biological origins of postpartum depression are now hard to dispute, no one is sure why it happens. The most widely accepted theory, that the depression is not a specific adaptation but a natural side effect of the hormonal changes that take place as a woman's body returns to its nonpregnant state, has been challenged by Darwinian theorists who doubt that such a strong and distinct emotional reaction could turn out to be accidental. Some biologists think that postpartum depression is related to lactation aggression, which causes females of many mammalian species to be especially defensive during the postpartum weeks as they keep watch over their newborns. While depression and aggression are very different feelings, it might be possible to explain away the discrepancy, since some experts on animal behavior believe that fearful animals are often mislabeled as aggressive when they panic. A more disturbing theory held by a small number of theorists stems from the indisputable record of infanticide in human history. According to this theory, the vulnerability to depression in the weeks after birth evolved so that mothers might abandon babies who were unlikely to survive. Horrific though it sounds, abandoning a baby who will never grow up makes perfect sense according to the amoral logic of natural selection, since the genes of parents who spent all of their time and resources raising children who failed to survive childhood would never reach future generations.

Whatever the cause of postpartum depression, Jennifer and I didn't feel we needed any theories at the time. Jennifer had plenty of practical reasons to feel overwhelmed. We were both responsible for our baby and both entirely freaked about it, but Jennifer was feeling that responsibility with a much greater intensity. I felt that if I didn't do my part, things would be harder for everyone else. Jennifer felt that if she didn't do her part, Isaac was going to die.

On the twelfth night of Isaac's life, Jennifer and I tried to go out to dinner at a restaurant a block from our apartment while my in-laws stayed with Isaac. I was thrilled to get out of the apartment, and so was Jennifer, at least at first. By the time we were a block away, Jennifer looked sick. She stopped walking.

"I feel like I left my kidney at home," she said.

We were lucky. After about a month, Jennifer began to feel much better. But there was little time to breathe a sigh of relief. Just when Jennifer started to cry less, Isaac began to cry more.

It wasn't only that Isaac's shrieks got louder or that they reached a higher pitch, although they did. It was that he didn't stop. Occasionally we'd enjoy a brief window of quiet after Isaac woke up from a nap, but once that window closed, usually after ten to twenty minutes, Isaac was usually either screaming or on the verge of screaming.

Jennifer and I now think that Isaac was suffering from infant colic. The label means little since there is no standard definition of colic. Some doctors diagnose it by the rule of three: crying that lasts for more than three hours a day, more than three days a week, for more than three weeks. The most salient feature of colic crying is that it is difficult, sometimes even impossible, to stop. Colicky babies are not necessarily crying because they are tired or hungry or experiencing digestive pain, as was believed by most doctors for the last five hundred years. They're just crying. No one knows why. In a *New Yorker* feature in 2007, Dr. Jerome Groopman described colic as a condition about which "medicine has almost nothing to say."

Isaac never cried for three consecutive hours in a single day, although I'm certain that on some days he would have if Jennifer and I had not worked so hard to calm him. At first I found that I could usually stop the crying by placing Isaac stomach-down on my forearm and bouncing my arm up and down. I'd seen another father hold a baby in the position, known as the football hold, before Isaac was born, and I was amazed by how well it worked. The problem was that it was the only calming technique that worked, and sometimes by the end of a day my arm would be so sore that I could barely lift it.

Then, a few weeks later, Isaac seemed to develop an immunity to my forearm. We went through several miserable days of screaming until Jennifer brought home a sling, strung it over her shoulder, and popped Isaac in. Snug in the sling, Issac looked like an unusually chubby fetus, but as long as we remained in constant motion, he would remain quiet. We were thrilled.

"I think it's going to get a lot easier now," I said. I wasn't just trying to make Jennifer feel better. I believed it.

Then the sling stopped working.

A few days later, on the advice of a friend of a friend, I brought Isaac into the bathroom in the sling and turned on the hair dryer. The instant the noise came on, Isaac stopped screaming and his eyes grew wider than I had ever seen them. It was as though he had been shocked into silence. The reaction was so sudden that it scared me. But the fear turned to delight in a matter of seconds. "Jennifer, you've got to come see this!" I yelled. Jennifer couldn't hear me over the hair dryer, and so I just stood there grinning to myself and thinking about how much better things were going to get now that we had a cure for the colic.

Then I realized that you cannot spend an entire day standing in the bathroom with your baby and a hair dryer.

I thought hard. A long extension cord for the hair dryer would allow me to move around the apartment but would pose a tripping hazard. The solution, it suddenly seemed obvious, was a portable, battery-operated hair dryer. I was pleased with this idea for a moment. I thought I might even get two portable hair dryers and wear them everywhere I went in a leather holster. Maybe, just to add to the shtick, I would even get a cowboy hat.

Then I thought about the financial analyst in Boca Raton who had invented a baby cry muffler. I can't become that guy, I thought. I can't become that guy.

Then I thought, The hell with it. I'm getting a holster and a cowboy hat.

Then Jennifer said the hair dryer could cause permanent hearing loss.

We grew desperate. One day I noticed that Isaac would smile when I made a loud Chinese-like sound and for the next several days I went around the house making profoundly offensive Chinese noises. It didn't help. When Isaac began to enjoy looking at his bumblebee mobile with spinning wings, Jennifer and I tried a two-person colic cure. Jennifer would carry Isaac in the sling, and I would chase after them, musical bumblebee in hand, like a crazed toy salesman. It didn't help.

We even tried some of the unlikely remedies we'd read about online. We rubbed olive oil into the bottom of Isaac's feet to relax him. When that didn't work we put a small serving of chamomile tea into a bottle. When that didn't work we drank the tea ourselves.

In the first months Jennifer and I could at least take solace in the knowledge that we were not alone, that, as difficult as it was to make it through a day, we were going through what all new parents go through. Then Jennifer went to a meeting of a local mom's group and we learned the truth: A few of the babies seemed like they might be serious criers, but most of them appeared to be able to remain awake for more than ten minutes without screaming. You could put them down on the floor or on your lap and they would just sit there and do nothing. You could bop them on your knee and they would not respond as though they were grenades whose pins had been loosened by the act of bopping.

"It's like observing a different species," Jennifer said.

"Damn those happy babies," I said.

We hated feeling sorry for ourselves. We were grateful to have a healthy baby and enough money to take proper care of him. We both knew how much harder some parents had it, how lucky we were that colic, which usually subsides after three or four months, was our major concern, rather than cerebral palsy, or a heart with a hole in it, or a breathing problem, or the countless other serious medical conditions a baby can have. And we knew that we were hardly unique even in our lesser suffering. An estimated 15 to 20 percent of all babies have colic.

But it is hard to relish your good fortune when someone in the room is screaming into your ear. It is hard to even be a decent human being when someone in the room is screaming into your ear. And the struggle to be decent was one of the worst parts of the constant crying. The stress brought out a part of me I had never seen before.

I reached my lowest point when Isaac was two months old. Jennifer had gone out to dinner with a friend. I encouraged her to go, but soon after she left, I was wishing I hadn't. Isaac started to cry and when the sling and hair dryer and pacifier all failed to put out the fire in my arms, I felt myself losing control. My chest was so tight with tension that it was hard to breathe.

I was hoping the worst was over when Isaac finally dozed off in the sling, but getting Isaac to sleep was only half the challenge. I still had to lower the sling onto the bed without waking him, a process that Jennifer and I referred to as "the transfer" and that we found as nerve-racking as anything we had ever done in our lives. On that night, knowing I couldn't take any more crying, I put the sling down even more slowly than usual. Probably a full minute passed from the time I lifted the strap over my head to the time Isaac made contact with the bed. But my caution was in vain. Isaac began to scream and as the noise echoed through my head, I did something I still can't believe. I looked down at my beautiful son and told him to "shut the fuck up."

I spent the next week debating whether I was the worst father of all time or only in the top ten worst. Then I said it again during another particularly bad crying spell.

I still feel terrible about those moments, but I now at least have a better understanding of what was happening. Crying is a serious health concern not because the babies are suffering permanent damage from their screaming but because their screaming leads adults to harm them, sometimes to shake them so violently that their brains bounce off their skulls and leave them dead or severely brain-damaged, a condition known as shaken baby syndrome. I never felt in danger of shaking Isaac, but it does not surprise me that one thousand to three thousand American babies die or sustain injuries from shaking every year, or that it's usually the father who commits the crime during a period of intense crying. Something about a particular cry made by some babies is uniquely unpleasant to the adult ear, so much so that the Bush administration reportedly blasted the sounds of screaming infants into the cells of prisoners at Guantánamo Bay in order to break them down.

Because colic poses risks to both babies and adults, Dr. Barry Lester, a professor of psychiatry and pediatrics and the director of a colic clinic at Brown University, insists that it should be studied and treated not as a passing medical problem but as a serious disorder that has the potential to wreak havoc on family life and create long-term relationship problems. Lester examines colicky babies at his clinic but his most upset patients are the parents. "Here is something that has no known cause and no known treatment," Lester told *The New Yorker* in 2007. "What could be more frustrating? For years and years, the mantra from doctors has been 'Bite the bullet.' The fact is, this message to mothers is devastating. The most common thing our patients say is, 'I must be doing something wrong.' It triggers a whole cycle: the mother feels inadequate and unable to parent effectively. And when these mothers get angry at their baby, they feel guiltier: 'How can I get angry at my baby?' The problem spirals out of control."

Jennifer and I did not have long-term relationship problems, but it wasn't hard to imagine it happening. At a moment when we needed to rely on each other most, we were arguing more than we had in years. Jennifer would tell me that I had put Isaac down on the wrong side of his baby bathtub, and I would respond as though there could be no greater crime against a person than to doubt his understanding of infant bathtubs. I would tell Jennifer that she was using too much A&D cream on Isaac's diaper rash and Jennifer would hand me the tube of cream and storm out of the room as though I had challenged her very right to raise a child.

When the arguments stopped, we could step back and see what was happening, and we tried to fight it. We did our best imitations of Isaac's postbreastfeeding face. We had family dance parties and mock family conferences at which Jennifer and I would have "serious talks" with Isaac about his behavior. We were grateful for whatever comic relief we could scrounge up, but the absurdity that had come to my rescue so many times before turned out to be no match for constant crying. By the end of the third month of Isaac's life, it was hard to escape the sense that something was fundamentally wrong. We had wanted a baby and we had known that it would be hard, but we had not signed up for this. I never admitted it at the time, but there were moments during those first months when I wondered if our decision to have a baby had been a mistake.

AMONG THE MOST FRUSTRATING ASPECTS of Isaac's colic were the well-intentioned comments from relatives who clearly thought that all our difficulties could be explained by our lack of parenting experience. It seemed that almost every time Jennifer and I described what we were going through, someone would smile and say something like "New parents are always anxious" or "You'll figure it out." I heard these comments so often that I was tempted to make a T-shirt that said "It's Not Me, It's Him" with an arrow pointing downward. Indeed I might well have made such a shirt if not for the problem that when I was not holding Isaac, the "him" in question might have been mistaken for my penis.

Even more frustrating than the comments were the various books and articles I came across that insist that extended bouts of crying are the product of the way we raise our babies in America. In *Our Babies, Ourselves,* an otherwise compelling book about parenting practices around the world, the anthropologist Meredith Small notes that on her many trips to Africa, she has never heard a baby cry, and claims that colic is a Western phenomenon. The problem, Small explains, is that we don't carry and feed our babies all day as mothers in other cultures do. "When an infant cries inconsolably for hours, when its tiny body arches in frustration, when its fist punches the air in anger," Small writes, "we see the clearest example of the clash between biology and culture."

The specific evidence cited for the cultural roots of colic is usually the !Kung San, a foraging population in southern Africa, and the explanation for why the !Kung San babies don't cry is always that they have exceptionally responsive parents. !Kung San mothers carry their babies at all times, react to their cries immediately, and breastfeed them constantly, as often as every fifteen minutes.

It makes sense that babies who are fed constantly won't cry much. After all, it's not particularly easy to cry when there is a breast in your mouth. But I was still convinced that Isaac would have found a way to cry even if we had fed him with !Kung San–like regularity, and the more I read about the !Kung San, the more I began to feel as though the entire population was a living indictment of my parenting skills. At my worst moments, I found myself fantasizing about walking into a !Kung San village, putting Isaac down on the ground, and shouting "Go for it," in the !Kung San's native Khoisan. At my even worse worst moments, I dreamed of sending letters to all the champions of !Kung San parenting. The letters would convey how grateful I was to learn that my son's crying was the result of my Western parenting techniques, and then end on a note of profound obnoxiousness: "P.S. Isn't it funny that the !Kung San practice infanticide?"

The biggest promoter of !Kung San parenting is the Los Angeles pediatrician Harvey Karp. Since the publication of his bestselling book and DVD, *The Happiest Baby on the Block,* Karp has become one of the most influential baby experts in America today. He regularly appears on national television to talk about his baby-calming techniques, and his advocacy of wrapping babies in blankets has given rise to a booming swaddling blanket industry.

Karp even has his own educator program and has certified hundreds of baby-calming instructors.

To quiet screaming newborns, Karp uses a combination of techniques he refers to as the 5 S's: Swaddling (wrapping babies tightly in blankets), Side/Stomach (turning babies on their sides), Shushing (using white noise), Swinging (jiggling the baby), and Sucking. While these techniques have been around for centuries, Karp's innovation was to use them all together, and he claims that when performed properly the 5 S's will work virtually every time.

In hopes of both learning more about how to soothe Isaac and talking about the !Kung San, I arranged a telephone interview with Karp. Karp's representative asked that I watch the DVD version of *The Happiest Baby on the Block* before the interview, and one night in the midst of the colic months, Jennifer and I sat down to watch it together. The DVD begins with a subdued Karp standing before the camera explaining the 5 S's. His thick mane of wavy brown hair and well-trimmed beard make him look the part of the celebrity he has become. As the video continued, we saw scene after scene of awed parents looking on as Karp calmed their screaming babies in a matter of seconds by tilting the babies onto their sides and shushing loudly in their ears. It was startling to watch: One second the babies look like mini, rage-filled Mussolinis—their faces are beet red, their fists clenched into tiny balls of fury—the next, they are peaceful little Buddhas in Karp's hands. The calming is so sudden and magical that I would hardly have been surprised if Karp had plucked hard-boiled eggs out of the babies' mouths or pulled an endless rope of swaddling blankets out of his shirtsleeve.

"If David Copperfield were a pediatrician he'd be Harvey Karp," I said.

"You talk about David Copperfield a lot," Jennifer said.

When I called Karp in Los Angeles, he told me that when he had trained as a pediatrician in the early 1970s, he'd been taught that colic was caused by gas pains and that if rocking a baby or car rides didn't work, the only remaining option was to prescribe strong sedatives like phenobarbital or opium. It was standard thinking on colic at the time, but by the end of the decade, the thinking was obsolete. Study after study had failed to prove the gas pains theory, and the practice of giving babies strong sedatives was no longer considered safe. "I would say to parents, 'I'm sorry. We just don't know how to make it better,' " Karp recalled.

It was only in the 1980s, when he began to consult on the cases of babies who had been badly abused during screaming fits, that Karp understood that something more needed to be done about crying. At the time Karp was a fellow in child development at the UCLA School of Medicine, and he found it hard to believe that modern science could do so little about excessive crying.

Karp began to read everything he could on colic, and his research led to two key findings. One discovery was that the !Kung San didn't experience colic. "I heard about these people in Africa who could calm their babies in under a minute," Karp told me. "So it was clear to me that either those babies in Africa were little mutant babies, radically different from our infants, or else their parents knew something that we had forgotten in our culture."

Karp's other discovery emerged from the new thinking about how childbirth evolved. Biological anthropologists had put forward the idea that for most of the first year of life, babies are, in a sense, still fetuses, born not because they are done developing but because if their heads grew any larger, they would never make it through the birth canal. With this concept in mind, Karp popularized the term *the fourth trimester* to describe the first three months of life.

For anthropologists the theory was of academic interest, but

Karp thought there might be a practical lesson for parents and doctors in the knowledge that babies are born in a fetuslike state. It was often said that babies were comforted and calmed by swaddling and jiggling because it made them feel like they were back in the womb, but Karp was interested in precisely what it was about the womb that helped babies to relax. "For hundreds of years we've known that some things work to calm babies," Karp told me. "But no one really ever knew exactly why. People kind of assumed swaddling was imitating the environment of the uterus, but what did that do? Were babies nostalgic for the womb?" Karp laughed. "Do babies go, 'Oh yeah. I'm back in the uterus. Far out.' "

As Karp's research progressed and he spent more time working with babies in his practice, he was struck by two observations. When babies were swaddled and jiggled and shushed in just the right way, they would calm down almost instantaneously, and virtually every baby would respond in the same way. Eventually it occurred to Karp that what he was really observing when the babies suddenly became relaxed must be a reflex, a response as involuntary and automatic as a leg jerking after a tap on the knee.

If a "calming reflex," as Karp dubbed it, is a real phenomenon—it's never been proven—it needs an evolutionary explanation, and Karp, an unusually broad thinker for a practicing pediatrician, has provided that as well. Karp told me that while others have theorized that babies evolved the ability to stop crying quickly so that prehistoric parents could quiet them when predators lurked, he thinks that the calming reflex evolved in the face of a different danger: childbirth. As the fetal brain grew larger, successful childbirth required fetuses to remain in a head-down position near the end of a pregnancy. The calming reflex evolved, according to Karp's theory, to keep fetuses from moving around too much inside the uterus and getting stuck in the wrong positions. "We're descendants of these Zen little babies who were put into a trance by these strong sensations in the womb and just kept their heads down for the last two months and relaxed," Karp said.

Karp said that he's waiting for someone else to do the research that will prove the calming reflex exists, since his own study would inevitably be received with skepticism. In the meantime, the "fourth trimester" and "calming reflex" concepts have helped him convince parents of the counterintuitive idea that to relax your babies you need to handle them in ways that seem decidedly unrelaxing to adults.

"When you understand that the sound inside the uterus is louder than a vacuum cleaner," Karp continued, "then it makes sense why being in a quiet room in a still bed by themselves is so utterly bizarre and unsettling for babies. The idea that babies cry because they are overstimulated is hardly ever the case. I mean, sure, if you've got blasting stereo music and banging pots and things like that, a lot of babies will startle awake. But if you take most babies to a noisy party or a basketball game, they usually go to sleep. They deal with that type of stimulation very well. What many babies have trouble dealing with is the absence of stimulation, the sensory deprivation that we expose our babies to once they are born."

"You have to elicit the calming reflex exactly right and then it works virtually every time," Karp continued. "If I hit your knee, and I'm off by an inch, absolutely nothing happens. Even if I hit it in just the right place and I do it too soft, nothing happens. But if I do it in the right place and with the right intensity, I can make your foot go out a thousand times in a row."

Karp said that some babies cry more readily than others. He referred to them as "more passionate" babies, but when I pressed him, he seemed unwilling to acknowledge that colic is an objective phenomenon outside a small percentage of medical cases. And, as I expected, he cited the !Kung San as his evidence.

"So is the implication that aside from these medical problems, there really isn't as much difference between fussy and nonfussy babies and that it's the techniques of—"

"Yes," Karp said. "The vast majority of colicky babies can be helped just by changing our parenting techniques."

I hung up thinking that Karp seemed sensible and that he was probably onto something with the calming reflex. Isaac's response to the hair dryer had certainly seemed like a reflex. I also think that in popularizing calming techniques like swaddling, he has done a nice thing for the babies of the world. Although we had initially failed at swaddling, after watching Karp's DVD, Jennifer and I bought a swaddling blanket and found that it did seem to make Isaac sleep a bit better.

But nothing Karp said changed my opinion that for more colicky babies, the calming methods are not quite as magical as he makes them seem. It's not that they don't work. I'm sure that in many cases they do. It's that if you have a real crier on your hands, the calming methods stop working the very second you take a break. And constantly soothing a baby on the edge of screaming is itself incredibly stressful, like walking around with a cup of boiling water filled to the brim.

My conversation with Karp had also failed to diminish my misplaced resentment of the !Kung San. So I was thrilled when, more than a year later, I learned that some !Kung San babies do cry. In the mid-1990s two researchers decided to take a closer look at the data Harvard anthropologists had gathered while closely observing the !Kung San from 1969 to 1971, and they found that the story was more complicated than had previously been reported. !Kung San babies do cry 50 percent less than Western babies. But even though they are constantly held and breastfed like all the others, a small percentage of !Kung San babies continue to cry on and on, just like colicky babies all over the world.

A more recent study by a group of European researchers came to the same conclusion about the universality of colic. The researchers studied infant crying patterns in London and Copenhagen. The researchers looked at three sets of parents and babies. One set held their babies for almost ten hours a day, the second group for eight and a half hours, and the third group practiced !Kung San parenting, holding their babies for sixteen hours a day and breastfeeding them all day long. The babies that were held for only eight and a half hours cried 50 percent more than the others but the "colicky crying" was the same for all three groups.

In 1999, James Leckman, a professor of psychiatry at Yale, asked parents to describe how they felt about their three-month-old babies. Considering how difficult parenting can be at three months, it would have been understandable if most of the parents had chosen not to respond. It would have been understandable if most parents had crossed out all of the choices and written "This sucks," or ripped up the survey and begun banging their heads against walls until Leckman was forced to call security. But parents, it turns out, aren't good at holding a grudge. Seventy-three percent of mothers and 66 percent of fathers felt that their three-month-old was "perfect."

I wasn't surprised when I read about Leckman's results. I probably would have said perfect as well. The single strangest part of Isaac's colic was that with each passing week, Jennifer and I were falling more and more in love with him. For each dark moment when I wondered if the decision to become parents had been a mistake, there would be two more moments in which I would be sure it was the best decision we had ever made.

It wasn't masochism. We took no pleasure in our torture. It was more like a severe personality disorder.

At times my love for Isaac felt almost romantic. The first time I noticed this, it bothered me. I expected to love my newborn son, not to have a crush on him. But a crush is what it felt like. Jennifer and I would usually be ready to collapse by the time we put Isaac to bed at night, but in the few hours we had before Isaac was due to wake up again, the one thing we wanted to do before falling asleep was to look at photos of him or discuss our current favorite parts of his body.

"I think right now it's the fat under his chin," I might say.

"I'm going through a thigh phase."

"Oh, you're right! I forgot about the thighs. Can I change my answer?"

It was enough to make even the most sympathetic of nonparents shoot themselves. And there was more. Some nights we would stand over Isaac's co-sleeper and admire him. No one's sleep has ever been so appreciated. Isaac would move his hand to his nose and I would run to get Jennifer as though he had just stood up in his co-sleeper and recited the Gettysburg Address. He would make an unusually sweet clucking sound and I would be racing to get the video camera as though the fate of the free world rested on my ability to capture those sweet clucks on film.

The only thing we appreciated more than watching Isaac sleep was watching him wake up. The wake-ups would begin with the slightest disturbance of the lips, a movement so subtle that you would never notice it unless you happened to be watching him. A quiet moment would pass and then the wet tip of Isaac's tongue would appear and disappear again, like a small crustacean peeking out from its shell and deciding the time was not yet right to take on the world. Then another, even longer, pause. You would think that the show was over. You would think that you had imagined the whole thing. And then, before you could catch your breath, the second act would begin with a dramatic rise and fall of the eyebrows. The eyelids would somehow remain closed but, as though the eyebrows' rising had flipped a switch, the rest of the face would now go into a flurry of motion. The nose would twitch. The forehead would wrinkle. The fat of the second chin would quiver like shaken Jell-O. The mouth would move left then right, sending ripples through the soft pink flesh of the cheeks. The second act might last anywhere from ten seconds to a minute. It was impossible to know. The only thing you knew for sure was that you had never seen anything so fascinating in your life. And then, just when you were sure it could not get any better, the dé-nouement: Like a magician's sheet being whisked away to reveal the impossible—the assistant's body split into two, the rabbit gone and replaced by a dove—Isaac's eyelids would flick open to reveal not pupils but two glowing white orbs. Your instinct would be to applaud but you would have no time because already the yawn would be starting, a yawn so gaping and enormous that it would seem somehow bigger than the face from which it arose. Sometimes the yawn would go on for so long that you would begin to worry that it would never end, that you would have to come to terms with the fact that your child would always have a large hole in the middle of his face. But eventually the mouth would close and the lips would seal. The face would quiet until it was as still as it had been during the peaceful sleep that had preceded the show. And then, and only then, would the eyelids open again to reveal two perfect brown irises staring back at you as though nothing out of the ordinary had just taken place.

THIRTEEN

Lactation

Freud, the Breast, and the Sea Squirt

LACTATION IS A FREUDIAN'S DREAM COME TRUE. It has everything the psychoanalytically inclined could ask for. Babies. Breasts. Sucking. Pain. The only things missing are the genitals.

Once Freud arrived at the idea that babies have sexual drives, it was almost a foregone conclusion that breastfeeding would become a central focus. Freud went so far as to suggest that a baby's blissful look after breastfeeding is the "prototype of the expression of sexual satisfaction in later life." And one of Freud's followers, Melanie Klein, took the argument a step further, claiming that the breast itself was the center of the baby's universe and that the infant's relationship to the breast existed independent of even the mother to whom that breast happened to be attached.

I can appreciate why Freudians would find it hard to think about breastfeeding without thinking about sex, but I was having no such problem in the first month of Isaac's life. To the extent that I was able to think at the time, I was wondering why, after so many millions of generations of being fine-tuned by natural selection, breastfeeding still ended up being so difficult.

Like any self-respecting dumb male, I'd always assumed that breastfeeding involved nothing more than picking up babies and letting them suck away. But that's not how things worked out for us. Sometimes Isaac would clearly want to eat but struggle to latch on to the breast. Other times—in what became known as Isaac's vaudeville routine—he would spend five minutes struggling hysterically to latch on and then fall asleep the very instant his lips touched the nipple.

The vaudeville routine should have been funny. But we were too worried and stressed to laugh. The struggle to get the feeding down had turned into a vicious cycle: The less Isaac ate, the more stressed Jennifer felt. The more stressed Jennifer felt, the less appetite she had, and the less appetite she had, the more nervous she felt about having enough milk for Isaac.

I have a long list of things I did wrong during my first months as a father, but my single biggest regret is that I added to the stress Jennifer felt about breastfeeding.

I wish that I had told Jennifer that it was no big deal if we had to use formula now and then. I wish that I would have said that the most important thing was for her to not feel so overwhelmed. Instead I told her that I was against the use of formula and encouraged her to keep breastfeeding. I even moved the bottles of formula we'd brought home from the hospital out of sight so that Jennifer wouldn't be tempted by them.

Jennifer said that I was making her feel trapped, and I felt terrible. But I also genuinely believed that by giving Isaac formula we'd be causing irreversible harm. I'd read and heard so much about the importance of breastfeeding that I forgot the lesson I'd learned again and again during my prebirth research: It's dangerous to believe in an idea too strongly—even when it's a good idea.

I wasn't the only person adding to Jennifer's stress. Every medical professional we encountered during the first month of Isaac's life seemed to have a different opinion on breastfeeding. The lactation consultant at the hospital urged us to immediately start Isaac on a three-hour schedule and to wake him up to eat if necessary. A nurse at the hospital said that there was no need to wake Isaac to eat unless he had slept for more than five consecutive hours. The instructor of the child-care class we took before Isaac was born recommended that we give Isaac as much milk as he would take as often as he would take it. Our pediatrician warned that if we fed Isaac all the time we risked expanding his stomach. "I know that you want me to tell you that it's okay to feed him more often," she said as Jennifer fought back tears, "but I'm just not going to do it."

Probably the logical thing to do when you are getting an endless stream of conflicting advice is to shut it all out and do your best by trial and error. Instead we called a lactation consultant.

Since the profession was formally created in 1985, lactation consultants have become the rising stars of the world of new parents. The International Board of Lactation Consultant Examiners has certified almost ten thousand consultants and the number is rising rapidly. Certification requires 2,500 hours of practice and forty-five hours of course work but it's also possible to be certified by smaller, less reputable organizations that offer degrees in a matter of days.

Rifka, the lactation consultant we called, was an energetic middle-aged woman. She arrived at our apartment in a long skirt—we later discovered she was an Orthodox Jew—and asked to observe Jennifer breastfeeding. After giving Jennifer a few pointers on how to position Isaac in her arms and recommending a better breastfeeding pillow, Rifka put on a pair of rubber gloves and asked to see one of Isaac's dirty diapers. I went to our diaper disposal system, removed the latest contribution, and brought it over. Rifka squinted her eyes and gazed into the diaper as though she were looking for a message in a crystal ball.

Jennifer and I said nothing as we awaited the diagnosis. "It's too green," Rifka said, shaking her head in disappointment. Rifka explained that babies who feed often but only take a little each time can fill up on the foremilk and won't manage to get to the good hind milk that makes their stools more yellow.

"The foremilk is the salad," Rifka said. "He needs to get the main course."

Rifka said that if possible we should wait an hour and forty-five minutes between the feedings.

Jennifer and I appreciated that *if possible*. Rifka was the first person we'd spoken to about breastfeeding who seemed to appreciate that not everything was possible.

Before leaving, Rifka recommended a cream that was supposed to make the breasts less sore. "Just a little is fine," she said to Jennifer. "You're not a bagel. You don't have to shmear it."

We followed Rifka's advice, but it was hard to know if it helped. One day Isaac would eat well and we would think Rifka was a genius. The next day the feeding would again be a struggle. In the meantime, Isaac began to cry more and more, which only added to our stress about the feeding.

Probably the logical thing to do when you have already spoken to a lactation consultant and are still not sure what you are doing is to shut out all the advice and do the best you can by trial and error. Instead I called another consultant.

The second consultant, Helen, was a postpartum doula and an expert in all newborn-related matters. I wasn't sure if I was going to hire Helen when I called, but I enjoyed our conversation. She told me that new babies were like immigrants who have come to a country where no one speaks their language, and it struck me as a nice image. I pictured Isaac wearing an adorable Russian cap and holding an antique trunk and then asked Helen to come by our apartment the following week.

I thought Jennifer would be pleased that I'd taken the initiative, but on the morning Helen was due to arrive, Jennifer was wishing I'd never called her. As it happened, the breastfeeding had been going much better in the previous few days, and Jennifer wasn't in the mood to have another person tell her what to do.

"You can just go in the other room and ignore her," I said. "I'll talk to her about the crying issues."

An hour later Helen was in our bedroom standing over Jennifer's bare shoulders and counting aloud every time Isaac swallowed.

Helen was an older, slightly rounded woman with wavy gray and black hair. She gave off an aura of warmth when she spoke, as though she were hugging you with her words. Jennifer played along with Helen's coaching, but I could tell that she was annoyed. And I suspected that Helen's unusually sexualized vocabulary wasn't improving Jennifer's mood.

In the course of an hour, Helen referred to Isaac as our lover several times and used the word *kiss* at least a half-dozen times. Isaac is a "living kiss," she said.

"Well, he's, um, living," I said.

"He was created from a kiss between you and Jennifer," Helen said.

The kissing was just the start. Helen said that babies are in a state of ecstasy the rest of us are always trying to reach and that babies can achieve a lingual orgasm, a process that apparently involves the rapid flapping of the tongue—what Helen referred to as a "flutter suck."

After describing the lingual orgasm in some detail, Helen moved on to soothing techniques and promptly put her pinky finger into Isaac's mouth.

I could see in Jennifer's eyes that she was not amused, and, recalling what I had already put Jennifer through with Sacha the water birth expert, I suggested that Helen and I continue to discuss soothing in the other room.

Helen followed me out of the room, her finger still lodged inside Isaac's mouth. But even before making it all the way to the couch, she stopped midstride, turned around, and rushed back to Jennifer.

"He's doing it right now!" Helen yelled out excitedly. "He's doing the flutter suck on my finger."

"Okay, well, we should probably let Jennifer get some rest," I said.

I HADN'T SPENT MUCH TIME thinking about babies and sexuality prior to Helen's arrival in our apartment, but with lingual orgasms on the mind, I decided it was time to explore the Freudian understanding of the infant. Since Jennifer had become pregnant, two different acquaintances had made the observation that a baby's first relationship is to the breast. I nodded when these comments were made, but I had no idea what they meant. I knew that babies and libidos were at the heart of psychoanalytic theory, but I didn't know much else, and the more I thought about it, the more bizarre it seemed that for much of the last century it was widely accepted that small children were tiny sex fiends moving through stages of oral and genital gratification.

As I began my research, I expected to discover that breasts play a central role in Freudian ideas about infantile sexuality, and they do. What I didn't expect to discover is that the story starts not with the breast or the genitals, but with the nose. And what I really didn't expect to discover is that the sea squirt, a potato-sized sea creature that grows on boat hulls, is at the center of the story.

According to classic Freudian theory, babies are born bisexual and develop through a series of sexual stages. The first stage of sexual development, lasting around eighteen months, is the oral stage, during which a baby seeks sexual gratification in the mouth. The second stage, the anal stage, begins in the second year and can last until age three or four, at which point the phallic stage sets in and babies begin to take pleasure in their genitals.

These stages weren't metaphors for Freud. They are a central component of Freudian personality development. A baby's ability to move through these stages in the proper way is the key to healthy psychological development and there are pitfalls at every turn. A baby who does not receive enough gratification from the breast might grow up to be manipulative and aggressive, always looking for a way to satisfy those early unmet oral needs. The baby who receives too much time at the breast might never grow out of the early dependency and struggle to become a self-sufficient adult.

According to the classic narrative of the origins of psycho-analysis, Freud arrived at the idea of infantile sexuality via his heroic self-analysis in late 1898, during which he explored his own dreams and realized that as a small child he had desired his mother. But the real story, as Frank J. Sulloway reveals in his groundbreaking work of Freud scholarship, *Freud: Biologist of the Mind*, is that Freud had arrived at infantile sexuality before his legendary self-analysis and that he took the idea from an ear, nose, and throat doctor from Berlin.

Freud met the doctor, Wilhelm Fliess, for the first time in 1887 when Fliess attended one of Freud's neurology lectures at the University of Vienna. Fliess and Freud took an instant liking to each other. Reading their correspondence it seems almost as if Freud was falling in love. "How much I owe you: solace, under-standing, stimulation in my loneliness . . . ," Freud once wrote to Fliess. "I know you do not need me as much as I need you. . . ."

Although Freud's supporters always dismiss Fliess as a crackpot, he was a widely respected doctor in the 1890s. And like the American doctors who became fixated on circumcision in the late nineteenth century, Fliess believed in the reflex neurosis. But in locating the origins of hysteria and other illnesses in the genitals, the American doctors were unknowingly borrowing from the ancients. Fliess, the ear, nose, and throat doctor, naturally believed that many physical and mental illnesses arose not in the genitals but in the nose, which was linked to the genitals through a reflex neurosis.

Freud came to believe in the nasal reflex theory wholeheartedly, writing to Fliess that the idea would one day be known as "Fliess's disease." In retrospect, then, the great irony of late-nineteenth-century medicine is that at a moment when puritanical Americans were tracing illness directly to the penis and clitoris, Freud was more focused on the nose.

If it seems odd that Freud, the great champion of the mind, could have put so much stake in a physical explanation of mental illness, it's only because Freud's background in neurology and anatomy has been edited out of the creation myth of psychoanalysis. Freud, in fact, was well entrenched in the same nineteenth-century scientific movement as Bekhterev and Pavlov, a movement of neurologists and physiologists who were intent on understanding humans in strictly mechanical terms. Freud and Bekhterev had both trained with the great French neurologist Jean-Martin Charcot in the mid-1880s, and just as Bekhterev had spent years cutting up cat and dog brains, Freud spent his early years as a scientist trying to understand the mechanics of the nervous systems of fish. Freud and Bekhterev even worked on the same neurological problem, distinguishing between the anterior and posterior roots of auditory nerves, and both experimented with hypnosis as a treatment for the mentally ill. (Although there is no evidence that they ever met, they also both once treated the same patient.)

In the mid-1890s Freud even worked on a grand unifying theory that would explain all of human behavior entirely in terms of biology, just as Bekhterev had attempted to do with reflexology. Freud referred to his biological reductionist project as "Psychology for Neurologists," and stated that his goal was "to furnish a natural-scientific psychology, that is, to represent psychical processes as quantitatively determined states of specifiable material particles, and thus make those processes graphic and consistent."

Unlike Bekhterev, Freud abandoned his reductionist theory after two years of frantic work. The project was taking a toll on Freud's health and Freud saw that it would be impossible for him to link specific mental states to specific physical states of the brain. But Freud's "Psychology for Neurologists" discussed many of the concepts, including the nature of biological drives, that would later become the foundation of psychoanalytic theory. And in light of his background in nineteenth-century physiology, it would have been entirely consistent for Freud to think that mental problems could arise from physical problems and that those physical problems might be linked through reflex reactions in the nervous system. In fact, Freud not only believed in the idea of a nasal reflex neurosis, but also thought that he himself might be suffering from neuroses that originated in the nose. On Fliess's advice Freud first treated his nasal reflex neurosis by padding his "genital spots" on his nose with cocaine, which was then used as an anesthetic. But Fliess saw cocaine as only a temporary solution. He thought permanent relief of Freud's symptoms required surgery and he would cut small pieces from Freud's nose when the two met in Vienna.

For obvious reasons, Freud's followers long downplayed his

interest in the nose. The idea of a nasal reflex neurosis now seems bizarrely unscientific. But Fliess's turn to the nose wasn't arbitrary. In fact, Fliess was following a chain of thought that was well within the bounds of mainstream Darwinian thinking at the time, and he was only one of a number of prominent scientists who believed in the link between the nose and the sexual organs. The theory emerged from the observation that smell was tied to sexual attraction in lower animals and was therefore part of humanity's evolutionary heritage.

A similar chain of evolutionary thought led Fliess and later Freud to infantile sexuality. In 1866 a Russian embryologist had made a surprising discovery: The embryos of sea squirts, the potato-sized creatures that were long thought to be plants, had primitive spinal chords. Darwin was thrilled. The sea squirt provided the missing link between vertebrates and invertebrates, and Darwin theorized, correctly, biologists now believe, that some sea-squirt-like creature must have been our earliest vertebrate ancestor.

The discovery made the sea squirt an important clue to understanding all of vertebrate evolution, and in *The Descent of Man*, Darwin suggested that the periodic nature of human gestation, growth, and disease might all be traced to sea squirts, which live in tidal zones and have vital cycles regulated by the changing tide. He also noted that sea squirts are bisexual.

Fliess, as Sulloway documents in great detail, was obsessed with male and female biorhythms and cycles and via a somewhat convoluted route he was able to derive infantile sexuality from Darwin's observation about the periodic attributes of the sea squirt. Freud accepted Fliess's arguments about biorhythms and used them to form many of his most famous ideas about the periodic development of the libido and childhood anxiety. In *The Interpretation of Dreams*, published in 1900, Freud explicitly stated that childhood anxiety can appear in periodic ebbs and flows because sexual libido can come in "successive waves of spontaneous developmental processes." Freud, in fact, became so interested in the importance of periods in human development and sexuality that he even began sending Fliess the dates of his wife's menstrual periods.

Fliess's Darwinian arguments for infantile sexuality also set Freud on the path to deriving his psychosexual stages. To a modern Darwinian the sexual preferences of the sea squirt might not seem particularly relevant to human sexuality, but in the late nineteenth century, Darwinism was still in its infancy. Biologists at the time had noticed that in the earliest stages of development, a human embryo resembles a tiny tadpole-like organism, and as embryos develop, they look similar to more advanced organisms. From this observation, they arrived at the "fundamental biogenetic law" which states that ontogeny recapitulates phylogeny, or, in other words, that in the course of development from embryo to adulthood a person progresses through the entire evolutionary history of its species.

This fundamental biogenetic law is now known to be wrong, but it was widely accepted well into the twentieth century. Freud adopted it as fact and believed that children were in the process of recapitulating the entire sexual history of human evolution. If sea squirts—or some early relative of the sea squirt—were bisexual, then babies had to pass through a bisexual stage and then progress toward later stages of sexuality. As Freud would explain it many years later, "Among animals one can find . . . in petrified form, every species of perversion of the [human] sexual organization." The oral stage seems to have come from Ernst Haeckel's idea that the very first sex in nature took place among multicellular saclike organisms that ate one another for gratification. The anal stage, in turn, could be explained by later organisms whose "genital apparatus," as Freud put it, "cannot be distinguished from the excretory apparatus."

When Sulloway published his biography of Freud, it was widely seen as one more attack on Freud's reputation. And there is good reason to be skeptical of Freud. The more scholars discover about his life, the more disturbing the story becomes. Freud repeatedly falsified his case reports, took ideas from others and claimed them as his own, and gave terrible advice. In one famous instance, Freud sent a woman who he believed was suffering from a nasal reflex neurosis to Fliess for surgery. Fliess's work on her nose left her bleeding and suffering from infections. After a while a strange smell began to emerge from her face. Freud sent her to another doctor, who discovered that Fliess had never removed the gauze from the inside of her nose.

Nevertheless, reading about the Darwinian roots of Freud's thinking made me admire him more rather than less. Freud's and Fliess's false beliefs about phylogeny might have caused them to get the specifics of infantile sexuality wrong, but in looking at sea squirts they were on the right track. The sea squirt fell out of fashion in biology labs in the thirties and forties, but in recent years it's become a popular research specimen again and is being explored for clues to understanding human immunology, developmental biology, and aging. And scientists are focusing on sea squirts for the same reason they interested Fliess and Freud: They offer clues to the origins of vertebrate evolution.

Freud's biggest mistake, arguably, was moving away from his Darwinian roots to more far-fetched theorizing that was based more in the imagination than in science. And there might have been a part of Freud that understood this. When in 1924 one of Freud's friends uncovered a paper on fish brains, which Freud had written as a young scientist in 1878, Freud seemed tickled by the discovery. "It is making severe demands on the unity of personality to try and make me identify myself with the author of the paper on the spinal ganglia of the petromyzon," Freud commented. "Nevertheless I must be he, and I think I was happier about that discovery than about others since."

FOURTEEN

Sleep Training

Little Albert and the Dark History of American Psychology

IN MANY WAYS American parents are like parents everywhere. I discovered this one day by watching an alarming number of baby videos on YouTube. Almost as soon as I started watching, one salient fact jumped out at me: A lot of the videos were just like my videos of Isaac. The babies, doughy and round, were doing more or less the same things: pawing at the air, laughing hysterically at decidedly unfunny things, clapping in celebration of nothing in particular. And the parents were even more predictable than the babies. No matter which country the videos came from, the parents made the same high-pitched sounds and goofy faces. I never imagined that I would see a Japanese or French or Argentinean version of myself, but they are on YouTube by the hundreds.

Still, if all parents are equally ridiculous, our cultural biases do sometimes lead to dramatic differences in parenting styles, and American attitudes about sleep are a good example. In surveying sleeping patterns around the world, cultural anthropologists have found that American parents are more likely than any others to put their baby to sleep in the child's own bed.

American babies shouldn't take their expulsion from the parental bed personally. The primary reason that American parents are less likely to share a bed, or a room, with their babies is that for the last hundred years almost every expert has told them to avoid doing so.

The case against co-sleeping was partially medical—doctors feared that babies could be smothered when a parent rolled over, an outcome that is now widely agreed to be unlikely. But as often as not, it was the psychological rather than the physical risks that the baby experts emphasized. The prevailing theory was that babies who shared a bed with their parents wouldn't grow up to be self-sufficient, independent adults, and in America, more so than in other places, failure to achieve self-sufficiency is a frightening diagnosis.

Before Isaac was born, Jennifer and I decided that it would be best to have him sleep next to our bed in a co-sleeper. I was still occasionally having nightmares that left me flailing about on the mattress and I didn't want to risk whacking Isaac in my sleep. But our decision ended up making little difference. Although we put Isaac down for the night in the co-sleeper, Jennifer would take him out of it for his first nighttime feedings and most of the time—even on the nights Jennifer could have sworn she had put him back—we would wake up to find him lying between us.

When he wasn't crying, it was a pleasure to share a mattress with Isaac. He was warm and mushy and sometimes his heavy breathing made him sound like a purring cat.

"If only he could use a litter box," I whispered one night as Isaac purred by my side.

"If only he could eat out of a bowl," Jennifer whispered.

"And catch mice," I said, my voice growing louder with excitement. "And leap onto counters."

His cat sounds notwithstanding, Isaac's presence in our bed wasn't usually a cause for celebration. On a bad night, he would be up almost every hour. I would fall back asleep within minutes but

Jennifer wasn't so lucky. Once he was on our mattress, Isaac ate nonstop and sometimes slept with his hand on Jennifer's breast, as if to ensure that I wouldn't take off with his loot. As he grew older, he began to pinch and claw as well.

"It's like going to sleep every night at an S&M club," Jennifer said.

If we failed to complain about our lack of sleep at first it was only because we were too overwhelmed by the crying and breast-feeding problems to worry about anything else.* But during Isaac's fifth month, with the breastfeeding going smoothly and the worst of the colic over, Jennifer and I began to talk about sleep training, the practice of letting babies cry until they learn to fall asleep on their own.

Neither Jennifer nor I particularly liked the idea of sleep training. We had worked so hard to calm Isaac during the day because we both believed that babies feel real anguish when they cry, even if they can't reflect on their unhappiness in the way that adults can. And, though we knew that letting babies scream at night

---

* One of the good things about the human brain, or at least my particular human brain, is that it's only capable of juggling a few major worries at once. Some years ago it occurred to me that the secret to happiness might lie in somehow tricking the brain into becoming preoccupied with subjects that lead to only moderate anxiety. If the moderate anxieties took hold, I reasoned, there would be no room left for the more potent worries. After giving the subject some thought, I decided that the thinness of my calves would be an ideal object for my obsessions, since I feel bad, but not terrible, about my calves. The next step was to figure out how to fool my brain into focusing on my calves. The only thing I could think of was to walk around all day with a photo, but then I would have to respond to questions about what I was doing, and there aren't so many good excuses for carrying around a picture of your calves. I could say it was "calvnitive behavioral therapy"—a play on "cognitive behavioral therapy"—but that's not funny and would explain nothing. I could say that I had taken the photo in order to examine my legs for ticks—which is exactly the sort of insane thing I might do at the height of a neurotic panic—but the very mention of ticks would make me think of Lyme disease, a more serious worry, and then I would be back to square one.

worked out well for many parents, it was hard for us to imagine Isaac wailing for a few minutes and then deciding that he should call it a night and catch some z's. If his daytime behavior was any indicator, Isaac was more than capable of crying all night long.

My resolve to try sleep training might have been stronger had I not remembered my own fear of sleeping alone. I shared a room with my older sister until age five, and when my father broke the news that Jessica was moving into her own room, it felt as though I were being placed in solitary confinement for life.

"You can't share a room with her forever," my father had said, trying to reason with me. "What would you do when one of you got married?"

"I wouldn't care," I said.

"But what if Jessica's husband cared? Or your wife?"

"I know they wouldn't," I said.

Jennifer could also remember her fear of the night—although, unlike me, she'd had a cadre of Cabbage Patch Dolls to protect her. And so after looking at a number of different books for advice, we settled on a middle-of-the-road approach to sleep training: We wouldn't let Isaac cry or put him in another room, but we would move him into a crib on the other side of our bedroom and stop offering him a meal every time he woke up. In time, we reasoned, he would learn that there was no food to be had in the night and would stop seeking it.

I thought the plan sounded great until we sat down to discuss the logistics. If Jennifer was no longer going to be feeding Isaac, someone was going to have to comfort him when he woke up in the middle of the night. And since Jennifer had already carried the burden for months, it was now my turn to not sleep.

I accepted my new responsibility without protest, and, as I expected, the transition to milkless nights did not go over so well with our new roommate. The first sign of Isaac waking up was typically the soft thumping of his swaddled feet against his mattress, and the sound alone could strike terror in our hearts.

"Oh God, please no," I would say at the sound of those first thumps.

"It can't be," Jennifer would say. "He's been asleep for less than an hour."

And then more thumps, now slightly louder—the footsteps of the approaching villain in the scary movie.

"It just can't be."

(Cue the haunting music.)

"No, no, no."

And then the desperate begging. But here the movie analogy breaks down because rather than begging for mercy from the approaching villain, I would be begging for mercy from my fellow victim.

"Please just wake up with him this time," I would say, fully aware that only hours earlier I had confidently assured her that I would be the one to get up and that it really wasn't a big deal.

"But you said—"

"I know. I know. But . . ."

"But what?"

"I'll give you twenty bucks."

"Sam, we share a bank account. You can't bribe—"

"One hundred dollars!"

Eventually Isaac's cries would drown out my begging, and I would give in and try to get Isaac to fall back to sleep by laying him down on my chest and rocking wildly from side to side—a technique Jennifer dubbed "the mental institution soothing method" because both Isaac and I looked as though we belonged in a padded cell.

When my rocking failed, as it almost always did, I would get up, grab the sling, and for the next few minutes pace around the apartment in the dark arguing so vociferously for Jennifer to feed Isaac that we both began to refer to me as "Isaac's agent."

"This is crazy," I would say. "He wants to eat."

"But I thought we agreed that he wasn't going to eat during these hours?"

"Yes, yes, but he really does seem hungry this time."

"I just fed him fifteen minutes ago. He's not—"

"Growth spurt."

"You say growth spurt every night. He should be twenty feet tall by now."

"Okay, how about this. We let him eat for five minutes. You know, just to sort of relax him."

"I don't even have any milk left."

"Two minutes and not one second more."

Sometimes I would win these battles, and sometimes not. When I didn't, my nights were maddeningly similar to my days. At four in the morning, I would often be standing in the bathroom with Isaac and a hair dryer, and as the noise whooshed through my numbed brain, I would wonder how it could possibly be that in the age of birth control, generation after generation of men and women continued to have babies. I knew that lots of parents experience some form of this 4 A.M. despair, and at the time, this thought depressed me even further. I was prepared to be a cliché in my happiness, but in my unhappiness, I wanted at least the Tolstoyan promise of exceptionalism.

I knew, of course, that it could be worse. It was worse, in fact, for our upstairs neighbor, Steve, who had to listen to Isaac scream throughout the night but got none of the benefits of parenthood. Almost every night we would hear Steve wake up after Isaac and then pace around his apartment. Sometimes we even heard his muffled groans. Jennifer and I both felt terrible about Steve's situation, and it made our stress significantly worse, particularly on the mornings that we saw him coming down the stairs looking as bad as us. After one particularly bad night, Jennifer emailed Steve an apologetic note, to which he replied kindly, and then asked if it would be possible for us to move Isaac to another room.

The next night we dragged Isaac's crib into the kitchen/dining area of our one-bedroom apartment. We were happy to experiment with the new arrangement for Steve's sake, but Isaac sleeping next to the kitchen created a new set of dilemmas, specifically, we could no longer eat after 7 P.M. We managed to avoid using the kitchen for the first few nights but soon Jennifer and I were making night raids to the pantry on our tiptoes, both of us feeling as though Isaac, stern-faced and huffing in his crib, were the parent, and we the mischievous children.

But the night raids weren't our biggest concern at that moment. Our more serious problem was getting Isaac to fall asleep in his crib. We'd always helped Isaac go to bed for the first time of the night by letting him hold on to one of our hands. But while it wasn't particularly difficult to offer him a hand when he was in the co-sleeper, giving him a hand in the crib meant standing hunched over the railing for as long as an hour. To escape from Isaac's side, Jennifer and I would try to inch our hands down his body, but even when Isaac's eyes were closed he remained on high alert for such shenanigans. Sometimes I would manage to slip my hand downward so that I was holding only the loose fabric on his pajama footsies and yet somehow he could sense when I let go. It was as though he had installed his own high-tech motion-detector security system in his crib.

Unwilling to cede defeat, one night I tried a new technique to escape Isaac's watch. Rather than standing hunched over the crib, I spread out on the hardwood floor and offered Isaac only a single finger through the slats of the railing. To my pleasant surprise, Isaac accepted my meager offering and I found that the finger trick allowed me to get away in less than half the time. I reported the good news to Jennifer and soon she too was lying on the floor every night with a finger in the crib.

We were delighted with our progress, but the finger trick also came with a problem of its own. Once we managed to work our respective fingers free from Isaac's clammy palm, it was far too risky to stand up and let him see us. It was too risky even to rise to our hands and knees. And so we did the only thing we could. We army-crawled back into our bedroom on our elbows.

Painful though it could be, a part of me enjoyed the crawling. For a few seconds I could forget that I was a thirty-year-old man on the floor of my own kitchen and pretend that I was a Navy SEAL on an undefined but extremely important mission. But with no military fantasies to fall back on, Jennifer found little to redeem the act of traversing her own apartment on her stomach. One night after crawling back into our bedroom, she stood before me, brushed the lint off her shirt, and spoke the six words that all babies would dread if they could understand them.

"I think it's time for Ferber," Jennifer said.

JENNIFER WAS REFERRING to Dr. Richard Ferber, the name that has become synonymous with the "cry it out" method of putting babies to sleep. In 1974, while a fellow at the Harvard Medical School, Ferber noticed the scarcity of research on the sleeping habits of small children and took it upon himself to fill in the gap. A decade later he published *Solve Your Child's Sleep Problems,* the book that would make him famous.

In his book, Ferber argues that if parents comfort them every time they cry in the night, babies will associate the comforting with falling asleep and become dependent on it. To break their nighttime comforting addiction, parents need to let babies cry themselves to sleep and should begin to do so as early as at three months, when infants begin responding to the circadian rhythms of day and night.

Ferber's research and Harvard degrees added authority to the idea that letting a baby shriek was the best solution to sleeping problems, but he was far from the first person to suggest the method. Baby experts, including Benjamin Spock, had been encouraging American parents throughout the century to let their babies cry. In fact, Ferber might be viewed as the final chapter in a much larger story about how Americans thought about babies in the twentieth century.

The Ferber method rests on two key ideas. One is that babies can learn by making associations—specifically, they can learn that comforting is associated with sleep and then refuse to go to sleep without it. The other idea is that babies are better off when they sleep alone. And in the 1920s and '30s, the name most associated with these ideas was John Broadus Watson, the founder of American behaviorism.

Watson was born in 1878 and grew up on a farm in South Carolina in a family of devout Baptists. Watson's mother took him with her to tent revivals but rather than inspiring him, the fiery pastors turned Watson off to religion for life, and he never lost his knack for rejecting authority. When he studied psychology as a graduate student at the University of Chicago, Watson was decidedly unimpressed. The psychology he encountered was classic introspective psychology, but to Watson it made no sense to try to understand a person's thoughts or feelings. Guessing at what was going on inside a person's mind seemed suspiciously like the religious worldview he had already dismissed.

Still, at the turn of the century, rejecting the study of human thought didn't necessarily mean rejecting psychology. The mechanistic outlook, the idea that humans could be understood in strictly physiological and material terms, had spread to America via German universities, and for a new generation of American psychologists the appeal of the idea was enormous. Psychology was still a young discipline struggling for credibility in an academic environment in which the physical sciences were regarded as far more prestigious. American psychologists were tired of wrestling with questions about minds and thoughts, as William James had done so elegantly throughout his career. They wanted to be more like physicists and less like philosophers, to make an impact on a booming America that valued productivity and efficiency above all else.

It was this new psychology that emerged from the new physiology that captivated Watson. In 1903, Watson completed his graduate work with a dissertation on the nervous system and behavior of the white rat and it established him as a rising star in the field. A decade later, in 1913, Watson published a manifesto that would change the course of American psychology. "Psychology is a purely objective experimental branch of natural science. Its theoretical goal is the prediction and control of behavior," Watson declared. "Introspection forms no essential part of its methods."

Watson's manifesto created the stir that Watson had hoped for, and the triumph of behaviorism in American academia took much less time than he could have imagined. Two years after his famous speech, Watson was elected president of the American Psychological Association, and behaviorism would go on to dominate American psychology for much of the next fifty years.

But in 1913, Watson still had a problem. He had made a public declaration that psychology should be a study of only behavior, rather than thoughts, but he still had no clear idea of how to go about turning the study of human behavior into a scientific discipline. "It is one thing to condemn a long-established method, but quite another thing to suggest anything in its place," Watson remarked several years after his famous speech.

The natural place for Watson to turn for his new science was Russia, where Pavlov and Bekhterev's work on behavioral conditioning was laying the groundwork for a more scientific psychology. Pavlov's experiments with salivating dogs had made him an international hero in the war against introspection, and to this day many accounts of Watson's life cite Pavlov as a key influence on Watson's thinking at this critical moment in his career. But in the end it was not Pavlov but Bekhterev whom Watson would turn to, the same Bekhterev who had indirectly given rise to hypnotized birthing and the Lamaze method. Both Pavlov and Bekhterev were focused on the idea that behavior could be reduced to a series of linked reflexes, but Pavlov was the more cautious scientist of the two. While Pavlov was narrowly focused on the secretions of dogs, Bekhterev was shocking dogs' paws to try to understand how the motor system was conditioned. Watson wasn't Bekhterev's intellectual equal, but he was a daring and far-reaching scientist in Bekhterev's mold, and it was Bekhterev's broad application of reflexes to every aspect of human behavior that Watson transformed into American behaviorism.

In a 1904 essay, Bekhterev had already put forth an "objective psychology" that spelled out many of the central ideas Watson would arrive at over a decade later. And though Watson would later downplay Bekhterev's influence on his thought, it's well known that Watson and his colleagues only began their conditioning experiments after translating Bekhterev from the French in 1914, and that they worked on the very motor experiments Bekhterev had described.

The similarities between Bekhterev and Watson extended beyond their science. Just as Bekhterev had tried to reconcile reflexology with Marxism, Watson was eager to use his new science to forward the American ideals of the day. The great appeal of behaviorism, after all, wasn't just that it turned psychology into a hard science by replacing the study of thought with the study of behavior. It was also that it came with the promise of shaping human behavior for the good of mankind. In Stalin's mind, the idea that you could shape people by tightly controlling their environment might have had a dark appeal, but behaviorism lends itself to utopianism just as easily.

And if you want to create a better world through conditioning, babies are the obvious place to start. "Give me a dozen healthy infants, well-formed, and my own specified world to bring them up in and I'll guarantee to take any one at random and train him to become any type of specialist I might select," Watson once famously declared: "doctor, lawyer, artist, merchant-chief and, yes, even beggar-man and thief, regardless of his talents, penchants, tendencies, abilities, vocations, and race of his ancestors."

In 1917 Watson and a colleague published a paper in which they argued both that humans were born with only three emotions—fear, rage, and love—and that the emotional lives of adults were dependent on how these three emotions were conditioned in infancy. But the paper was purely speculative. To prove this theory, Watson would need to experiment with a baby, and in 1920 he found a poor wet nurse to let him experiment with her nine-month-old son, Albert.

Watson first wanted to see if he could condition Albert to fear a stimulus and then decondition the fear out of him. Working with his assistant, Rosalie Rayner, Watson began by testing Albert's initial responses to different stimuli. According to Watson and Rayner's account of the experiments, the first time Watson introduced Albert to a white rat, Albert gurgled happily and reached out to touch the animal as it moved around him. By contrast, when Watson took a long metal bar and struck it with a claw hammer just behind Albert's back, Albert would become upset and cry. Convinced that Albert feared the noise but not the rat, Watson moved on to the second stage of the experiment. He brought the rat to Albert just as he had done before, but this time struck the metal bar with the hammer every time Albert reached for the rat. Watson repeated the pairing of the rat and the noise on seven different occasions. By the eighth time he brought the rat to Albert, there was no longer a need for the hammer and bar. The sight of the rat alone brought Albert to tears, and the fear wasn't restricted to rats. Watson claimed that Albert now feared every furry animal, even a sealskin coat. Thirty-one days later, Albert was tested again. He still feared the rat and the sealskin coat, although he was willing to touch the coat with hesitation.

The next step for Watson was to see whether he could remove the fear of rats in Albert, and he had a number of ideas as to how he might do this. He thought he might reintroduce the rat while giving Albert a bottle of warm milk or candy, or perhaps allow the rat to stay with Albert until he became habituated to it. If these methods failed, the backup plan was to show Albert images of the rat while stimulating his lips and nipples, and, if need be, his genitals.

But the Little Albert experiment, as it is now known, was never completed. Albert's mother, not surprisingly, decided to remove her son from the hospital, and the next year Watson's academic career came to a sudden end when Watson's wife discovered his love letters to Rayner. The scandal that ensued forced Watson to retire from academic life and Albert was lost to history. To this day, no one knows what became of him, and it's possible, if unlikely, that even now there is a very old man named Albert who has spent his life in terror of rats.

It might have seemed like good news for the babies of the world when Watson gave up his research, but it turned out that Watson wasn't done with babies. From academia Watson moved seamlessly into the role of popular scientist and his influence continued to grow. He wrote articles for parenting magazines and in 1924 brought his scientific thinking to the mainstream with his book *Behaviorism*. On January 4, 1925, *The New York Times* ran a blaring headline across an entire page: MAN AT BIRTH HAS NO FEAR, TESTS REVEAL: DR. WATSON'S EXPERIMENTS SHOW THAT MOST SUPPOSEDLY FUNDAMENTAL INSTINCTS ARE ACQUIRED BY THE CHILD AFTER IT HAS BEGUN ITS LIFE. The 6,500-word feature on Watson's ideas included a photo of him holding back a large dog, its snout just inches from a baby's face.

Three years later, in 1928, Watson published his own parenting guide, *Psychological Care of Infant and Child*. At the time, the parenting expert was a growing phenomenon in American life. Just as academic psychologists were anxious to bring the rigor of science into their field, many American parents were anxious to bring the promise of the new scientific age into their homes. The advice books of the period are filled with almost comically detailed feeding charts and sleep schedules. "Your child will never know that there are laws that govern the universe unless he knows that there are laws that govern the home," Ada Hart Arlitt wrote in her 1930 guide, *The Child from One to Six*. "It was formerly believed that mother was the simple and safe basis for the problems of training; it is now known that a much more adequate guide is the kitchen timepiece."

At the turn of the century, the most well-known baby expert to tap into this longing for a more scientific parenthood was Dr. Luther Holt. In his bestselling *The Care and Feeding of Children* Holt provides detailed diets for babies—at approximately five months, they should receive four ounces of barley gruel a day—and warns parents against excessive emotion. "Never give a baby what it cries for," Holt insists, later adding that "[b]abies under six months old should never be played with."

Holt's antisentimentality might sound extreme by contemporary standards, but compared to Watson, Holt was a softy. In the first page of his book, Watson suggests that the ideal scenario for babies would be to abolish motherhood altogether. Babies would instead be raised by rotating foster parents who would be much less likely to show them any affection.

Recognizing that motherhood wasn't going away in the near future, Watson went on to describe an emotion-free parenting program. "When you are tempted to pet your child remember that mother love is a dangerous instrument," Watson wrote. Even allowing a baby to sit on your lap was forbidden. If parents felt they absolutely had to show a child some sign of love, Watson allowed for one kiss on the forehead at bedtime and a handshake in the morning.

From Watson's perspective, affection itself wasn't the problem. The problem was that by showing their children affection, parents were conditioning an emotional reflex that would cause the children to remain dependent on affection for their entire lives, a fate similar to the Freudian baby who spends too much time at the breast. And as if Watson's message were not frightening enough, he also insisted that babies were permanently conditioned by age two and that in a matter of days parenting mistakes could set children on the wrong path. "Mother love could inflict a never healing wound," Watson wrote in a typical passage, "a wound which may make infancy unhappy, adolescence a nightmare, an instrument which may wreck your adult son or daughter's vocational future and their chances for marital happiness."

Considering Watson's extremism, the most surprising thing about *Psychological Care of Infant and Child* may be how well it was received. In its review, *The New York Times* credited Watson with beginning "a new epoch in the intellectual history of man." *Parents* magazine wrote that it was a must-have for "every intelligent mother's shelf."

IF FERBER SHARES Watson's belief in conditioning babies at an early age, he is far from a 1920s antiaffection extremist. In fact, Ferber maintains that he created a program to reduce the amount of time babies cry at night precisely because he takes crying and infant suffering seriously. But, in the earlier editions of Ferber's book, at least, it was still possible to see traces of the ideas of the harsher baby experts. Ferber argues that sleeping alone in cribs teaches children to see themselves as independent individuals, and that even if babies seem happy sleeping in bed with their parents, it's probably not a good idea to allow it to continue.

In drawing this link between sleeping alone and independence, Ferber was perhaps unknowingly regurgitating a uniquely American myth. In a 1997 attack on Ferber, the science journalist Robert Wright makes a good point that somehow rarely came up in twentieth-century America. "It isn't obvious to me how a baby would develop a robust sense of autonomy while being confined to a small cubicle with bars on the side and rendered powerless to influence its environment," Wright notes. ". . . I'd be willing to look at the evidence behind this claim, but there isn't any." Nor, for that matter, is there any reason to assume, as Ferber does, that the fear of sleeping alone indicates an emotional problem. Wright can barely contain his dismay at Ferber's insistence that "there must be a reason" why babies are afraid of sleeping alone:

Yes, there must. Here's one candidate. Maybe your child's brain was designed by natural selection over millions of years during which mothers slept with their babies. Maybe back then if babies found themselves completely alone at night it often meant something horrific had happened—the mother had been eaten by a beast, say. Maybe the young brain is designed to respond to this situation by screaming frantically so that any relatives within earshot will discover the child. Maybe, in short, the reason that kids left alone sound terrified is that kids left alone naturally get terrified. Just a theory.

But then Wright, who writes regularly about morality and evolution, would be the first to say that there is no reason to assume that what's natural is also what's good.

And this is where Jennifer and I found ourselves during Isaac's fifth month: on the one hand thinking that sleep training was not only harsh and unnatural but also a product of an outdated individualistic ethic we didn't subscribe to, and on the other hand desperately needing to sleep.

In the end exhaustion prevailed. We decided to Ferberize our son. The key to the Ferber method is letting your baby cry for increasingly long intervals and resisting the urge to pick him or her up. On the first night, you can go into the baby's room after three minutes, but then should not return again for five minutes, and so on. The next night the intervals should be longer.

Jennifer and I decided that we wouldn't ever let Isaac cry for more than fifteen minutes. If he passed the fifteen-minute mark, we would just accept army crawls as part of life.

On the first night of Ferber, we prepared ourselves with a pep talk, like a sports team before a big game.

"We can do this," I said.

"And in the long run, he's going to cry less," Jennifer said.

"Much less," I said. "We just need to take things one day at a time."

Jennifer kissed Isaac good night, and then I carried him into the other room and put him down in his crib, feeling like Abraham putting Isaac's namesake down in the sacrificial pit.

"I love you so much," I said, bringing my hand to Isaac's face so that he might experience one little gesture of warmth before being left to fend for himself in the dark of our kitchen. I meant to just glance his cheek, but before I could pull my hand away from his soft skin, Isaac reached up and clutched it.

Two minutes later Jennifer walked out of the bedroom and found me hunched over the crib.

"What's going on?" Jennifer whispered, clearly exasperated.

"He caught me."

"He caught you?"

"He's got my hand. I can't get it out." I shrugged with my free arm. "We'll start tomorrow."

The next night, knowing that I couldn't let Jennifer down again, I put Isaac in his crib and raced back into the bedroom, as though I were running from enemy fire.

"Quick, turn up the TV," I said. "We can't listen to the screaming."

Jennifer turned the volume almost all the way up, but behind the roar of *The Simpsons* we could still hear our son wailing.

"I can't do this," Jennifer said. "I'm going out on the balcony."

"Okay," I said. I spread out on the floor and tried to watch *The Simpsons*. Then I got up and opened the door to the balcony.

"I think it's been five minutes," I said.

Jennifer checked the time on her cellphone. "It's been less than two minutes," she said.

"Right," I said. I lay down again, listened to Isaac, and got back up.

"Is it five minutes yet?" I asked.

"It's not even three," Jennifer said.

"All right, well, maybe I should just go. I mean, by the time I get there . . ."

We both appreciated that it took only ten seconds to walk to his crib but Jennifer could hear Isaac through the open door and she was breaking down along with me.

"Okay, just go," she said.

I returned to Isaac's crib. My plan was to reassure him that he was not alone, put his pacifier back in his mouth, and then walk away.

Two minutes later, Jennifer appeared and found me hunched over the crib.

"He got me again," I said, grateful that I could not see Jennifer's expression in the dark. "We'll start tomorrow night."

The next night it seemed as though Isaac might not be feeling well and we both agreed that we couldn't let him cry. And then we lost our momentum. Isaac might have been ready for Ferber but Jennifer and I weren't ready to Ferberize.

We didn't give up altogether. Every month or so, after a bad night, I would catch Jennifer flipping through Ferber's book and joke that Isaac was in big trouble. And midway through the ninth month of Isaac's life, we decided to give it one more shot. Jennifer went out onto the balcony again and I turned up the TV.

I only made it to four minutes, but after giving Isaac his pacifier, I managed to get away. Isaac cried for a total of thirteen minutes that night, much less than I had expected. On the second night he cried for a total of ten minutes.

On the third night, he was silent even before the initial five minutes were up. And on the fourth night, when I put Isaac down and walked away, he didn't make a sound.

I stood by the door and waited for the scream for another minute but there was only silence. It felt so miraculous that I wouldn't have been surprised to see a rainbow when I walked back into our bedroom.

Jennifer and I hugged, and then looked at each other.

"I'm worried something is wrong," I said.

"Me too," Jennifer said.

"Maybe I should go check?"

"No," Jennifer said.

A minute passed, and still silence. "Okay, maybe you should go check," Jennifer said.

I waited a few minutes and then opened the door and stepped out. Isaac was standing in his crib in silence, gazing at me. I could barely breathe.

"Okay, just, um, uh, good night," I said. I turned around and raced back to the bedroom.

"What's he doing?" Jennifer asked.

"He's just standing there."

"Just standing there?"

"Yeah."

Jennifer looked like she might faint from amazement.

"We're parenting geniuses," I said.

FIFTEEN

Child Care

The Nanny Spy

AMERICANS USED TO LIKE happy nanny stories. Walt Disney had to soften the edges of the original Mary Poppins of Pamela Travers's books before putting her on film. But times have changed. Now we are more interested in bad nannies. If Disney were creating Mary Poppins today, he would probably have to make her even nastier than the original. He would probably have to include a new ending in which Mary Poppins is caught on a nanny-cam beating the Banks children over the head with her magic umbrella.

The tide might have turned against nannies with the case of British nanny Louise Woodward. In 1997, Woodward was convicted in the killing of an eight-month-old baby in Newton, Massachusetts. The case became a media sensation and Woodward became the embodiment of the worst fears of the American parent. By the time the conviction was reduced to involuntary manslaughter and Woodward was released from prison, it was too late. Our image of the nanny was already stained with blood, and American parents were already rushing to buy cameras to spy on their children's caretakers.

The rising sales of spy equipment might be the best indicator of how American parents feel about their nannies. Tiny wireless cameras that sell for under a hundred dollars have become popular items at Radio Shack and spy shops around the country. One market research firm found that nearly 40 percent of households with children in 2004 expressed interest in spy cameras, up from 16 percent in 2000. In 2006, Pat Palmer of Spy Chest, an Internet company that sells spy cameras, told *The Arizona Republic* that the market was "exploding," and that sales of hidden cameras had doubled the company's growth for four consecutive years.

When Jennifer and I began our search for a nanny in the last month of her pregnancy, our goal was to find someone so transparently trustworthy that we wouldn't even be tempted to spy.

The first nanny to come to our home for an interview, a large jolly woman in a blue jumpsuit, insisted that we call her Nana Jane. She seemed warm and loving and my first impression was that she would make an excellent nanny. Then, several minutes into the interview, Nana Jane paused in the middle of a sentence and looked at me.

"I know, Daddy," she said. "I'm tired, too."

I smiled. I felt fine, and I didn't particularly appreciate Nana Jane suggesting that I looked worn down. "I'm actually not—"

"Boy am I tired," Nana Jane said, leaning back in her chair.

If her insistence that I looked tired had been her only offense, I would have been happy to overlook it. But Jennifer and I were both also troubled by the way Nana Jane gossiped about her last employer, a mother in the neighborhood. When the subject turned to feeding schedules, Nana Jane shook her head. "Donna just couldn't get any milk out," Nana Jane said, lifting her hands to her breast. "She was just pumping and pumping."

I nodded. From that moment on almost everything Nana Jane said made me pause. When I asked her if she had experience giving babies tummy time—for a several-week period prior to Isaac's arrival, I had come to believe that putting newborn babies on their stomachs was the single most important thing a parent could do—Nana Jane nodded.

"Sure," she said. "I like to grease the baby up and move it around. It's boring for a baby to sit there like this." Nana Jane dropped her head as though she were dead, then lifted it back up and laughed.

By the time Nana Jane revealed that she had once yanked the arm of a toddler in her care so hard that the child had to be taken to the hospital, I had already decided that she was not the nanny for us. "It was an accident," Nana Jane said. "I cried all weekend."

The next nanny we interviewed, Mary, was in her twenties and going to school in the evenings. She had braided hair and braces. She seemed competent, but also stern: "I can only work with you if there's cooperation and communication," she said. By the end of the interview, it felt as though she were interviewing us, rather than the other way around, and I could already imagine her becoming the dominant figure in our home.

"I'm slightly scared of her," I said after Mary left.

"She'll probably be putting us in time-out," Jennifer said.

Her sternness notwithstanding, we might well have hired Mary had she not broken the first rule for nanny job applicants, which is that they should never set up their cellphones so that when you call them you hear the song "Sexual Healing" in place of ringing.

The next nanny we interviewed, Natasha, had dyed red hair and black sunglasses resting on her head. She was an ethnic Russian from Azerbaijan and she impressed us by talking lovingly about the children she had cared for in the past. She even carried photos of them in her wallet.

After speaking with her references and hearing only good things, we hired Natasha to take care of Isaac on Tuesdays and Thursdays. (I would take care of Isaac on Mondays and Wednesdays, and Jennifer would handle Fridays.)

Natasha started to work for us when Isaac was five months old. It was good timing. Our nights were still a disaster but the worst of the daytime colic had passed, and Isaac was on something resembling an eating and sleeping schedule. On a good day, we could even get him to fall asleep by putting him in his stroller and jiggling it, as opposed to pacing with the sling. (It's perhaps the best testament of all to the difficulty of the colic months that the prospect of jiggling a stroller until our arms became numb seemed like a dream come true.) When Isaac wasn't crying, he was also becoming much better company. He was smiling more and more, sometimes even breaking into the sort of full-fledged chuckle that has turned many a happy baby into a YouTube celebrity. And he was also gazing at us with something that looked like real affection. So what if his bumblebee mobile received even more loving looks. One of the hardest parts of the first months was that, for all our efforts, we got almost no affection back from Isaac. Now we were happy to take what we could get.

Every now and then we would even have a moment that felt downright tranquil. Isaac would be sitting in his bouncy chair gazing at the dangling plastic fish and Jennifer and I would feel almost jolted by the peacefulness.

"Isn't this what you imagined parenthood would be like?" Jennifer asked one day during one of these peaceful moments.

"Totally," I said.

We laughed. Then I told Jennifer that I thought we had turned a corner.

"You always think we've turned a corner," Jennifer said.

It was true. In the first six months of Isaac's life I had falsely proclaimed turned corners almost every week. But this time I was sure of it.

I'd like to think that we would have turned that first corner on our own, but having Natasha in our lives made a big difference. Sometimes she seemed too good to be true. She held Isaac all day and sang "Baa Baa Black Sheep" in a high operatic voice. I thought that she had to be putting on a show, that no person could possibly sustain that much warmth and energy for so many hours, but one day when I came home from work early, I paused at the door and heard her belting out "Baa Baa Black Sheep" like usual.

Another day Jennifer came home and found Isaac on his back on the couch. Natasha had one of his feet in each of her hands and was flexing his knees. "We are making calisthenics," Natasha said. "He *iz* getting little bit heavy."

Not everything about Natasha was perfect. There were occasional communication problems that gave us pause, such as the time Natasha announced that she had taken Isaac outside in a plastic bag—it took us a minute to figure out that she meant the plastic rain cover on his stroller—but we were not about to complain, particularly when Natasha was filling our refrigerator with the best borscht and kasha you've ever tasted. In fact, the only real downside to our nanny situation, as far as Jennifer and I could see, was that Natasha was making a mockery of our own child-rearing skills.

And yet, even with our very own Azerbaijani Mary Poppins it was hard not to worry sometimes, particularly during the first weeks, when we still didn't know Natasha very well. One night, during the second week of Natasha's tenure, Jennifer raised an issue that hadn't occurred to me. The only things we really knew about Natasha were what her references had told us. We didn't even know where she lived.

We decided that we would get more information from Natasha, but with our paranoia in the air, we also talked about whether we should get a nanny-cam.

It wasn't an easy decision. On the one hand, it seemed intuitively wrong to me to spy on someone without permission. On the other hand, it seemed insane to leave your baby with someone you knew so little about.

I could see that in even considering a camera we were being paranoid, and it struck me that we were experiencing the dark side of parental love. I am always on the lookout for a good response to existential despair, and the intense love that coursed through me when Isaac slept in my arms was probably as good a response as I will ever muster. It was only after Isaac was born that it even occurred to me that meaning might be a feeling rather than a fact.

Still, if love is profound, it isn't bliss. Sometimes the love I felt for Isaac was overwhelming. Worrying about the health and happiness of Jennifer and the rest of my family was already a full-time job, and now there was another person to worry about with even more intensity. Sometimes it felt as though in becoming a father I had opened a new border to invading armies of disease and accidents and violence. And the new border was even harder to protect than the old border. The new border was vulnerable to everything and sometimes you had no choice but to abandon the watchtower to someone you barely knew.

WE DECIDED AGAINST A CAMERA, but to learn more about nanny and baby safety I contacted Tamara Pilblad, founder of a nanny surveillance outfit called Whereismybaby.com, which provides GPS tracking of nannies, background checks, and nanny-cam installation.

Tamara invited me to her Manhattan apartment, where she lived with her seven-year-old daughter, Lily, and her dog, Riley. The apartment was decorated with an unusual mix of antique furniture and quirky knickknacks. In the foyer, a footstool stood on two plaster feet. A clock that looked as if it had once been in an old European train station jutted out from the entry to the living room. Tamara was thirty-seven and petite with straight brown hair. She has a soft, slightly raspy voice that sounds subdued until she begins to talk about the safety of small children, at which point her entire body becomes animated. She told me that she had wanted to hide video cameras to see if I could find them, but a client had rented most of the cameras the day before. Instead, Tamara led me through the rooms and pointed out all the places a camera could be.

"See that globe on the cabinet? It would be easy to punch a camera through there," Tamara said. "See that big hand?" Tamara pointed to one of those large foam hands with a "We're #1!" index finger pointing up. "I had a camera in there yesterday."

I followed Tamara into her living room, where she pulled a book—Chinua Achebe's *Things Fall Apart*—off the shelf and showed me how she had taken out the insides and made a hole in the cover for a camera. In Lily's bedroom, Tamara picked up a teddy bear.

"I could put one in here, but I don't like to use teddy bears," she said. "Kids like to touch them. A clown doll is better. Kids are scared of clown dolls."

Tamara tapped a small boom box on Lily's cabinet.

"Is that a camera?" I asked.

"No, but it could be," Tamara said. "At the spy shop they sell a camera that looks exactly like it. You can't tell the difference." I asked Tamara how anyone has time to watch all the tapes from their nanny-cams, especially people like Tamara's clients, who have multiple cameras set up in different rooms. It seemed that someone would have to spend all night watching the footage.

Tamara didn't seem to see the problem. "You can watch four cameras at once on a split screen and fast-forward through the slow moments," she said.

We sat down in the living room, where I noticed a suspicious-looking Rubik's Cube on a stand on the coffee table.

"I bet that Rubik's Cube is a camera," I said.

"No, that's a Rubik's Cube," Tamara said.

"What about that antique phone?"

"That's an antique phone."

I asked Tamara how she had ended up in the nanny spying business and she told me that she had graduated from George-town Law in 1997 and spent the next five years in the Army's Judge Advocate General's Corps, where she achieved the rank of captain. She then moved to New York, and, after a stint as a labor and employment attorney, Tamara took a position in Citigroup's ethics and compliance division.

At Citigroup, Tamara saw firsthand how a large company monitors its workforce, right down to reading private emails and instant messages. "Every job these days has a built-in way of monitoring their employees, especially the high-stakes ones," Tamara said, her voice picking up steam. "The highest stake for me is the well-being of children but that's where we have the least amount of safeguards and protection."

Yet what really motivated Tamara to start a nanny surveillance company wasn't what she witnessed at Citigroup but what she witnessed at a dance class. On Fridays Tamara would leave work early to pick up Lily from her ballet lessons. Most of the little girls in the ballet class were met by their nannies and while Tamara waited for the class to end, she would sit in a small room with the nannies and listen.

Some of what Tamara heard was troubling: nannies talking about dropping off their charges with other nannies and going shopping; nannies visiting boyfriends or taking babies to their own apartments in other boroughs. And some of what she heard was horrific: One nanny admitted that she'd given a child a big dose of Nyquil so she would sleep all day. Another claimed that she used the gas on the stove to get the child to go to sleep, figuring that since she weighed three hundred pounds and the child weighed thirty-five, she'd have plenty of time to turn the gas off before it knocked her out.

Tamara said that the nannies often spoke only in Spanish, and I can't help but wonder if she misunderstood the gassing story. But whatever she heard, it resonated with her. Tamara had had her own bad nanny experience when Lily was two. A nanny had asked for several weeks of advance pay and then disappeared with the cash.

It was with these nanny memories in mind that Tamara took an exam to become a licensed private investigator and then left her job to start Whereismybaby.com, originally incorporated under the name Merry Pop-ins, LLC, in May 2005.

I asked Tamara if she ever felt bad about her spying. I could understand why some parents felt the need to do it, but I couldn't entirely rid myself of the feeling that it was wrong to watch other people without their knowledge.

"I tell parents that the best thing to do is tell the nanny before they hire her that she'll be monitored. It protects the nannies, too," Tamara said. "People are people and nannies are human. They have lives. They get upset. They make mistakes."

Tamara explained that the Nyquil and gassing were extreme cases. The bigger problem was the well-intentioned nanny having a bad day and lashing out at the child in a moment of stress. "People are people," she said again.

I scanned the room for more cameras. Tamara disappeared into her bedroom for a moment, then returned with a box of baby wipes. "Look at this," she said. She opened the box, removed a thick layer of wipes, and pulled out a rectangular GPS tracking device. "You can put this in a diaper bag and then track your baby on a map."

ooo

Usually the cameras and GPS devices were enough to answer parents' questions about their nannies, but sometimes there is no substitute for live nanny surveillance. I asked Tamara if I could join her on a stakeout. It was part professional curiosity and part realization that it was the only chance I would ever have to live out the universal male fantasy of being an undercover agent.

When I met with Tamara she was sitting on a green bench in the park reading *The New York Times*—or at least pretending to read *The New York Times*. I sat down next to her. There was no need for pleasantries. We both understood why we were meeting in the park on New York's Lower East Side that morning.

"The subject's over there," Tamara said, gesturing with her head.

I didn't look. It was my first stakeout and I wasn't going to blow it by gawking at the subject.

"It's okay, you can look," Tamara said.

I turned my head and there, about thirty yards away, was the nanny. She had a full, curvy figure and straight brown hair that fell over her shoulders. She was talking on her cellphone and pushing a baby in a swing.

I turned back to Tamara. She saw the nervousness in my eyes. "Try and relax," she said.

We continued to wait in the park. The nanny pushed the swing. The baby swung back and forth.

"Do I look okay?" I asked Tamara. I had thought a lot about what to wear to the stakeout before deciding that my usual attire— jeans and a short-sleeved collared shirt—would be sufficiently inconspicuous.

"Your clothes are fine, but that big blue recycling bag isn't helping," Tamara said.

I wanted to kick myself. Probably somewhere there is a rule-book for spies and on the first page it says, "Whatever you do, don't show up for a stakeout carrying an enormous blue bag." I knew the bag was a bad idea, but I needed to bring my computer—box and all—to a nearby store for repairs and it was the only large bag I had.

"Try and relax," Tamara said.

I asked Tamara why this baby's mother was suspicious of the nanny. All Tamara knew was that the mother had been having doubts about the nanny for some time, and now she wanted the hard facts.

Tamara took out a manila folder and showed me an email the mother had sent her. The mother described the nanny as "a little thing, but curvy" and the baby as "pale-skinned, with blue-gray eyes and chubby cheeks—not much hair yet." Then the mother listed what she wanted for the fifty dollars an hour (the price has since gone up to eighty-five an hour) she'd be paying for Tamara's services:

I pretty much want to know everything . . .

What time does she leave the apartment?
Where does she go?
Does she put her on the swings?
Does she ignore her?
Is the baby ever crying?
Is she on the phone the whole time?
Does anyone join her?
Does she stop for food?
Is the baby sleeping at any time? If so, where? On her, in the
    stroller?
Is the stroller seat laid back or upright?

Does she feed her anything or give her any bottles?
If it's sunny, does she have her hat on at all times?
Exactly what time does she get home?

Having more experience at this than I do, you may be able to
suggest other things to note. I can also call or text you in the
morning to let you know what both of them are wearing.

Ten minutes passed.

"Okay, let's move," Tamara said.

I looked up. The subject was leaving the park. By the time I
gathered my recycling bag, Tamara was off. I ran down the street
to catch up.

Tamara was on her cellphone. "She's walking toward Rivington
Street," she said. "Hurry."

"Who was that?" I asked, still struggling to catch my breath.

"Matt," Tamara said. "He's driving the van."

The van? There was no time for questions. The nanny was
keeping a quick pace. We stayed about twenty yards behind. Now
and then Tamara took a pad of paper out of her purse and jotted
down the nanny's coordinates.

At Ludlow Street, the nanny turned the corner. We were suddenly in peripheral vision. Tamara hooked my arm in hers. I
wasn't sure why. Presumably she wanted us to appear as a couple
in case we were spotted, but it wasn't clear that appearing as a
couple would make us any less conspicuous.

I decided to play along, hoping no one I knew would see me
walking arm in arm with a woman who was not my wife.

The nanny turned another corner. Tamara stopped and looked
up at me.

"Kiss me," she said, her voice urgent.

I looked into her eyes. Was she serious? I didn't want to ruin the mission, but I also didn't want to jeopardize my marriage so that Tamara could keep her cover. I pictured myself telling Jennifer what had happened. "The good news is that I helped a nanny spy keep her identity a secret. The bad news is that I had to make out with her to do it."

Tamara, meanwhile, was moving ahead as if nothing unusual had just happened. I caught up to her and we followed the subject down another block. The nanny turned again and Tamara looked up at me.

"Kiss me!" she said.

I saw then that this was not a joke. I tried to think of something, anything, to say.

"So the idea is that you don't want her to have a chance to see your face, right?"

"I have to use whatever resources I have," Tamara said, already heading down the block.

We tracked the nanny three blocks back to the apartment building where the mother and baby lived. Matt's van was parked in front of the building. I stepped into the passenger seat and Tamara scooted into the back.

Matt sat smoking a cigarette in the driver's seat. He had long wavy hair streaked with gray and wore black jeans, black cowboy boots, and a black leather vest with a barely visible tank top beneath. Had a team of experts traveled the world in search of someone who looked exactly like what you would expect an eighties rock star to look like today, they couldn't have done better. Every touch was perfect, right down to the dirty bandana hanging from the knob of his turn signal.

Matt told me he was a carpenter who worked with Tamara on the side. He had a New York accent. I asked him if he enjoyed working with Tamara and then he launched into a short speech, somewhat less articulate than Tamara's, about why it's important to keep tabs on nannies. "Someone's gotta watch out for the kids," Matt said.

"Matt cried once," Tamara called out from the back of the van.

I looked at Matt.

"I didn't really cry."

"Remember that one time when we saw the nanny shake the kid?" Tamara said. "You were tearing up."

"Okay, I was tearing up," Matt said.

As he spoke, Matt fingered a rubber chicken that was attached to a long pole. The chicken pole was a prototype of a device Tamara had invented to attach to strollers. The idea, as I understood it, was for the chicken to stick out in front of a stroller so that oncoming traffic would see it before the stroller made its way into the street. It seemed unlikely to me that many parents would want to put poles with rubber chickens on their strollers, but I didn't say anything.

Tamara reappeared between Matt and me with a cooler full of snacks. I took a bottle of water and some salt-and-vinegar potato chips. The conversation drifted off. I tried to think of something to offer. "It's a shame that I didn't bring a disguise and pretend to be a deliveryman," I said. "I could walk right into the apartment." I added a slight chuckle to indicate I was trying to be funny.

"Why? Were you planning to chloroform the nanny and rape her?" Tamara said.

"Ummm . . . uh, no," I said. "I was just thinking that for all this work of following the nanny, we don't have any idea what's going on in the apartment."

"The mom's got nanny-cams," Tamara said. "She knows what's going on in there."

The van was sweltering and Tamara said that if the nanny stuck to the schedule the mom had given her, we wouldn't see her again for several more hours.

I decided to drop off my computer and then go to my office, only a few blocks away, to cool down. When I returned a few hours later, I spotted Matt hurrying down the street on foot. "She's on the move," he said under his breath.

For the first time, I felt nervous for the nanny. Tamara and I didn't make the most intimidating duo, but it would be scary if she realized Matt was following her.

Up the street, I saw the nanny adjust the stroller's umbrella to keep the sun out of the baby's face. The poor woman, I thought. She's taking perfectly good care of that child and this is how she's being rewarded.

Then the nanny, who apparently had told the mother she spent the afternoons in the park, pushed the stroller inside a New York University dorm and didn't emerge until it was time for her to bring the baby home.

I have no idea what the nanny did inside that college dorm for two hours, but it didn't seem like a good place for a baby.

Tamara waited in the van, now parked just behind us, and I stood next to Matt on the corner. Matt didn't say much, and pretty soon my exciting stakeout didn't feel so exciting anymore. The weirdness of the moment—I was stalking a woman and a baby with a man who looked like a member of Journey—was no longer obscuring the depressing story beneath the surface. We've somehow arrived at the point where overburdened parents are hiring strangers to watch their children and then hiring additional strangers to monitor the first strangers.

At one point during the afternoon, Matt went back inside the van, and the responsibility for the stakeout was mine alone. The excitement returned. If I lost my focus for even one second, the subject could lose us and the entire mission would be a failure.

My pulse quickened. My breaths grew short.

But the thrill of being a lone spy was short-lived. When I glanced over my shoulder at the dark window on the van's back door, I could just make out Matt's peering eyes.

SIXTEEN

Baby Classes

Mommy and Me Yoga, Loneliness, and the Growth of the Infant Brain

IT'S A GOOD TIME to be a studious baby. American babies today can take a class in just about anything: music and rhythm, dancing, Chinese, yoga, gymnastics, sign language, even cooking.

The classes aren't cheap. In New York, a yearlong music program can cost up to six thousand dollars. But the expense doesn't seem to be slowing demand. Music Together, a franchise of music classes for young children, has expanded to 1,700 communities around the country, and the number of teacher-training sessions has doubled since 2000. Some New York baby classes are so highly sought after that parents add their baby to the waiting lists on the day of their birth. The hottest class of the moment, Little Maestros, a music class for children as young as six months, is so popular that some parents are reportedly trying to bribe instructors for a spot.

The brochures for baby classes are usually filled with the same claims about stimulating or developing infant minds that are now found on almost every baby product—in addition to exposing children to music, Little Maestros includes "language development activities." Music Together emphasizes that the classes offer a "research-based, developmentally appropriate early childhood music curriculum." And while many parents no doubt ignore these claims, for some parents the educational benefits of the classes are the main draw. "I want my child to have any edge another child has," one father told *The New York Times* in 2006, explaining why he spends six thousand dollars a year on classes for his three-year-old. In New York, in particular, where preschool enrollment is often a highly competitive process complete with intelligence tests, getting a baby into the right class can feel like a high-stakes proposition. "Fail to provide the right stimulation during early childhood and your child will suffer devastating consequences," Sara Mead wrote in a 2007 Education Sector report on the false claims about infant education. "Pass on baby water aerobics, in other words, and you can say goodbye to college."

The classes and products might be entertaining for babies, but as the Education Sector report makes clear, that doesn't mean that babies gain any developmental benefits from them. In fact, much of the science behind the claims for baby classes and products relies upon the same creative interpretations of brain research that inspired Brent Logan to invent the BabyPlus Prenatal Education System.

The enthusiasm for stimulating baby brains can be traced back to the last decades of the twentieth century. Logan was seemingly interested in the growth of neurons—the cells of the brain and nervous system—but the parents, educators, and policy makers hoping to stimulate babies have been more focused on synapses, the chemical junctions that connect one neuron to another.

Neurologists have long known that cognitive development depends upon neurons making connections with one another—but it was only in the 1970s, when a handful of researchers undertook the painstaking task of dissecting animal and human brains and counting the synapses under microscopes, that we began to discover when the networks are formed. And perhaps more so than any other scientists in recent decades, those synapse-counting neurologists changed the way we raise our children today. Before synapse counting began, brain researchers assumed that the adult brain was much more dense in synapses than the infant brain, since adults are capable of much more complicated cognitive tasks. But the opposite now appears to be true. Right around the time of birth, synapses begin to grow at an astonishing rate, trillions of them, and the spectacular growth continues in spurts throughout the first two years of life until the brain has many more synapses than can ever be used. As the brain continues to mature, the active synapses are strengthened and the unused synapses begin to die off—a process known as synaptic pruning, which continues throughout adolescence.

It's easy to see why the findings about the growth and decline of synapses captured the public's imagination as the studies were written up under provocative newspaper and magazine headlines. If synapses in the brain grow rapidly only in the first years of life, and if the synapses that aren't actively used die off, then it takes only a small leap to arrive at the idea that the more our brains are stimulated in the first years of life, the more synapses we will have, and the more powerful our brains will be. And these links—between stimulation and more synapses and between more synapses and more brain power—looked even stronger after a handful of rat studies found that raising young rats in enriched environments could not only make the rats better at solving tasks but could also increase the number of synapses in adult rat brains.

The excitement about synapses also fit together well with another line of research that was generating excitement during the same period. Neurologists at the time knew that if adults developed cataracts and lost the ability to see, their vision would return if the cataracts were removed. But if a child was born with cataracts that were not removed by age five or later, the blinded eye or eyes would remain blind for life.

Because of the ethical problems, it was hard for neurologists to study sensory deprivation in humans. But in the 1960s, attempting to better understand the phenomenon, David Hubel and Torsten Wiesel found that if they placed a patch over a kitten's eye for the first three months of its life, the cat would remain permanently blind in that eye. And when Hubel and Wiesel dissected the cats' brains, they saw that without incoming data from the eyes, the visual cortex failed to develop properly. Eyesight in both cats and humans appeared to be dependent upon a critical period very early in life, and if the critical period passed without proper environmental stimulation, the damage was permanent.

Hubel and Wiesel's famous research—they later won a Nobel Prize—had focused on the visual cortex of cat brains, but the implications were tantalizing for anyone interested in how the human brain develops. Perhaps, the reasoning went, it wasn't just vision that was subject to critical periods. Perhaps if children didn't receive the right stimulation in the first years of life, their brains would forever be as useless as the eyes of those blindfolded kittens.

The move from stimulated rats and blind kittens to the intelligence of babies is one that few scientists have ever been willing to make. But the absence of conclusive research did nothing to stop the flow of popular articles about the new brain studies that began to emerge in the 1980s. In one typical example, a 1986 article in *Parents* magazine titled "Brain Power: You Can Make Babies Smarter," the educational psychologist Jane M. Healy cited the same studies on the stimulation of infant rats that Logan had mentioned to me and argued that the new neuroscientific research implied that if infants were not stimulated from an early age it could affect their lifelong ability to learn.

By the 1990s, the hype about making connections between children's neurons before it was too late had reached a fever pitch. In a 1996 *Newsweek* cover story, "Your Child's Brain," Sharon Begley wrote that a baby's experiences can wire neural circuits just as a programmer uses a keyboard to reconfigure the circuits of a computer. "Which keys are typed—which experiences a child has—determines whether the child grows up to be intelligent or dull, fearful or self-assured, articulate or tongue-tied," Begley declared. ABC, for its part, aired a celebrity-filled prime-time special on the importance of early stimulation. And Hillary Clinton, then the first lady, organized the Conference on Early Childhood Development and Learning in 1997 so that leading scientists and pediatricians could come together to discuss the implications of the latest research on neurons and synapses.

Meanwhile the discussion of brain development in the media was moving beyond claims about intelligence to more dramatic claims about the social implications of failing to stimulate babies. "Unfortunately, for a growing number of children, the period from birth to age three has become a mental wasteland," the Pulitzer Prize—winning science journalist Ronald Kotulak writes in his 1997 book *Inside the Brain*. "Society needs to focus on this period if it is to do something about the increasing rates of violent and criminal acts."

In the face of so much hype, it was easy to forget that none of the studies being touted in the press had shown that babies benefited from early stimulation of their senses. Neurologists and developmental psychologists now believe that, while the early findings about blindfolded cats oversimplified a very complicated process, some fundamental, species-wide human abilities, such as the ability to see and hear and use language properly, are subject to critical periods. But the research had found only that complete sensory deprivation could impede development. There has never been good evidence that extra stimulation—beyond the sights and sounds that all babies hear in the course of daily life—enhances infant development.

The good news for all of us is that, for most of the ways that we learn, critical periods don't appear to exist. The thrust of the most recent brain research points in the opposite direction. Rather than remaining frozen in time after age three, the human brain is amazingly plastic and continues to change—and even grow new neurons—into adulthood. With the notable exception of the ability to perfect foreign accents, the type of learning we do in school or throughout our daily lives has little to do with critical periods, which is why adults can still master complicated cognitive tasks such as reading. As John T. Bruer notes in his book *The Myth of the First Three Years,* "Binocular vision might only develop during a certain period, but we can learn algebra at any point in our lives."

Moreover, as Bruer also makes clear, even if we somehow could stimulate babies and prevent synapses from dying off, we have no idea how additional synapses would affect intelligence, if at all. Some neurologists think that synaptic pruning is the key to intellectual development. Even the rat-stimulation studies turned out to be misleading. Further research found that the synaptic growth in stimulated rats only took place in the visual areas of the rats' brains and, since the same changes would occur when older rats were stimulated, the rat studies said nothing about critical periods.

Perhaps because they don't make for good journalism, the later findings that dimmed the hopes of would-be baby stimulators received almost no attention in the media. Meanwhile, in the early nineties, enthusiasm for critical periods and synapses still on the rise, a single study of thirty-six college students further muddled the public's understanding of infant brain development. The study, published in *Nature,* found that college students did better on tests of spatial imagery if they listened to a Mozart sonata. The effect wore off after a few minutes, and a number of efforts to repeat the results failed, but by then it was too late. The Mozart Effect had been released into the zeitgeist. In a 1999 review of the most cited studies in the top fifty U.S. newspapers, Stanford researchers found that the Mozart study was cited 8.3 times more than the second most popular paper at that time.

The Mozart Effect generated so much excitement that states across the country drew up legislation to expose children to classical music. Georgia governor Zell Miller asked his state legislature to put aside $100,000 so that every newborn in the state could receive a classical CD or cassette. The state of Florida passed a law that required state-run schools to play classical music to toddlers every day.

And among the people to take note of all of the latest studies about baby brains was a mom in Colorado named Julie Aigner-Clark, who tapped into the baby stimulation craze more successfully than anyone else when she videotaped a handful of toys, set the footage to classical music, and then, in a final brilliant stroke, called her creation Baby Einstein.

PERHAPS NOT SURPRISINGLY, there is now a small but zealous backlash against the obsession with infant stimulation. And for any parents hoping to build better baby brains, infant classes and products are probably an enormous waste of money. Even more disturbing, educators and policy makers who believe that the first years of life are the key to intellectual development risk de-emphasizing education programs that focus on the following years of childhood, which, the current evidence suggests, have a bigger impact on a child's academic success.

Still, while there is no solid evidence that music classes or Baby Einstein videos help babies develop, there is also no solid evidence that too many products or classes harm babies. And whether or not baby classes have any developmental or educational value, there are plenty of good reasons to sign up for them. I suspect that, like Jennifer and me, a lot of the parents take the classes for a much more practical reason: They have no idea what to do with their time.

As I adjusted to parenthood, my new understanding of time felt almost as profound as when I first pondered the theory of relativity—perhaps even more so, since I actually understood what I was thinking about. Before parenthood, time was elusive. I could get out of bed, have brunch with a friend, and somewhere along the way the day would slip away. But when I was taking care of Isaac during that first year, time was never slippery, no matter how much fun I might be having or how much love I might be feeling. Time was slow and sticky. It clung to the skin like wet paper. When I was a nonparent, I would often start a Sunday at noon. But when I woke up with Isaac at 5:30 in the morning, noon was a million miles away. Noon was like a desert mirage that I could only dream of reaching. Sometimes, to pass the hours and to keep myself awake, I would sing "Ninety-nine Bottles of Beer on the Wall," all the way down. Other times, I would lie on the floor and let Isaac claw at my eyes for sport. (It occurred to me during one of these sessions that this is the real Oedipus complex—*they want to claw our eyes out!*)

The difference in my perspective on time only hit me fully one Sunday while Jennifer and I were shopping at Target. It was around four o'clock. We had already been at the store for several hours and had visited every section at least once.

"I guess we should head home," Jennifer said.

I had spent my entire life trying to avoid shopping trips and yet at that moment, I realized something incredible: I did not want to leave Target. During the winter, when it was too cold to go to the park, leaving Target meant going home, and the one fundamental law of parenting during the first year is that time moves more slowly inside the home than outside.

"Let's just hang around here a little more," I said.

"You want to hang around at Target?"

"Yeah. I think so."

"But we already have everything we need."

I thought for a moment. "Let's look at the DVDs again," I said.

We continued to walk around the store, and as the other shoppers hurried past us, my childhood began to make more sense. I had remembered spending a lot of time at Target while growing up in Houston. But until that afternoon it had never occurred to me that my father couldn't possibly have needed to make that many trips to the store, no matter how wide the selection or reasonable the prices. We had been at Target because Target was a place to be on the weekends. In Houston you went to Target for the air conditioning. In New York you went for the warmth. But the principle was the same.

Jennifer agreed that it was important to get out of the apartment with Isaac, but she wasn't thrilled with the prospect of spending our weekends looking at the same DVDs over and over. Probably we should have just organized a new parents' group or arranged more get-togethers with the new friends Jennifer had made in her moms' group. Instead we decided to spend several hundred dollars on a Music Together class.

The Music Together class was Jennifer's idea, but I was all for it. I liked the idea of sitting and singing as babies crawled around a tambourine-covered carpet and slapped at drums. The problem with Music Together, I soon discovered, is the seriousness with which the company takes this educational mission. Each week the instructors would urge us to practice at home with the CD that

we'd been given at the first class—one of the instructors even referred to the CD as homework.

In fairness, it's possible that older children who take the
classes get something out of them. Many children who begin
playing instruments at a young age do excel. Because musical development is so complicated from a neurological perspective and
involves so many different areas of the brain, it's particularly difficult to determine whether a critical period exists. A 2005 review
of the literature on critical periods and musical development in
the *Journal of Developmental Psychobiology* concluded that "the effects of early enrichment or early deprivation on the emergence
of sensitivity to . . . various aspects of music pitch structure remain largely unknown."

In any case, our Music Together teachers were much more focused on the participation of the parents than the babies. Part of
the company's educational philosophy is that babies learn from
watching their parents. As one of the founders of Music Together
once put it in an interview, "It's an educational tragedy, really, an
educational disaster, musically speaking, for one's children, if
you just sit on the couch and consume music. They need the
model of your musical doing in order to get the disposition to be a
music maker."

I had no problem with Music Together's parent-centered educational philosophy, and I was more than happy to sing along. But
the instructors' almost militant insistence that parents stay involved even when their children are nowhere to be found led to
the same unfortunate scene repeating itself week after week:
Isaac would crawl away, or Jennifer would take him into an adjacent room to feed him, and the next thing I knew I would be running in circles and waving chiffon rainbow scarves over my head
with a group of strangers.

Music Together was only the beginning of our time-filling activities. We also attended a "Sign and Sing" baby sign language class during which Isaac and the other babies sat and watched as the parents sang about baby kangaroos and learned to sign "I want milk." And one Sunday afternoon, we attended a Baby Loves Disco party at a local rock-and-roll club.

Baby Loves Disco, a series of dance parties for babies and parents that have sprung up around the country, sounded like a great idea to me when I first heard about it. The parties have become part of a larger hipster parenting trend that has swept through New York and across the country in recent years. Critics of the trend have complained that young parents are trying to push back adulthood by dressing their babies in heavy-metal onesies, but, though I've tried, I can't see the downside to ironic onesies. If anything, the right to dress your child in ridiculous outfits struck me as fair payback for all parents do during the first year—or, at least this is what I was thinking when we dressed Isaac as a French painter for his first Halloween and taped a paintbrush and a piece of baguette to him.

Baby Loves Disco lived up to my expectations for a few minutes. I was amused by the scene when I stepped into the dark dance hall. As a DJ spun records onstage, toddlers with juice boxes mingled with beer-guzzling adults.

But the charm of the scene wore off once Jennifer and Isaac and I made it onto the strobe-lit dance floor. At that point Baby Loves Disco became a haunting reminder of my junior-high dances. Jennifer was bopping around and holding Isaac so that he was facing her, and I was left with the unfortunate choice that every awkward twelve-year-old boy knows too well: Either dance by yourself in the vicinity of a female and pretend as though you don't mind dancing alone or hurry to the food table and pretend as though you don't mind drinking twenty consecutive cups of

Pepsi. The female sex has ingeniously solved this dilemma by joining together and dancing in groups, but the guys are on their own; like wild apes who have been evicted from the troupe by the high-status males, we can do nothing but lurk and hope—although, unlike wild apes, we can also fantasize about taking over the dance floor with John Travolta's *Saturday Night Fever* routine.

After a minute or so of lumbering awkwardly around my wife and child as "Billie Jean" blasted from the speakers, my inner twelve-year-old returned and I headed to the bar, where I spent the next twenty minutes sucking down juice boxes and feeling sorry for myself. And as I watched the others dance, I realized that the real problem with Baby Loves Disco was the babies. The painful truth is that babies are not that into dark clubs. What parents really need, I thought, is a nightclub with a special sound-proofed room in the back full of Pack 'n Plays and nannies. For a moment I imagined how incredible this parenting club would be and how much fun Jennifer and I could have there. Then I re-membered that we didn't particularly like clubs and never went to them before Isaac was born.

If I wasn't always at ease during our weekend baby activities, I at least had Jennifer with me. Even though Isaac was becoming better company every month, it was even harder to fill the hours on the two days a week that I took care of him by myself. Because it was closer to our apartment than Target, we spent a lot of time in the supermarket. While the rest of the shoppers rushed by, Isaac and I would fondle the fruits and tip over cereal boxes as though it were a carnival game. Isaac particularly liked looking at the Quaker Oats guy, and, inevitably, from time to time someone I vaguely knew would stroll by and be surprised to find me sitting on the floor of the supermarket with a baby and an armful of oat-meal canisters.

When I would begin to fear that the supermarket management

might be taking notice of our prolonged presence, Isaac and I would move on to a café or to Barnes & Noble, where we spent so much time during the winter that I almost felt obliged to begin paying rent.

One particularly lonely day, I had the idea that I would integrate myself into one of the cliques of Caribbean nannies on the playground benches. I had the entire white-liberal fantasy mapped out in my head. I would ask them for advice on some sort of baby issue, and within a few weeks, I would not only be a regular part of the group at the playground but also be good friends with the nannies. Soon the Caribbean nannies and I would be breaking down social barriers right and left with heartfelt cultural exchanges. They would come back to our apartment and teach me how to cook flavorful rice dishes and I would give them thick chunks of store-bought challah and talk to them about forming a union or gaining legal immigration status—that I know nothing about either subject had no bearing on this particular fantasy.

It was a nice, if vaguely offensive, fantasy, but then, I was pretty sure that the nannies didn't like me. Once I got Isaac's foot stuck in a bench at the playground. And as I spent two minutes trying to wrestle it free, I could see the nannies looking at me and shaking their heads. I knew they were thinking, "amateur," but I felt I could do no right in their eyes. Sometimes I would take Isaac out in his fluffy bear suit on a lukewarm day, and as soon as Isaac cried, the nannies would shake their heads and tell me he was hot. Another time, I was wheeling Isaac around in only a T-shirt and diaper, and a nanny stopped and looked at Isaac without even acknowledging me. "Daddy took you out naked?" she said, the disdain visible on her face.

○○○

ONE NIGHT, after a particularly lonely day in the supermarket, I complained to Jennifer that Isaac and I needed a new activity. Jennifer suggested Mommy and Me Yoga. She had taken the class before going back to work and had a few passes left.

It didn't seem like a good idea. I'd tried yoga once in high school. I had been going through a bad anxiety spell, and my father thought that yoga might help relieve my stress. When I pointed out to him that I could barely touch my knees, let alone my feet, he said not to worry.

I worried. I knew yoga was wrong for me from the very first *ommm*. The two teachers were a mother and son team, and the son took his yoga seriously. He had a goatee and a ponytail, and I can still see the baffled expression on his face as he tried to wrestle my limbs into places they had no intention of going. I don't think he had ever seen such an inflexible human before.

"Just stretch," the son said.

"That's as far as I go," I said.

I am even stiffer now than I was then, but what really made me nervous about Mommy and Me Yoga was the potential for emasculation. I have always been proud of my stereotypically feminine attributes. When guy friends made fun of my interest in feminist folk music or pointed out that my winter coat was actually a woman's coat—I was aware of this, but it was unusually warm— I always insisted that my womanly ways were really a testament to how profoundly secure I was in my manhood. And yet by attending Mommy and Me Yoga classes, I thought I might be taking it to another level. I wondered if I might be crossing an inviolable line into a realm where no heterosexual man could safely travel.

In the end I decided I would rather be emasculated than lonely. And that is how I found myself walking through Brooklyn with Isaac Björned to my chest, a Starbucks skim latte in one hand and a rolled-up purple yoga mat in the other.

When I arrived at the yoga studio, a dozen or so moms had already unrolled their mats onto the hardwood floor and placed their babies in front of them on blankets. In the center of the room—the mosh pit, I would later hear it called—a few of the more mobile babies were manhandling a small mountain of toys.

As I had expected, no other dads had shown up, and I felt increasingly anxious as the instructor, Trish, stepped in front of the mosh pit and introduced herself. Trish had short red hair and thin muscled arms. She looked tough.

I glanced down at Isaac, lying on his back on a blanket, and suddenly longed to be back at home playing *Claw Daddy's Eyes Out.*

Trish asked us to close our eyes and *ommm*. The sound echoed through the sunlit room, and for a brief moment, I allowed myself to relax, one deep breath at a time.

Then Isaac freaked out.

I felt guilty. The world must have seemed strange and surprising enough without all the people in the room suddenly closing their eyes and humming in unison.

Trish waited for Isaac to calm down and then began to bark out impossibly long Sanskrit words. The moms, to my amazement, seemed to speak Sanskrit. No sooner would Trish say *"Parivrtta Ardha Chandrasana"* than the moms would be balancing on one leg and turning their bodies parallel to the floor. I did my best to keep up, but with each additional *Parivrtta Ardha Chandrasana,* it became increasingly obvious that in a roomful of mothers, many of them still recovering from the physical trauma of labor, I was without question the least physically fit student.

Trish occasionally stopped by to adjust me this way and that, but her efforts were no match for my rigidity. The Tin Man from *The Wizard of Oz* could have made me look bad on a yoga mat. By the fifteen-minute mark, I was drenched in sweat and exhausted.

And my desperate situation was only made worse when one of the more mobile babies crawled over to say hello and then—even as I waved my cutesiest wave—took off with my water bottle.

With the exception of this one tiny hooligan, the babies remained mostly calm, including Isaac, who had become otherwise engaged with a crinkly-paper-filled caterpillar. But the tranquility came to an abrupt halt during a grueling round of *Bharadvajasanas*. A baby on the other side of the room began to shriek as if it were he, and not I, who was being asked to rotate his torso 180 degrees. The shriek set off a chain reaction, and soon all of the babies were grunting and crying in unison, a discordant mockery of the *ommming* adults.

I'd like to think that babies cry in response to one another's cries out of empathy, that in their shared tears they reveal something profound about the innate capacity of humans to feel the pain of others. And it might be the case. But I also can't help but wonder if what appears to be empathy is anxiety. Judging by the volume of Isaac's screams, he is either the next Mother Teresa or he was genuinely terrified.

Even as the other babies calmed down, Isaac continued to fuss in my arms. After the colic months, I never thought the time would come when I wouldn't mind Isaac's crying. But the longer he complained, the longer it would be until I had to do another downward dog. So I wasn't thrilled when Trish came by and offered to take him off my hands for a few minutes. I reluctantly handed over my son and then looked on in horror as he began to suck on Trish's bare shoulder.

I knew from experience what was coming next, and I should have stopped it. Instead, I collapsed onto my mat and looked on as Isaac gave Trish a bright red arm hickey.

Trish took the hickey as well as a person can take an unsolicited hickey. "I'd rather get one from him than a lot of other guys," she said. She handed Isaac back to me and then asked us all to lie down with our babies and to position foam bricks under our backs so that they were aligned with our "bra straps."

With those two words, my emasculation was nearly complete, but as I lay down with Isaac and waited for our next instruction, I saw an opportunity for redemption. I began to bench press Isaac up and down, ostensibly to entertain him but really to demonstrate that there was at least one physical feat at which I could outdo a mother who was still recovering from giving birth.

To my frustration, no one seemed especially interested in my great show of virility, and after about fifteen Isaac reps, I joined the others in what struck me as the weirdest exercise of the afternoon. Trish asked us to form a circle, hold our babies in front of us, and then swing them right to left so that they came face to face with the babies on either side of them.

I could almost hear the "Check, please!" on Isaac's lips.

After about five minutes of baby-swinging, Trish told us to return to our mats. There was still half an hour left in the class, and I felt as though I was one *Bharadvajasana* away from passing out.

I picked Isaac up and approached Trish at the front of the room. "I should probably go," I said. "He looks like he's getting tired."

○ ○ ○ SEVENTEEN

Attachment Parenting

The Importance of a Mother

IN HER BOOK *Raising America*, the journalist Ann Hulbert documents how parenting trends have moved back and forth throughout the twentieth century, like a pendulum swinging from side to
side. If Watson's behaviorist approach to parenting was the top of
the pendulum's arc on the strict approach, attachment parenting,
today's most influential parenting philosophy, is the top of the arc
on the other side.

Jennifer and I first learned about attachment parenting at the
baby care class we took before Isaac's birth—the same class at
which we learned about the many varieties of newborn rashes.
When we moved beyond the horrific appearance of newborns to
different parenting styles, our teacher, Diane, noted that we'd be
hearing a lot of strong opinions about parenting in the coming
months and also that it was a good idea to tune the opinions out.
She then proceeded to give us her own strong opinions. Diane
encouraged us to respond to our child's crying as much as possible. She said that trying to put a baby on a sleeping schedule could
be dangerous during the first twelve weeks and that it was "inap-
propriate" up until around nine months.

The "never let a baby cry" approach also applied to feeding.
"How would you like to be told to wait twenty minutes every time

you got hungry?" Diane asked. "You have to listen to your babies. They will tell you what they need, and then you have to trust your instincts."

I'd brought a pen and notebook to the class, and I scribbled down "listen to your baby," as though it were an entirely novel concept.

I didn't realize it at the time, but Diane was essentially repeating the ideas of Dr. William Sears, a California pediatrician who coined the term "attachment parenting." Sears is best known as the bestselling author of *The Baby Book: Everything You Need to Know About Your Baby from Birth to Age Two,* but he has published dozens of successful parenting books and is arguably the most well-known baby expert in America today. He is sometimes referred to in print as "the new Dr. Spock" but refers to himself as "America's pediatrician."

Not to be outdone by Harvey Karp's 5 S's, Sears and his wife, Martha, a nurse who has cowritten many of his books, have condensed attachment parenting to a series of B's: birth-bonding, breastfeeding, bed-sharing, baby-wearing, and "belief in the signal value of an infant's cry." As the B's indicate, attachment parenting calls for as much holding of a baby as possible and emphasizes the importance of responding quickly to a baby's physical and emotional needs. "Imagine how you would feel if you were completely uncoordinated—unable to do anything for yourself— and your cries for help went unheeded," Sears writes in *The Baby Book.* "A baby whose cries are not answered does not become a 'good' baby (though he may become quiet); he does become a discouraged baby. He learns the one thing you don't want him to: that he can't communicate or trust his needs will be met."

Although Harvey Karp has made his name by soothing infants, he has also become associated with attachment parenting. (The best testament to the ascendance of attachment parenting may be

that, with the exception of Dr. Ferber and other sleep training advocates, the most famous baby experts today—Brazelton, Karp,
and Sears—have made their names by urging parents to be super
attentive to the emotional needs of their babies.) When I interviewed Karp about crying, he told me that when children's needs
are met early in life, it makes them less stressed. "I often think of
it as there are two kinds of people in the world," Karp said. "Pes-
simists who go around saying, 'I knew it wasn't going to work,'
and optimists who go around saying 'I just think it's all going to be
okay.'

"And part of that is built into early infancy," Karp continued,
"when hundreds and hundreds of times a baby cries, and over
and over again arms come to pick them up and a breast comes to
feed them, they just learn that this is a cool place—'whenever I
have a need it's met.' "

Like Karp, Sears was influenced by African mothers, specifically two women from Zambia whom he and Martha met at an international parenting conference. The Zambian women carried
their babies in a sling at all times, and the Searses noticed how
content babies seemed when parents raised them the way that
nature intended.

Diane's advice notwithstanding, Jennifer and I hadn't set out to
practice attachment parenting. We had been holding Isaac all day
out of necessity—or, at least, what felt like necessity during Isaac's
colic phase—and in practicing sleep training and letting Isaac cry,
we had moved decidedly away from attachment parenting. But
though we broke the cardinal rule of attachment parenting, if
someone had asked me to spell out my intuitions or philosophy
about babies at the time, it probably would have been fairly similar to the Sears approach. Comforting babies as much as possible
seemed intuitively right, and it fit well with my personal philosophy, which boils down to something like, be as nice to others as

you possibly can, because even if you can't see it or don't understand it, there's a good chance they're struggling on the inside.

And so I was surprised to discover that while the health benefits of breastfeeding—an important component of attachment parenting—are no longer in dispute, there is no evidence that being extremely attentive to the needs of a baby or holding a baby a lot provides any psychological benefits. I was even more surprised to discover that attachment theory, the widely researched psychological theory from which attachment parenting emerged, rests on extremely shaky intellectual foundations.

THE ORIGINS OF ATTACHMENT PARENTING can be traced to British psychiatrist John Bowlby. Bowlby's father, Major Sir Anthony Bowlby, was King George V's surgeon, and John Bowlby thought that he too would be a doctor. But while studying medicine at Cambridge, his interest turned to child psychology, and after graduating in 1929, he volunteered at a progressive school for maladjusted children.

The six months the twenty-one-year-old Bowlby spent at the school would change the course of twentieth-century psychology and parenting. Bowlby wasn't at the school only to lend a hand. He had always had a strong scientific curiosity, and the troubled students at the school presented him with an intellectual puzzle: What had gone wrong? What was different about these children that prevented them from functioning in society? Why was an aloof adolescent thief whom Bowlby found particularly fascinating incapable of forming emotional bonds?

Bowlby suspected that some experience in infancy was at the root of abnormal psychology, and in that intuition he was hardly alone. The belief that our first years shape who we are as adults dates back at least to Plato, and it was among the few principles that all of the major schools of twentieth-century psychology agreed on. Bowlby didn't yet know which early experiences had the greatest impact on how we turn out, but when he discussed the case of the affectionless adolescent with school officials, he uncovered a clue: The boy had never had a stable mother figure in his early years.

Bowlby decided to return to school to study child psychiatry and psychotherapy. He enrolled in medical school and was accepted into the British Psychoanalytic Society, where Melanie Klein, the famous Freudian theorist and child psychology pioneer, was one of his advisors. But even as he trained in psychoanalysis, Bowlby was bothered by the strange paradox at the center of Freudian thinking. Freud had argued that infancy and parents were the key to psychic development, and yet most Freudians seemed strangely uninterested in moving beyond theory to observing how real mothers and babies interacted. And when Freudian thinkers in the mid-twentieth century did offer their insights on how mothers affected their babies, they tended to agree with the behaviorists that a mother's love was a dangerous tool that should be used with caution. The antimother sentiment in the air was so great in mid-twentieth-century America that in 1945 *Ladies' Home Journal* ran an article under the headline "Are American Moms a Menace?" that questioned whether mothers might be "a threat to our national existence."

Bowlby thought there was much more to the story of infant-mother relationships, but there was no obvious place for him to turn for information. When he reviewed the Western medical literature on the relationship between maternal care and mental health, Bowlby found fewer than thirty papers from the twenties and thirties. One popular textbook on developmental psychology in the 1930s didn't even include a chapter on parent-child relationships.

In the mid-1940s, Bowlby, by then a trained psychiatrist and psychoanalyst, began the project of filling in the gaps himself. In 1946, he wrote a paper on forty-four juvenile thieves whose cases he had studied while working at the London Child Guidance Clinic. Among the forty-four criminals, Bowlby noticed that a subset of fourteen had a "remarkable lack of affection or warmth of feeling for anyone." When Bowlby searched for a common thread in the backgrounds of these affectionless teens, he found what he thought he might: Twelve of the fourteen had experienced a "prolonged separation" from their mothers or foster mothers. Here was a first bit of evidence of the phenomenon Bowlby had first glimpsed at age twenty-one. When young children didn't have a stable mother figure, it seemed to damage them psychologically for years to come.

To Bowlby, as well as to the handful of other researchers now thinking along the same lines, the study of what he began to refer to as "maternal deprivation" wasn't just another academic inquiry. It was a matter of life and death. In the first half of the twentieth century, it was still regular practice for hospitals, fearful of spreading diseases, to isolate sick babies from all visitors. And it was still regular practice for these babies to die. Antibiotics had eliminated most of the germs that once routinely killed small children in orphanages and hospitals, but they hadn't eliminated the high infant-mortality rates. Otherwise healthy babies who had little contact with other humans seemed to be withering away, as though literally starving for affection.

The tragic situation of isolated children became harder to ignore after World War II. The war had separated millions of children from their parents, and if Bowlby was right about maternal deprivation, the fate of these children was in real jeopardy. In 1950, the World Health Organization hired Bowlby to study the psychological impact of homelessness on children. In the revised popular edition of his report, which was translated into ten languages and sold 450,000 copies in English, Bowlby made no effort to hide the moral underpinnings of his message. "The proper care of children deprived of a normal home life can now be seen to be not merely an act of common humanity," Bowlby concluded, "but to be essential for the mental and social welfare of a community."

More recent scholarship has found that the situation at hospital wards and orphanages that inspired Bowlby and the handful of other early activists to advocate for more maternal affection was not as clear cut as the psychologists thought. In some cases, children who were thought to have died from isolation had in fact died from a measles epidemic. But by the time Bowlby published his report in 1951, he had little doubt about the effects of maternal deprivation on infants. What Bowlby still lacked was a way to explain the phenomenon, and in his search for a theory, he turned his attention to animal studies.

Austrian scientist Konrad Lorenz's work with newborn geese was the first animal research to interest Bowlby. Lorenz demonstrated that after hatching, a baby gosling will imprint on the first moving object it sees and will follow it like it would its mother. Lorenz's work intrigued Bowlby because it indicated a critical period for emotional development. Lorenz claimed that if the gosling didn't imprint in the first thirty-six hours of life, it would never be able to imprint on a mother figure. Bowlby later determined that for humans the first three years of life make up the critical period for a child to attach to a mother or caregiver.

But if Lorenz's gosling inspired Bowlby, it was the monkey studies of Harry Harlow that would have the greatest influence on Bowlby's thinking. By placing infant macaques in isolation chambers he called "pits of despair," Harlow showed that denying a monkey any social contact for an extended period would destroy them emotionally. When released from the pits of despair, the monkeys would be in a state of shock, clutching themselves and rocking back and forth. "Twelve months of isolation almost obliterated the animals socially," Harlow wrote. In another series of experiments, Harlow put rhesus monkeys in cages with two fake monkey mothers, one made of wire and one made of terry cloth. When Harlow would terrify the young monkeys (sometimes by placing comically psychotic-looking dolls in their cages) they consistently turned to the cloth monkey for comfort. More revealingly, the scared monkeys went to the cloth mother even when they had already grown accustomed to eating from a bottle attached to the wire monkey. At the time, it was widely believed that infants were drawn to their mothers only out of an instinctual need for food or oral gratification. But Harlow showed that the frightened monkeys wanted much more from a mother figure. They also had a biological need for the security and comfort of a soft, warm touch.

Harlow's monkeys helped convince Bowlby that psychological need for a mother's care was a part of our evolutionary heritage. Just as infants who didn't seek food, for example, would never have been favored by natural selection, so infants who didn't have a powerful desire to cling to and bond with a mother would also have been at a tremendous disadvantage in trying to survive a dangerous environment. The damage to the body when a baby's biological need for food went unmet was obvious. The psychological damage to the mind when the baby's biological need for a mother's comfort went unmet was less visible but devastating just the same.

In her book *Love at Goon Park*, the journalist Deborah Blum traces Harlow's influence on the development of attachment theory. And what Blum makes beautifully clear is that while Bowlby was a typically reserved British scientist trading in clinical terms like *maternal deprivation* and *failure to thrive,* at the heart of his research and theorizing was a powerful idea about love. "What attachment theory essentially says is that being loved matters—and, more, that it matters who loves us and whom we love in return," Blum writes. "It's not just a matter of the warm body holding the bottle. It's not object love at all; we love specific people and we need them to love us back. And in the case of the child's tie to the mother, it matters that the mother loves that baby and that the baby knows it."

Bowlby, in other words, was never satisfied with the Freudian dogma of the day. But in the end, he never fully rejected his Freudian roots so much as expanded upon them. Object-relations theorists like Bowlby's Freudian advisor Melanie Klein believed that infants create internal mental representations of the people and things they encounter and that these representations have a profound effect on their development. And Bowlby's thinking never strayed too far from this theory. But Klein had emphasized the role of the fantasy life in the developing mind. Babies could form relationships with breasts even before they formed a relationship with the whole mother. Bowlby, in essence, had said that focusing on fantasies and breasts misses the larger story. It's the mental representations the baby makes of the real relationships with the whole mother that lay the foundation for psychological development.

As Bowlby's theory grew in fame, the attention of researchers, including Bowlby himself, moved away from the extreme cases of motherless and neglected infants to the attachment needs of babies in more typical home environments. After all, if the absence of a mother had such a profound effect on a child, it seemed likely that the day-to-day differences in maternal care could also influence psychological development.

In 1963, psychologist Mary Ainsworth, who had researched maternal deprivation with Bowlby in the fifties, took the next step in attachment research. Ainsworth spent a year periodically observing twenty-three sets of mothers with their new babies. When the babies turned one, Ainsworth asked her subjects to come to a lab where she attempted to measure their levels of attachment in an experiment known as the Strange Situation. Ainsworth first watched the mother and her baby together in a room to see how comfortable the baby felt playing in the mother's presence. Then she watched the babies' responses to a series of different scenarios in which the mother and a stranger entered and left the room.

Ainsworth paid particular attention to how the babies reacted when their mothers returned to the room. Some of the babies were anxious for their mothers' comfort. Ainsworth deemed these babies securely attached. Other babies didn't seem especially interested in greeting their mothers when they returned to the room. Ainsworth called the attachment level of these babies insecure-avoidant. Babies who showed resistance or distress upon being reunited with the mother were deemed insecure-resistant.

The differences between the babies were obvious to Ainsworth, and she also thought she knew how to account for them. During her year of observation, Ainsworth had watched the mothers as closely as the babies, watched which mothers hurried to their babies at the first sign of unhappiness and which let their babies cry. She kept track of how the mothers played with their babies—whether they were smiley and talkative or not—and how often they fed them. As Ainsworth saw it, the doting made the difference. The most securely attached babies were the ones with the most attentive moms. The insecurely attached babies had mothers who were either insensitive and inept or angry and rejecting.

In the following decades, the Strange Situation became the foundation for an entire field of attachment research and gradually moved from the periphery to the center of American psychology. Securely attached babies, the thinking went, were more psychologically healthy and would be more likely to grow up to form secure and successful relationships. The internal representation of their comforting mother would remain with them and help them manage the stresses of adult life. The insecurely attached, in turn, would be vulnerable and struggle to form lasting bonds with others.

The rise of attachment theory is full of parallels with the rise of the baby-stimulation craze. The baby-stimulation craze began with the belief that if the first years of life, a critical period for intellectual development, passed without proper intellectual stimulation, the brain would never recover. Attachment theory told the same story about emotional development. And as with the baby-stimulation craze, the sensational nature of the claims almost guaranteed that they would make their way into the public consciousness via the media and prominent baby experts. In their 1988 book *High Risk: Children Without a Conscience,* Dr. Ken Magid and Carole A. McKelvey argued that putting a child in day care without a chance to bond might be thought of as child abuse. An alarm-sounding piece in a 1990 issue of *The Atlantic Monthly* warned that the babies in one third of middle-class American homes were insecurely attached.

As in the case of the brain-stimulation theories, the thinness of the science behind the attachment claims rarely came up for discussion. But despite the thousands of studies and papers on attachment theory, more than forty years since Ainsworth first introduced the Strange Situation, attachment researchers have never been able to definitively show that the insecure and secure attachment categories are meaningful. As Diane Eyer explains in her book *Mother Guilt,* drawing conclusions about human relationships, where so many variables come into play, is inherently problematic under the best social-science research conditions, let alone in the course of a twenty-minute experiment. In some cases, studies found that babies who went to day care were slightly less attached than babies whose mothers stayed home. The findings led to dramatic articles about the possible risks of mothers going back to work too soon, but the researchers hadn't considered that babies who went to day care might be less anxious about separations from their mothers because they had a lot of practice at separating. And while the better studies are carefully controlled, the controlled variables change from one study to the next, making it nearly impossible to draw conclusions from the larger body of research.

It's no surprise, then, that while some long-term studies have found that babies deemed securely attached end up being more well adjusted and forming better relationships than insecurely attached babies, many other long-term studies have failed to show any correlation between attachment status in infancy and adult personalities or behaviors. One attachment researcher, Jay Belsky, who had made sensational claims about the risks of mothers going back to work too soon, found that when he repeated the Strange Situation tests on the same children three months after the initial test, half of them received a different classification, raising the question of whether the studies might reflect nothing more than a child's mood at the time of the test. Other studies have found that, despite having grown up with the same parents, a third of siblings end up with a different attachment status after going through the Strange Situation.

Even if it could be shown that securely attached babies have better relationships as adults, the mystery of which particular parenting techniques or behaviors determine a baby's attachment status remains unsolved. Despite Ainsworth's initial findings, no one has been able to show that super-attentive mothers lead to super-secure attachments or that less-attentive mothers end up with insecurely attached babies.

But if the story of attachment theory resembles the infant-stimulation craze in the ways that the science behind the claims has been exaggerated or misinterpreted, the social implications of the attachment hype are arguably worse. The misconceptions about brain development have led parents to spend money on products and classes that won't make their children any smarter. But the extreme claims of attachment theorists and attachment-parenting advocates—T. Berry Brazelton once suggested that children who fail to bond in the first year because their mothers are working will become delinquents and terrorists—have left both mothers and fathers (but especially mothers) feeling guilty every time they put their babies down or leave them at home to go to work. As Judith Warner explains in her book *Perfect Madness,* attachment parenting has become a contributing factor to the "caught-by-the-throat feeling so many mothers have today of *always* doing something wrong."

To its credit, Attachment Parenting International, a nonprofit network of parenting support groups, encourages parents to set realistic goals, and Martha Sears, for her part, has begun speaking about the "Myth of Perfect Mothering." But at times, Dr. Sears has seemed strangely unsympathetic to how his calls for more attachment parenting can make overworked parents feel. In books and interviews, Sears has cavalierly called on mothers to bring their babies to work in slings, as though it were a viable option for most American workers. He's even suggested that a mother's guilt can be healthy at times. "Guilt is an inner warning system," Sears writes in *The Baby Book*, "a sort of alarm that goes off when we behave in ways we are not supposed to."

In an anti-Sears essay in *Brain, Child* magazine, one mother described how the pressure builds when an anxious new mother reads Sears for the first time. "Through Dr. Sears's eyes, I could see that my frequent desire to escape from my screaming infant meant that I was insufficiently bonded with her," the mother writes. "That was a horrible thought. But I also knew the cure prescribed by Dr. Sears: Ask those around me to lift some of the burdens of cooking and laundry from my sagging shoulders, so I could spend more time breastfeeding and sleeping with the baby. Then undoubtedly I would begin to love her the way nature intended me to: sublimely, unfailingly, with all my other interests in life falling away like dandruff to leave only the single pure desire to give my daughter everything she needed, everything she wanted, everything that every baby should have."

Still, if attachment parenting can't live up to the claims of its strongest advocates, that doesn't mean it needs to be abandoned by the lucky parents who have the time and patience for it. Considering that studies of infant crying have found that babies who are held more spend less time screaming, attachment parenting might well add to the day-to-day happiness of babies. And just as baby classes might be worthwhile for their entertainment value even if they don't make babies any smarter, minimizing the crying of babies is a nice thing to do, even if it won't make them more secure adults.

OOO

As it happens, even as Bowlby's attachment theory was gradually growing in popularity and influence, another theory about how we develop was also slowly gaining ground in psychology departments. It was an idea that had been around in one form or another for thousands of years and yet it had almost entirely disappeared from the landscape of American psychology in the first half of the twentieth century. The idea was that we can't explain how people turn out only by what happens to them as they grow up. The idea was that we all come into the world with inherited dispositions, or temperaments, and that these temperaments remain more or less fixed throughout life.

The most prominent champion of temperament theory over the last forty years has been Jerome Kagan, a professor emeritus of psychology at Harvard. When I called Kagan to discuss his research, he told me that throughout his early life, he had wholeheartedly believed that humans were the products of their environments. Kagan even remembered arguing with his mother about it when he was a teenager.

"I was an egalitarian as a young scientist," Kagan told me. "I believed the Bowlby message and the Freudian message."

It wasn't until 1972, when Kagan spent a year in the Guatemalan village of San Marcos, that he began to seriously question the orthodoxies of American psychology. The Mayan Indians of San Marcos believe that infants are vulnerable to the evil eye and, to keep their babies safe, they leave them in hammocks at the back of their huts and never take them out.

Kagan performed cognitive tests on the Mayan babies at age one and found that remaining isolated in a hut for a year took its toll on a baby. At age one the babies seemed to be in great trouble. "They're retarded," Kagan said. "They look terrible."

But the surprise for Kagan wasn't that the babies looked terrible at age one. The surprise was that the older children in San

Marcos looked fine. All of the Mayan Indian children had gone through the same year of isolation in the hut and yet when Kagan tested the six-year-olds, he saw that they were developmentally normal. "I said, oh my god," Kagan recalled. "What happens in the first year can be easily changed. It's not all that important."

In another unlikely twist in Kagan's path to temperament theory, one of the first papers he happened upon after returning from his year in Guatemala was about Harlow's monkeys, the same monkeys whose plight had made such a strong impression on Bowlby. This study looked at how monkeys who had experienced Harlow's pits of despair later reacted when placed with infant monkeys. It turned out that the monkeys who had become famous for their psychological devastation treated the infants more or less like any normal monkey would.

When Kagan and his co-author, Robert Klein, published their findings about the Mayans of San Marcos, they came under heavy fire from their academic colleagues. In his memoir, *An Argument for Mind,* Kagan recalls being surprised by how upset his paper made other psychologists. The idea that the first years of life were crucial to how children turned out was so deeply woven into the reigning narrative of the era that Kagan's colleagues didn't even want to consider the possibility that it might be wrong.

But if the anger of his colleagues gave him pause, the evidence kept pushing Kagan back to the conclusion that the experiences of infancy couldn't, by themselves, explain our adult personalities and proclivities. In the early eighties, while working on a study of infant behavior, Kagan tested the reactions of about one hundred sixteen-week-old babies to different stimuli. After first determining that all the babies were healthy and well fed, Kagan played tapes of different voices to the babies and showed them mobiles and videos. Observing the babies' reactions in real time was difficult, but Kagan had videotaped the experiments (by giving researchers the ability to study babies' reactions more closely, the video camera revolutionized the entire field of developmental psychology) and he later took the tapes into a quiet room and watched them. The first eighteen babies Kagan viewed varied in small ways from one another, but not in ways that seemed unusual. Then Kagan put in the tape of the nineteenth baby and the experiment suddenly became much more interesting. The difference between the nineteenth baby and the first eighteen babies was immediately apparent. The first eighteen babies had moved around in response to the voices and mobiles, but the nineteenth baby, a girl, wasn't just moving. Her arms and legs were thrashing. Just putting a little mobile in front of her face gave her a pained expression and made her cry.

Kagan knew he was on to something as he watched the tape of that nineteenth baby. And he was even more convinced the next day when he saw the tape of another baby on the opposite end of the spectrum. In response to the very same stimuli that had made baby nineteen so upset, the other baby hadn't moved a muscle.

"After four or five days, I was convinced by looking at the films that yes, there really were two very clear groups," Kagan told me. "One group—about twenty percent of the babies—were extremely arousable, while the majority were not. The babies were all healthy and well fed. There was absolutely no reason why twenty percent should be so hyper."

No reason, that is, other than that the babies had inborn temperaments that caused them to react differently from the other babies. That Kagan had found that there are two categories of people wasn't especially new. Kagan called the fearful babies "high reactives" and the less fearful ones "low reactives." Jung had called the more or less same categories "introverts" and "extroverts." What was new was that Kagan thought he could see temperament as early as four months. If the different temperaments of the babies remained fixed, if the fearful babies continued to be more fearful and the calmer babies continued to be more calm, then Kagan would be able to trace temperament to a point in life so early that it could only be explained by genetic inheritance.

The next obvious step for Kagan was to determine if the behaviors he was seeing at four months did, in fact, remain fixed. To that end, in 1986, Kagan and his colleagues Nancy Snidman and Doreen Arcus began a long-term study of more than 450 babies. They observed the babies first at four months and then at various intervals for seventeen years. And the longer the study went on, the clearer it became that Kagan's initial suspicion had been correct. Temperament was real. The high-reactive four-month-olds were more likely to be inhibited toddlers and shy adolescents. The low reactives were more likely to be calm and social.

Kagan isn't a determinist. Temperament doesn't replace the idea that environment is everything with the idea that biology is everything. If biology is everything, then identical twins would end up with identical personalities, but they don't. (Behavioral geneticists now believe that about half of our personality differences can be explained by genes.) The renewed interest in temperament only moved biology back into the discussion of human behavior and development.

"What we had seen was temperament, not personality," Kagan stressed. "Not all the high reactives become shy and cautious."

But Kagan also told me that when the high reactives overcame their inhibitions and became more social, the change was often on the outside rather than the inside. When Kagan did brain scans and heart-rate analyses on the high reactives who were more social, they tended to show similar biological reactions to the more inhibited children. And in interviews, these children would often reveal that beneath the surface they were riddled with tension.

"The human is an onion," Kagan said. "You can easily change

the outside layer. Easy. Therapists do that, and life does it. A good marriage does it. Success in life does it. But now as we go deeper, as we peel away the layers of the onion, it's harder."

Recognizing the biological core of our behavior wasn't just a blow to attachment theory. It was a blow to every psychologist—the Freudians and the behaviorists alike—who claimed that what happens to us early in life determines how we end up later in life. But the idea of temperament is particularly problematic to attachment theory because it exposes the biggest flaw of the Strange Situation—as well as of the more sophisticated experiments attachment researchers have created in their efforts to move beyond the Strange Situation. All of the attachment experiments begin with the dubious assumption that how a mother or caretaker treats a baby is the key to the relationship. What Bowlby and Ainsworth failed to consider is that the babies' own behavioral tendencies might play an equal role in how the relationship unfolds. In fact, some researchers now think that if the Strange Situation measures anything at all, it's the baby's temperament. The children who were dubbed "insecurely attached" by a generation of attachment researchers because they didn't clamor for the attention of their mothers might just have been the less anxious low reactives. This would help explain why when one researcher in 1998 tracked down and interviewed eighty-four people who had undergone the Strange Situation test seventeen years earlier as one-year-olds, he found that the babies who had been labeled insecurely attached were actually more likely to be well-adjusted at age eighteen than the babies who had been labeled securely attached.

AFTER READING ABOUT BOWLBY, I could see why attachment parenting had felt intuitively right to me. I had unknowingly believed in attachment theory for my entire life. The idea that losing a mother at a young age had a long-lasting psychological impact on how I had turned out seemed so obvious that I had never bothered to question it.

I am not sure when I began to assemble the various moments of my life into a narrative, but by the time I was a teenager, I knew my own story well.

I was three and wild when my mom's rapid decline began and my wildness made her dizzy and sick. My father had no choice but to drag me away from my mom's sickbed, and I responded, as any three-year-old would, with fury.

We had a very small tree in our backyard at this time, not much taller than I was, and I began to kick and beat it on a daily basis. My goal was to knock this young tree down, and when, after months of hard work, I succeeded, I was surprised and disappointed that no one was proud of me. The beating of this tree and my reaction to its fall are among my earliest memories. My father doesn't remember it. I think that it happened, but it is possible that it didn't, that at some point along the way, I had constructed a useful metaphor, a small tree to stand in for the mysterious disease that had taken my mother from me.

Whether the tree was real or not, the memory took root. Long after my mother was gone, I still understood myself as that confused little boy flailing at the tree. I was older and bigger, but the motherless little boy lived on inside me. And so when, at twelve, I began to worry obsessively about my father's safety—began to worry so much that if he was five minutes late in returning home I would be sick with fear, gazing out the window for the first sign of his return—I had a ready explanation: I had lost my mother at a young age, and now I was terrified of another loss. When I began to suffer from hypochondria around the same time, I understood it as the natural outgrowth of my firsthand experience with disease and loss at age three. When, at seventeen, my first romantic relationship fell apart, and I found myself feeling so alone and broken up that it was impossible to imagine that I would ever feel whole again, I assumed, just as Bowlby might have predicted had he known my story, that I would always struggle in my relationships with women.

I am not sure how this one particular theory about small children and mothers became so entwined with my sense of self. I imagine it happened because attachment theory was in the air and because we all take the scattered moments of our lives—the chaos inside and out—and assemble them into narratives that make sense to us.

I also suspect that, in making my mother central to my life even in her absence, the narrative I created became perversely comforting. It's hard to know this for sure, and I certainly wasn't consciously comforted by it. But the theory would explain, as my research progressed and I grew increasingly skeptical of the ideas of Bowlby and Ainsworth, why I felt a strange sense of loss.

EIGHTEEN

The Baby Brain

On Rubbing Baby Shampoo into My Own Eyes

IT MIGHT BE A GOOD THING that babies can't talk. Probably if babies could talk they would be unbearably repetitive. Probably they would say, "I would like to suck on a breast now," over and over; or "I am tired and should get some sleep, but first I would like to suck on a breast for a bit."

Still, boring as it would be to listen to babies talk about breasts all day, there would be some advantages. It would be nice, for example, if babies could calmly request food rather than going cuckoo-bananas at the first hint of hunger. And it would be fascinating to know how babies think and learn about the world.

It would also be helpful if babies could tell us if they actually liked or wanted all the products we blow their college savings on.

Jennifer and I had been warned by other parents that it would happen, but the transformation of our apartment from a mess of our own things to a mess of Isaac's things was still startling. By the time Isaac was four months old, it was already hard to walk from one end of our apartment to the other without accidentally stepping on a toy and setting off an electronic jingle.

I assumed that most of Isaac's baby toys had turned out to be a waste of money, since he was usually more interested in the tags than the toys themselves. But some of the things we bought turned out to be useful. Because it occasionally allowed us to put Isaac down for a few minutes during the colic months, I consider the twenty dollars I spent on a used bouncy chair to be the best money I've ever spent. And because it helped him sleep a bit better, I have no regrets about spending thirty dollars on a swaddling blanket that was little more than a thin piece of cloth with a few cloth flaps stitched to its sides. The real challenge for new parents is to figure out which products are worth the money, and it's not an easy task—both because there are so many products and because children respond to toys differently.

As it happened, at the very time I was thinking about Isaac's toys, the media company I work for launched a parenting website and invited me to write about the ABC Kids Expo, an enormous baby products trade show in Las Vegas. I wasn't sure about going to Vegas. Isaac was still colicky, and it seemed cruel to leave Jennifer on her own even for one night. But the trade show's website promised "the premier juvenile products specialty show in the nation," with 460,000 square feet of exhibition space and nearly seven hundred registered vendors—not to mention an all-attendee reception featuring the music of the Desperate Dads. If I was ever going to get a sense of what the baby industrial complex was all about, the trade show seemed like the place to do it.

My cab pulled up to the enormous convention center at about noon, and over the next six hours, I explored almost all of the 460,000 square feet of baby products. I ran my finger along the spokes of three-thousand-dollar Silver Cross carriages and sipped wine with a fashion designer whose exhibit included a naked mannequin wearing a faux-suede infant carrier. I had an intense discussion about the war in Lebanon with an Israeli inventor holding his portable toddler toilet—as far as I could tell, the toilet was nothing more than a cardboard box with a hole in it—and argued with a man who insisted that he had come up with the first innovation in the spoon since 4782 B.C. ("But what about the spork?" "The spork is not a spoon. It's a combination of fork and spoon." "It's still a spoon!") I met an ultra–Orthodox Jewish owner of a stroller company who was much more interested in wrapping traditional Jewish leather cords around my arm than in talking about his strollers. I met a Mormon from Utah who had invented a wristwatch with a toilet-shaped face to assist children with potty training and who smiled politely as he sang "Look at me, it's potty time, potty time," to the tune of "London Bridge Is Falling Down." I met a pediatric urologist, a.k.a. the Potty MD, who had invented a toy monkey that calls out to be taken to the bathroom every half hour, and I listened as the Potty Monkey calmly announced that he'd had an accident. I accepted repeated offers of fresh-baked chocolate chip cookies from a woman selling cloisonné IT'S A BOY and IT'S A GIRL lapel pins and washed them down with a sample of a nutritional shake for pregnant and nursing mothers. I twice tried to look at Fisher-Price's products, which had been barricaded behind movable walls, and was twice told that I could not see them without the Fisher-Price press liaison—who had already left town. I admired painted plaster casts of pregnant bellies and sucked on anti-nausea Preggie Pops. I began to count the companies that claimed Angelina Jolie used their products, then lost track when the number got too high. I searched for and struggled to find toys that did not have the words "development" or "developmental" on their packaging.

Then I returned to my hotel room and collapsed.

Despite my failure to penetrate fortress Fisher-Price and the pang of regret I felt upon learning I had missed the Desperate Dads, I enjoyed much of my time at the trade show. But not all of it. The baby products trade show, after all, is about more than scatological humor and free food. It is also about death.

The Earth Mama Angel Baby display included the company's

Healing Hearts Baby Loss Comfort Kit, which comes complete with tea, aromatherapy mists, and Seeds of Hope—a packet of organic herb-blossom seeds that includes a "special blessing." A woman pitching a monitoring device that attaches to a car seat reminded everyone who passed by her exhibit that every nine and a half days an American child dies after being forgotten in a car. The inventor of CPR Teddy, a teddy bear that doubles as an unconscious infant, handed out literature on choking hospitalization rates. At the Pure Plushy exhibit, I learned that plush toys can have "up to fifty times more serious germs" than a toilet seat in the same home. Even the products that weren't explicitly about sickness and death were often so decorated in the morbid graffiti of warnings and hazards that I found it hard to look at them without envisioning a tragic accident.

The trade show was a lot to process in a day. Later that night, after briefly playing blackjack with the marketing team for Skip Hop diaper bags, I headed over to the Venetian hotel to take in the sights and sounds of a fake Italian city. I was hoping to not think about baby products for a few minutes, but as I walked up and down the banks of the faux canals and admired the plaster cobblestone roads, the baby industrial complex suddenly made sense in a way it hadn't before.

All along I'd been operating under the assumption that new parenthood was a uniquely transcendent experience—that no matter how hard advertisers tried, parenthood would somehow remain outside of the commercialism that infects every other part of American life. But in the Venetian hotel, that thought seemed hopelessly naïve. American capitalism makes no exceptions for transcendent emotion, and no part of American life is beyond the long reach of the marketer.

But then, the ABC trade show also told a happier part of the American story. As I walked around the convention center, I'd asked the vendors how they had arrived at their ideas, and their stories impressed me: One mother had dreamed up disposable potty mitts when her toddler took to touching public toilets; an uncle had created germ-resistant plush toys after his niece returned home from preschool with a cold; the Potty MD had seen the need for a Potty Monkey by working with bedwetting children.

It wasn't the ideas for the products themselves that I admired. In fact, I doubted that most of the products at the show would ever make a profit. But that was the astonishing thing about American optimism. It persists in the face of all the evidence against it. The great thing about America, I thought, as a group of drunk tourists stumbled out of a gondola, is that we can still believe in our own bad ideas.

Of all the people I spoke to at the trade show, the mother who had invented a spoon with a small airplane on the handle captured this wonderfully delusional American entrepreneurial spirit best of all. The airplane spoon seemed like a fairly simple and obvious idea, so much so that I almost felt silly in asking her how she came up with it. But there was nothing silly in the woman's response. She explained that she had seen an episode of *Oprah* about following your dreams and had decided to go ahead and invent the spoon. I think there may have even been tears welling up in her eyes. Never mind if she never earned a dollar from her invention. The spoon with the airplane handle had been her dream, and now she was at the trade show turning that dream into a reality.

A country that still believes in *Oprah,* I thought, was a country with hope.

○○○

IF I SYMPATHIZED WITH THE INVENTORS at the trade show, it might have been because I am not immune to the dream of creating a ridiculous baby product. Among the many inventions I dreamt up during Isaac's first months, my favorite was the Baby Reader, a soft baby helmet with a little magazine or newspaper stand on top so that you can read while you hold your sleeping child. But there were plenty of others: the sling that generates loud white noise, the supersoft earmuffs that generate loud white noise, the metal frame that allows you to put a sling down so that the sleeping baby remains suspended and doesn't wake up, the pacifier that sticks to the side of a baby's face, the diaper that plays C & C Music Factory's "Everybody Dance Now" whenever a baby pees.

Because I have no understanding of how things work, I have never thought seriously about creating a prototype for one of my baby product ideas. But several months after my return from the ABC trade show, I did pursue what might well be the most idiotic idea I've ever had.

The idea first came to me while washing Isaac's hair with a "no tears" shampoo. I began to wonder why, if it's possible to make shampoo that doesn't hurt your eyes, adults continue to buy the stinging variety. Pondering this important question, I found myself wondering if baby shampoo really is so gentle on the pupils. After all, most babies will cry if shampoo gets in their eyes, whether it stings or not. I realized that for all these years, parents have been trusting the makers of these no-tears shampoos without a shred of evidence.

I finished giving Isaac his bath, but I was no longer focused on removing the mysterious gook that collected in the folds of his skin. I had a plan. Babies might not be able to tell us what they think of the products we buy for them, but I could. I would answer questions once thought to be unanswerable by testing the products on myself.

"I'm going to become a baby guinea pig," I told Jennifer that night, and then realized how bad that sounded. "I mean, not literally."

Jennifer didn't think I was serious as I explained my plan, and neither did I. Mostly I was relishing the sheer stupidity of it all. But when I mentioned the idea to my editor at *Parents* magazine, she thought it sounded stupid but also fun.

"I mean, you're not going to diaper yourself, right?" she asked.

"I , er . . . of course not," I said.

With my editor's encouragement, I decided to go for it. After all, it is tempting to carry out bad ideas even when I am not getting paid. At a dollar a word, stupidity is irresistible.

Over dinner that night, I told Jennifer that I was going ahead with my baby guinea pig plan. Jennifer is used to my weird plans and has even had a few weird plans of her own over the years. But there is a limit to her tolerance.

"Please just don't diaper yourself," she said—apparently this is the first thing people think of when you tell them you are going to test baby products.

"Give me some credit," I laughed. Then I thought for a moment. "Maybe I'll just press the inside of a diaper against my groin to see if it feels soft."

The next evening I started with the baby shampoo and immediately had my first important insight: Pouring shampoo directly into your own eyes is not as easy as you'd think. Unable to stop myself from instinctively twisting my face away from the bottle, I finally had to pour the shampoo onto my hands and rub it into my eyes.

I appreciate that rubbing shampoo into my own eyes is probably enough to qualify me for involuntary institutionalization in some states, but I did make an important discovery: Baby shampoo stings. I tried two different brands, and both left me wincing—so much so that the babies of the world might have a strong case if they got together for a class-action suit.

When the pain in my eyes died down after a few minutes, I put on my underwear, spread a quilt across the living room floor, and lay down on it. Jennifer was watching TV on the couch.

"Is there a reason you're lying on a quilt in your underwear?" she asked, reasonably enough.

"Would you mind just quickly swaddling me during the next commercial break?"

Jennifer looked like she might be ill.

"Um, I'd really rather not."

"Please?"

"No."

It took ten minutes of my whining on the floor and then threatening to invite my friend Brad over to swaddle me before Jennifer got down on the carpet and began to bind my limbs with our bedspread.

Fully swaddled on the floor of my living room, a big unshaven baby, I felt as uncomfortable as I had expected. Jennifer had wrapped me so tightly that escaping on my own was not going to be easy. After trying and failing to break out of the swaddle by extending my arms, I realized the trouble I'd be in if a fire broke out. Jennifer would grab Isaac and head for the door, and I would end up with the single most embarrassing obituary of all time.

But then, to my surprise, the feeling of constriction went away, and a few minutes later, my body, somehow sensing that it couldn't beat my mind's idiocy, decided to join in. After five minutes, I felt calmer than I had in some time, so much so that I began to wonder if I should give up writing and open a relaxation-swaddling studio. I could charge thirty dollars for an hour of swaddling. For an additional fee, I could sing "Rock-a-Bye Baby" to the customers as they lay helpless on the floor. I could even change the lyrics to make the song less terrifying: "When the wind blows, the cradle will inexplicably remain motionless in the treetop."

"It sounds like the plot of a horror movie," Jennifer said.

"No swaddling for you," I said.

I thought a swaddling studio was a genuinely good plan, but I had another plan to finish first.

I moved on to my most masochistic experiment of all: watching an entire Baby Einstein DVD.

If I could ask babies only one question, it would probably be "What's with all the Baby Einstein nonsense?" At times Isaac was so transfixed that it was almost impossible to distract him. I probably could have dangled from the ceiling by a bungee chord and performed an upside-down robotic dance while shouting "Vive La France!" and it probably wouldn't have been enough to get Isaac to turn away from the plastic mobile going 'round and 'round on the screen.

If adults don't get Baby Einstein, it may be because it's impossible for an adult to watch the videos without thinking about how many millions the company has made by setting footage of cheap toys to classical music. In one video, *Baby Noah*, half of the footage is nothing more than a camera moving around a single board book. It's so outrageous that I'm convinced that the heads of the company produced this particular video not out of cheapness or laziness but to let the rest of us know that we might as well give up because nothing is beyond their powers. Probably the company will one day produce a video with nothing but footage of a single cardboard box—*Baby UPS Guy*—and probably I will buy it.

Still, I was determined to at least try to watch Baby Einstein with fresh eyes. I thought that if I stared at it long enough, I might be able to experience something akin to Isaac's trancelike state.

Not wanting to be distracted, I waited until Isaac had gone to sleep and then sat down on the floor in front of the TV to watch a full Baby Einstein DVD.

It was no use. All I could think about was the money. At one point I even found myself imagining the company's founder diving into a sea of gold coins like Scrooge McDuck on *Duck Tales*.

It was time to move on to taste tests. I started with infant formula. At the time, Isaac was still breastfeeding, but we were also supplementing his diet with formula, and I was surprised by how much he seemed to love the formula, considering the metallic odor it gave off.

I poured two ounces of water into a glass, mixed it with a full scoop of baby formula, and took a sip. It was only slightly more pleasant than shampoo in the eyes.

After struggling for several hours to describe the taste and coming up only with "seriously crappy," I decided to ask my friend Zoe Singer, a professional food critic and cookbook author, to help out. Zoe was surprisingly willing to taste an assortment of baby foods, and a few days later I showed up at her Brooklyn apartment with a bagful of baby foods and a translucent plastic teething ring, which Zoe put into the freezer so that she could try it as it was intended to be used.

We started with a premixed liquid formula. (I'd wanted to bring breast milk as well, but Jennifer had decided that she didn't particularly want me carting her breast milk around town for our friends to taste.) Zoe poured a glass of the formula, sniffed it as though she were about to taste a fine wine, and took a sip.

"A little malty. A little sweet," Zoe said. "It leaves a chalky, almost soapy feeling in the mouth."

Zoe took a second small sip. There was a brief pause, and then a look of total disgust overtook her face. "Oh, I don't like it," she said. "Something in the middle of my stomach just said stop."

She took a swig of seltzer, then tasted a glass of powdered formula. This time she looked more concerned than disgusted. "This one has a thinner body," she said.

I nodded knowingly. I had no idea what that meant. "I don't get that plastic, sour tang with this one," Zoe said. "It's like a really poorly made vanilla milk shake."

Zoe downed another shot of seltzer and moved on to the food. The stage-one organic sweet peas weren't bad but left her with "a chalky mouth feel." The stage-two chicken and gravy smelled and tasted like "cafeteria turkey" and had the texture of cornstarch pudding. The stage-two lamb was "meaty" and "mild" and had a metallic aftertaste that Zoe didn't like. The stage-one zucchini, which mysteriously said LATIN RECIPE on its label, despite containing only zucchini and water, had a bitter aftertaste. The rice cereal with mixed fruit both looked like "the paste you'd use to make papier-mâché" and tasted like what Zoe thought papier-mâché paste would taste like.

When we arrived at the squash-corn-chicken, something interesting happened: Zoe salivated. She said that it was the first time she had salivated since we started the tasting, suggesting that her brain hadn't really recognized the other items as food. And not only was the squash-corn-chicken actual food, it tasted pretty good. "I could imagine making it into a nice bisque," Zoe said.

I remembered the plastic teething ring only that night. I probably should have let it go. Instead I emailed Zoe and asked her if she would mind sucking on the teething ring and then sending me an email with her thoughts.

Zoe wrote back later that evening.

I'm teething right now. It doesn't feel that cold, and it's got sharp seams that bother the corners of my mouth. It seems not full enough unless I squeeze it at the same time, which is hard because I'm typing. The little toy shapes inside are toothsome (gumsome?) and pleasing. I think my mouth is just too big and toothy for this. I feel like I'm slobbering all over a deflated mini inner tube. Okay, I have to go wipe off my chin. Bye.

Zoe was a true friend, even if in the end she did go back on her offer to taste a breast milk sample that I had planned to purchase on Craigslist. But as I thought more about testing baby products, it occurred to me that the entire concept was even dumber than I had first thought. All of my testing was predicated on the belief that adults experience the world in essentially the same way as infants, yet I had no reason to make that assumption. It seemed possible that no amount of testing I could do on myself—or my friends—could get me close to the truth of what it's like to be a baby.

I'M NOT SURE WHY I didn't spend more time thinking about the differences between the adult and infant before conducting the experiments. After all, the question I had arrived at—how babies take in the world—had been on my mind in one form or another since the day Isaac was born. If I had been able to avoid the question, it was in part because the subject rarely comes up in the history of thinking about babies. For most of the last millennium, Western thinkers tended to view babies as retarded adults. William James, the founder of American psychology, referred to the baby's mind as "one great blooming, buzzing confusion."

To better understand the infant mind and to learn if there's any way for an adult to understand what it's like to be a baby, I called Alison Gopnik, a developmental psychologist at the University of California at Berkeley and the author of *The Philosophical Baby: What Children's Minds Tell Us About Truth, Love and the Meaning of Life*. Gopnik explained that babies process and learn much more, across a much wider range of information, than adults, and that all this information-processing makes babies vividly aware of what they're doing.

"But is there any way for an adult to get a sense of what it's like to be so vividly aware?" I asked.

"Most of the time adults don't go through the world like a baby because adults have the ability to mentally tune out things that they're already familiar with," Gopnik said, explaining that an adult might barely see the kitchen cabinet door that a baby wants to open and close one hundred times.

Still, there was hope. According to Gopnik, there are moments when an adult may be able to experience something akin to a baby's hyperawareness. "When you're traveling, or when you're in love, or when you're doing certain kinds of meditation, you can sometimes leap out of the usual state that you're in of 'what do I have to do now?' or 'how do I get to work?' " said Gopnik. "You suddenly get very vividly aware of everything that's going on around you because you're in a situation in which you're taking in a lot of information."

Gopnik told me that for adults these moments of awareness are often accompanied by a sense of exhilaration, but that we shouldn't assume that a baby's life is all exhilaration all the time. There can be a downside to the tremendous amount of information-processing babies do. Gopnik said that babies sleep so much in part because the brain needs sleep to consolidate new information.

That influx of information might even play a role in colic. Babies take in so much, the theory goes, that they become overstimulated and fussy. And just as adults might be able to experience a little bit of a baby's awareness, they might also be able to get a small taste of a baby's overstimulated state. Gopnik recalled once attending an academic conference and then lying in her hotel room at three in the morning, exhausted but unable to sleep. "I suddenly realized that basically I was suffering from colic," she laughed.

My conversation with Gopnik had begun with broad questions about how babies experience the world, but as our conversation continued, my mind wandered back to parenting. I asked Gopnik what lesson parents could glean from her knowledge of the infant mind.

"When you're a developmental psychologist, the question parents invariably ask you is, 'How can I do it better?' but developmental psychology itself suggests that this is not a sensible question to ask," Gopnik said. "In America, especially, parents think of parenting as a job. They think that their job is to do a bunch of things that will end up making this person end up as a better adult. So when they read developmental psychology, very often it's with that kind of view in mind. But, for the most part, the things that parents are doing that are having an effect on their babies are not the sorts of things that they are sitting down and consciously deciding to do. For example, one of the things we know is that parents are good at adjusting their behavior to their babies' particular temperaments."

"But, as a parent yourself, were you able to resist the urge to try and turn your baby into the best possible person?" I asked. "Isn't it instinctive?"

"It's not instinctive to begin with," Gopnik said. "It is very much a product of a particular place and a particular time. But no, of course I didn't resist it. I don't resist to this day. I can't get out of this culture any more than anyone else can. And, of course, I feel guilty when things go badly with my children and feel proud when things go well with my children. It's hard to get out of that way of thinking. But I did try to think about it differently.

"The different way to think about it is that it's like a marriage," Gopnik continued. "Like a deep relationship with another person. You do have a sense of what makes a marriage go well or what doesn't make a marriage go well. You have a sense of responsibility about your relationship with the other person. But you don't think that you're somehow shaping the person or that there's some formula you could use to come out with a better person. If you asked people about getting married and they said, 'What I really want is for my husband or wife to be good and better after twenty years of marriage,' you'd say, 'What? That's an incredibly weird way of thinking about the most intimate relationship between two people.' And, from my perspective, it's just as weird a way of thinking about the relationship between parents and children. I think it would be helpful if parents could think more about the process—'Are my child and I thriving?'—rather than thinking, 'What's the outcome of this going to be?' or, 'What's he going to be like when he's twenty-five?' Frankly, we have no idea what makes people be the way they are when they're twenty-five. It's complicated. There are lots of other factors, and there isn't very much we can say at the level of individual parents. What you can do is ask what it is like for me right now with my baby. Is that a relationship that's working?"

I LIKED GOPNIK'S WAY OF THINKING about parenthood, but I also found it a little frightening. Maybe I was just being too American, but I wasn't ready to accept the idea that there was little I could do to shape how Isaac ended up at age twenty-five. I could accept that biology accounted for at least half of the outcome, but surely parenting had to count for something.

I decided to get a second opinion and traveled to New Haven to meet Paul Bloom, a psychologist at Yale who studies how babies make sense of the world and what our knowledge of children reveals about human nature more broadly.

Bloom is in his forties, but his shaggy blond hair gives him a youthful appearance. Over lunch at a Vietnamese restaurant near campus, I asked him what parents could take away from the latest research in developmental psychology.

"That's an easy one," Bloom said, "nothing."

Perhaps seeing the dejection on my face, Bloom continued, "I think there is a real exciting science of what kids know and what babies know, and there are some really exciting discoveries that are interesting to parents. But I don't think the science has much to say, maybe anything to say, about parenting, beyond what's common sense. In fact, one of the contributions of behavioral genetics is that in the normal range of how you treat your kids, parenting doesn't have much effect on the kid's personality or intelligence or proclivities."

"Does that mean you think that Judith Harris is right when she says that parents don't really matter?" I asked.

Judith Harris is perhaps the most controversial person in the world of developmental psychology. In her 1998 book, *The Nurture Assumption,* she argued that parents can't shape a child's personality. It wasn't just the attachment studies that were problematic in Harris's view. There have been plenty of critics of attachment theory in recent decades. Harris took the argument a step further to argue that the vast majority of parenting studies were useless, and usually for the same reason: They failed to control for genetic factors. Children who grow up in a home with depressed parents might be depressed due to the unhappy home environment or they might be depressed due to the genes for depression they inherited from their parents. Without controlling for genetic factors, it's impossible for a researcher to learn anything about how parental behavior influences children. And what Harris noticed was that whenever researchers did conduct controlled studies of parenting and looked beyond genetic inheritance, they came up empty. The personalities and intellects of adopted children are no more similar to their adopted parents than to any two strangers. Harris argues that psychologists have made an enormous oversight in failing to see that children have a second environment outside of their homes, an environment of their peers, who influence them most of all. But despite her many critics, Jerome Kagan among them, who continue to insist that parents have a significant influence on their children, no one, thus far, has been able to prove Harris wrong.

"Well," Bloom said. "Judith Harris argues that parents have a huge influence, but it's all that moment of conception. But yes," Bloom continued. "I think the evidence [for Harris] is quite strong. I think anyone who has more than one kid is often struck by how different the kids are even though they might treat them pretty much the same.

"There's also a point on which Judith Harris is extremely clear, and people who don't like her often ignore this, which is that, of course, you treat your kids well. You treat them with love because you love them and want them to be happy," Bloom said. "You want to have a good relationship with your children, but you shouldn't expect to mold their personalities by treating them in certain ways." Bloom paused to take a bite of food and then went on. "And there is a domain in which parenting does have an effect. If you raise your kid Catholic, he's more likely to be Catholic when he grows up than Jewish. On the other hand, how religious somebody is when they're an adult doesn't seem to have much to do with how they're parented."

I thanked Bloom for his time and headed back to Brooklyn.

AFTER TALKING TO GOPNIK AND BLOOM, it was hard not to wonder whether my relationship with Isaac was working, and the more I thought about it, the more I thought that it was.

In the first months of Isaac's life, the relentless crying had almost banished humor from our lives. Now the trend was reversing itself. It seemed like almost every day Isaac was doing something new and hilarious—why had no one told me that babies do tribal squatting dances? I realized that Jennifer and I might have been in a parenting sweet spot between colic and the terrible twos, and I no longer had any illusions about the life of a father—even in the sweet spot Isaac had new behavioral issues for Jennifer and me to work through each week, including his unfortunate habit of slapping me across the face every time I started to sing. But, for the moment at least, we were having fun. Ron, the instructor of my fatherhood workshop, had been right. Something different had happened, and then life had gone on. Beneath my Björn, I was the same dork I had always been.

My conversations with Gopnik and Bloom and my readings about contemporary cognitive science had also made me feel as though my intellectual journey was coming full circle. Again and again, throughout my research I'd unexpectedly come across the name of Vladimir Mikhailovich Bekhterev, a mostly unknown—in America, at least—early-twentieth-century Russian neurologist. If someone had told me at the start of my research that an early-twentieth-century Russian neurologist would turn out to be a central figure in my book, I probably would have said, "cut it out"; I probably would have scrunched my face and said

"Whatchu talkin' 'bout, Willis?"—and then been disappointed when no one laughed. But Bekhterev's fingerprints show up on modern American parenting again and again, from sleep training to HypnoBirthing, to Lamaze and the rise of childbirth education classes.

Still, the most surprising thing I discovered about Bekhterev came only at the end of my research, as I began to read about how cognitive scientists today look at brains and minds. What gradually became clear is that Bekhterev—along with Pavlov, Watson, and the early Freud—got a big part of the story right. Without modern scientific tools like the functional MRI scans that are now used to measure neural activity, they had no way of understanding the intricacies of the brain—even now neuroscientists know relatively little. And they got human behavior entirely wrong in their assumption that everything we do can be explained as reflex responses to our environments. But in their reductionism, in their broad belief that it is a mistake to try and understand our thoughts and feelings as an independent realm, separate from our brains, they have been vindicated. As the Harvard cognitive scientist Steven Pinker puts it, "Scientists have exorcised the ghost from the machine not because they are mechanistic killjoys but because they have amassed evidence that every aspect of consciousness can be tied to the brain."

But more than anything, it was what Bloom and Gopnik had said about the limits of parents to shape their children that had me feeling as though I had arrived at the right place to finish my research. Not long after I set out to make sense of parenting, my research on water babies had led to a frustrating realization: If I wanted to understand who my mother really was, I had to stop imagining a perfected version of myself. My mother had been like me but she had not been me.

Now I was beginning to see that I would need to learn the same lesson again, not as a child but as a parent. I'd never doubted that I would love Isaac regardless of the person he grew up to be, but already in his first year I had caught myself imagining that he would be like me, that he would not only appreciate silliness for its own sake but also see irony as a survival strategy; that he would come to see that wrestling with his Jewish identity was not a bad thing but among the best parts of being Jewish; that he would feel an allegiance to the Houston Rockets that transcended any rational explanation.

And because half of his genes would come from me, and because he would grow up in the same home as me, there was a good chance that he would have some or all of these attributes. But I was also beginning to understand that there was a very good chance that he would have none of them, that he might one day see irony as nothing but a distraction from an earnest quest for spirituality, that he might decide to become a religious fundamentalist, that he might even, God forbid, root for the Knicks. And there would be nothing I could do but continue to love him with the same all-consuming love that had overpowered me in his first months.

My mother had been her own person and Isaac would be his own person. The thought was maddening and liberating at once.

And Then There Were Three

I WAS WORKING ON THIS BOOK at Starbucks when I got the message. "Call me as soon as you get this," Jennifer said. "Everything is okay. Just call me."

I could hear in Jennifer's voice that everything was not okay, and I was scared. I knew Jennifer had just had her first doctor's appointment since we'd found out that she was pregnant with our second child.

I held my breath and dialed her number.

"What's wrong?"

"Everything's okay. It's just that . . ."

"What?"

"It's twins."

"Twins?"

"Twins."

"Are you serious?"

"I'm serious." And then Jennifer started to cry—and not out of happiness.

I let the news sink in for a moment. "Oh my God," I said. "I'm so excited."

I was horrified. At least a dozen times during the first year of

Isaac's life I'd commented on how incredible it is that some parents manage two babies at once.

Jennifer and I met back at the apartment. By then I was thinking more clearly. "I know it's going to be insane," I said. "But we're so lucky. Just think about how amazing and fun Isaac is now. Imagine two more at his current age."

"You're right," Jennifer said. "I know it will be fun. And we're lucky to even be able to have children." Jennifer paused. "All I really want is for the babies to be healthy."

"Me, too," I said.

I hugged and kissed Jennifer. Then I slumped down on the couch so that my back was on the seat cushion and looked up at the ceiling.

"We are so screwed," I said.

I WAS LUCKY TO HAVE two unusually nice and talented people in my corner as I wrote this book. My editor, Jill Schwartzman, is everything a writer could ask for in an editor. She was patient when I needed patience, and inspiring and insightful when I needed inspiration and insight. My agent, Dan Lazar, was a great source of encouragement and support at every stage of the process.

This book would be much worse if not for the following people who read parts of the manuscript and shared their thoughts: Jessica Apple, Max Apple, Rebecca Jacobs, Lydia Musher, Hasdai Westbook, and Linda Yellin. Other people who helped and inspired me along the way: Talya Fishman, Elisheva Apple, Leah Apple, David Kaplan, Adam Korn, Lea Beresford, Binnie Kirshenbaum, Patty O'Toole, and Cuttino Mobley.

My life would be much worse if not for Jennifer Fried and Isaac Apple. I love them so much it's not even funny.

A NOTE ON MY SOURCES: This book is not a work of scholarship, and while I relied on a wide range of sources in the course of my writing, the following books were especially important to my research: *Love at Goon Park: Harry Harlow and the Science of Affection* by Deborah Blum; *Birth: The Surprising History of How We Are Born* by Tina Cassidy; *Mother Nature: Maternal Instincts and How They Shape the Human Species* by Sarah Blaffer Hrdy; *The Myth of the First Three Years: A New Understanding of Early Brain Development and Lifelong Learning* by John T. Bruer; *Parenting, Inc.* by Pamela Paul; *Better: A Surgeon's Notes on Performance* by Atul Gawande; and *Freud, Biologist of the Mind: Beyond the Psychoanalytic Legend* by Frank J. Sulloway. I recommend all of these titles for further reading on the subjects in this book.

Allen, Greg. "BabyPlus Prenatal Audio System Makes Normal Babies Look Like Geniuses Compared to Their Stupid Parents." daddytypes.com, August 30, 2007. http://daddytypes.com/2007/08/30/babyplus_prenatal_audio_system_makes_normal_babies_look_like_geniuses_compared_to_their_stupid_parents.php.

Alter, Alexandra. "The Baby-Name Business." *The Wall Street Journal*, June 22, 2007.

Andrews, Edmund L. "Patents: A Device to Muffle the Cries of an Infant." *The New York Times*, December 24, 1988.

Angier, Natalie. "Why Babies Are Born Facing Backward, Helpless and Chubby." *The New York Times*, July 23, 1996.

Bazelon, Emily. "To Snip? Help Slate's Circumcision Research Project." Slate.com, August 23, 2005.

Beck, Neils C., Elizabeth A. Geden, and Gerald T. Brouder. "Preparation for Labor: A Historical Perspective." *Psychosomatic Medicine* 41, no. 3 (May 1979): 243–57.

Beck, Neils C., and Lawrence J. Siegel. "Preparation for Childbirth and Contemporary Reasearch on Pain, Anxiety, and Stress Reduction: A Review and Critique." *Psychosomatic Medicine* 42, no. 4 (July 1980): 429–47.

Beekman, Dan. *The Mechanical Baby: A Popular History of the Theory and Practice of Child Raising*. L. Hill, 1977.

Begley, Sharon. "Your Child's Brain." *Newsweek*, February 29, 1996.

Bekhterev, Vladimir. *General Principles of Human Reflexology*. Leningrad: Government Publication, 1926.

Bell, John D. "Giving Birth to the New Soviet Man: Politics and Obstetrics in the USSR." *Slavic Review* 40, no. 1 (Spring 1981): 1–16.

Blakeslee, Sandra. "Doctors Debate Surgery's Place in the Maternity Ward." *The New York Times*, March 24, 1985.

Block, Jennifer. *Pushed: The Painful Truth About Childbirth and Modern Maternity Care*. Cambridge, Mass.: Da Capo Press, 2007.

Blum, David. "When Lullabies Aren't Enough: Richard Ferber." *The New York Times Magazine*, October 9, 1994.

Blum, Deborah. *Love at Goon Park: Harry Harlow and the Science of Affection (Science Matters)*. New York: Penguin Group (U.S.A.) Inc., 2004.

Boncompagni, Tatiana. "Baby Shall Enroll: Mommy Knows." *The New York Times*, May 11, 2006.

Bowden, Kelley, Dale Kessler, Mike Pinette, and Elizabeth Wilson. "Underwater Birth: Missing the Evidence or Missing the Point?" *Pediatrics* 112 (October 2003): 972–3.

Bowlby, John. *Child Care and the Growth of Love*. World Health Organization Report on Maternal Care and Mental Health. New York: Penguin Books, 1963.

Bradley, Robert A. *Husband-Coached Childbirth: The Bradley Method of Natural Childbirth*. New York: Bantam Books, 1996.

———. "What Is Husband-Coached Childbirth?" Address to Western Regional Conference of the ICEA. Los Angeles, March 1965.

Bruer, John. *The Myth of the First Three Years : A New Understanding of Early Brain Development and Lifelong Learning*. New York: Free Press, 1999.

Cassidy, Tina. *Birth: The Surprising History of How We Are Born*. New York: Grove Press, 2006.

Chertok, L. *Psychosomatic Methods in Painless Childbirth*, trans. D. Leigh. New York: Pergamon, 1959.

Coates, Susan B. "John Bowlby and Margaret S. Mahler: Their Lives and Theories." *Journal of the American Psychoanalytic Association* 52, no. 2.

Cohen, David. *Watson: The Founder of Behaviourism*. London: Routledge & Paul, 1979.

Cyna, A. M., G. L. McAuliffe, and M. I. Andrew. "Hypnosis for Pain Relief in Labour and Childbirth: A Systematic Review." *British Journal of Anaesthesia* 93, n. 4 (2004): 505–11; doi:10.

Dick-Read, Grantly. *Childbirth Without Fear: The Principles and Practice of Natural Childbirth*, 3rd ed. London: Heinemann, 1956.

Donkin, Pam. "Music Together: The Joy of Family Music: An Interview with Kenneth K. Guilmartin and Lili M. Levinowitz." Children's Music Network: *Pass It On!* (2005): 2–40.

Ellison, Peter Thorpe. *Reproductive Ecology and Human Evolution*. Aldine Transaction, 2001.

Eyer, Diane E. *Mother-Infant Bonding: A Scientific Fiction*. New Haven: Yale University Press, 1994.

Finger, Stanley. *Origins of Neuroscience: A History of Explorations into Brain Function*. New York: Oxford University Press, 1994.

Flanagan, Owen J. *Science of the Mind*, 2nd ed. Cambridge, Mass.: MIT Press, 1991.

Gawande, Atul. *Better: A Surgeon's Notes on Performance*. New York: Picador, 2008.

Gladwell, Malcolm. "Baby Steps." *The New Yorker*, January 10, 2000, p. 80.

Glick, Leonard B. *Marked in Your Flesh: Circumcision from Ancient Judea to Modern America*. New York: Oxford University Press, 2006.

Goleman, Daniel. "When a Baby Cries: Researchers Seek Clues to Potential Problems." *The New York Times*, April 14, 1988.

Gollaher, David L. *Circumcision: A History of the World's Most Controversial Surgery.* New York: Basic Books, 2001.

——. "From Ritual to Science: The Medical Transformation of Circumcision in America." *Journal of Social History* 28, no. 1 (Autumn 1994): 3–36.

Goode, Erica. "Mozart for Baby? Some Say, Maybe Not." *The New York Times*, August 3, 1999.

Gopnik, Alison, Andrew N. Meltzoff, and Patricia K. Kuhl. *The Scientist in the Crib: What Early Learning Tells Us About the Mind.* New York: HarperCollins, 1999.

Gould, Stephen Jay. *Ever Since Darwin: Reflections in Natural History.* New York: W. W. Norton & Company, 1992.

Grady, Denise. "Study Urges Early Painkillers in Labor for First Deliveries." *The New York Times*, February 17, 2005.

Grant, Michael, and Rachel Kitzinger. *Civilization of the Ancient Mediterranean: Greece and Rome.* New York: Scribner's, 1988.

Groopman, Jerome. "The Colic Conundrum." *The New Yorker*, September 17, 2007.

Gutmann, Caroline. *The Legacy of Dr. Lamaze: The Story of the Man Who Changed Childbirth.* New York: St. Martin's Press, 2001.

Harris, Ben. "Whatever Happened to Little Albert?" *American Psychologist*, February 1979: 151.

Hrabi, Dale. "Ringing Up Baby." Salon.com, February 2, 2006.

Hrdy, Sarah. *Mother Nature: Maternal Instincts and How They Shape the Human Species.* New York: Ballantine Books, 2000.

Hulbert, Ann. *Raising America: Experts, Parents, and a Century of Advice About Children.* New York: Knopf, 2003.

Iovine, Vicki. *The Girlfriends' Guide to Pregnancy: Or Everything Your Doctor Won't Tell You.* New York: Simon & Schuster, 1996.

Joravsky, David. "The Mechanical Spirit: The Stalinist Marriage of Pavlov to Marx." *Theory and Society*, no. 4 (Winter 1977): 457–77.

——. *Russian Psychology: A Critical History.* Ames, Mass.: Blackwell Publishing, 1989.

Kagan, Jerome. *An Argument for Mind.* New Haven: Yale University Press, 2007.

Kagan, Jerome, and Nancy C. Snidman. *The Long Shadow of Temperament.* Cambridge: Harvard University Press, 2004.

Kalonyme, Louis. "Man at Birth Has No Fear, Tests Reveal." *The New York Times*, January 4, 1925.

Karmel, Marjorie, and Alex Karmel. *Thank You, Dr. Lamaze.* Pinter & Martin Ltd., 2005.

Karp, Harvey. *The Happiest Baby on the Block: The New Way to Calm Crying and Help Your Baby Sleep Longer.* New York: Bantam Books, 2002.

Kotulak, Ronald. *Inside the Brain: Revolutionary Discoveries of How the Mind Works.* Kansas City: Andrews McMeel Publishing, 1996.

Kramer, Peter. *Freud: Inventor of the Modern Mind.* New York: HarperCollins, 2006.

Lamaze, Fernand. *Painless Childbirth: Psychoprophylactic Method.* H. Regnery Co., 1956.

Leckman, James F., L. C. Mayes, R. Feldman, D. W. Evans, R. A. King, and D. J.

Cohen. "Early Parental Preoccupations and Behaviors and Their Possible Relationship to the Symptoms of Obsessive-Compulsive Disorder." *Acta Psychiatrica Scand* 100 (1999): 1–26.

Levitt, Steven D., and Stephen J. Dubner. *Freakonomics: A Rogue Economist Explores the Hidden Side of Everything*. New York: HarperCollins, 2005.

Logan, Brent. *Learning Before Birth: Every Child Deserves Giftedness*. La Vergne, Tenn.: Lightning Source, Inc., 2003.

London, Ivan D. "Contemporary Psychology in the Soviet Union." *Science*, n. s., 114, no. 2957 (August 31, 1951): 227–33.

Loudon, Irvine. *Death in Childbirth: An International Study of Maternal Care and Maternal Mortality, 1800–1950*. Oxford: Oxford University Press, 1992.

Mead, Sara. "Million Dollar Babies: Why Infants Can't Be Hardwired for Success." *Education Sector*, April 3, 2007.

Melzack, Ronald. "Labour Pain as a Model of Acute Pain." *Pain* 53 (1993): 117–20.

Melzack, Ronald, and Patrick D. Wall. *The Challenge of Pain*. New York: Penguin Books, 1988.

Melzack, R., P. Taenzer, P. Feldman, and R. A. Kinch. "Labour Is Still Painful After Prepared Childbirth Training." *Canadian Medical Association Journal* 125, n. 4 (August 15, 1981): 357–63.

Micale, Mark S. "Charcot and the Idea of Hysteria in the Male: Gender, Mental Science, and Medical Diagnosis in Late Nineteenth-Century France." *Medical History* 34 (1990): 363–411.

Michaels, Paul A. "Childbirth Pain Relief and the Soviet Origins of the Lamaze Method." Title VIII project, University of Iowa, 2007.

Mongan, Marie F. *HypnoBirthing: The Mongan Method: A Natural Approach to a Safe, Easier, More Comfortable Birthing*, 3rd ed. Deerfield Beach, Fla.: Health Communications, Inc., 2005.

Nguyen, Sarah, Carl Kuschel, Rita Teele, and Claire Spooner. "Water Birth: A Near-Drowning Experience." *Pediatrics* 110 (August 2002): 411–3.

Odent, Michel. *The Farmer and the Obstetrician*. London: Free Association Books, 2002.

Orenstein, Peggy. "Where Have All the Lisas Gone?" *The New York Times Magazine*, July 6, 2003.

Osnos, Peter. "Childbirth, Soviet Style: A Labor in Keeping with the Party Line." *The Washington Post*, September 2, 1970.

Paul, Pamela. "And the Doula Makes Four." *The New York Times*, March 2, 2008.

——. *Parenting, Inc*. New York: Times Books, 2008.

Pinette, Michael G., Joseph Wax, and Elizabeth Wilson. "The Risks of Underwater Birth." *American Journal of Obstetrics and Gynecology* 190 (2004): 1211–5.

Pinker, Steven. "The Blank Slate." *The General Psychologist* 41, no. 1 (Spring 2006): 1–8.

Rayback, Matthew, and Michael Sherrod. *Bad Baby Names: The Worst True Names Parents Saddled Their Kids With, and You Can Too!* Provo, Utah: Ancestry Publishing, 2008.

Razran, Gregory. "Soviet Psychology and Psychophysiology." *Science*, n. s., 128, no. 3333 (November 14, 1958): 1187–1194.

Reed, Richard K. *Birthing Fathers: The Transformation of Men in American Rites of Birth.* New Brunswick, N.J.: Rutgers University Press, 2005.

Remondino, Peter Charles. *History of Circumcision from the Earliest Times to the Present: Moral and Physical Reasons for Its Performance, with a History of Eunuchism, Hermaphrodism, Etc., and of the Different Operations Practiced Upon the Prepuce.* California: Davis, 1891.

Schroeter, Ken. "Water Births: A Naked Emperor." *Pediatrics* 114, no. 3 (2004).

Sears, William, and Martha Sears. *The Attachment Parenting Book.* New York: Little Brown, 2001.

Sears, William, Robert Sears, and James Sears. *The Baby Book: Everything You Need to Know About Your Baby—from Birth to Age Two.* New York: Little, Brown, 2003.

Shea, Christopher. "The Temperamentalist." *The Boston Globe*, August 29, 2004.

Sidenbladh, Erik. *Water Babies.* New York: St. Martin's Press, 1983.

Small, Meredith F. *Our Babies, Ourselves: How Biology and Culture Shape the Way We Parent.* New York: Anchor Books, 1999.

Stanley, Alessandra. "A Birth Method Stirs a Debate." *The New York Times*, June 8, 1995.

Stodder, Gayle Sato. "Have It Your Way." *Fit Pregnancy*, 2008.

Sulloway, Frank J. "Freud and Biology: The Hidden Legacy." In *The Problematic Science: Pyschology in Nineteenth-Century Thought*, ed. William R. Woodward and Mitchell G. Ash, 198–227. New York: Praeger, 1982.

———. *Freud, Biologist of the Mind: Beyond the Psychoanalytic Legend.* Cambridge, Mass.: Harvard University Press, 1992.

Thomas, A. Noyes. *Doctor Courageous: The Story of Dr. Grantly Dick-Read.* New York: Harper, 1957.

Todes, Daniel P. "Pavlov's Physiology Factory." *Isis* 88, no. 2 (June 1997): 205–46.

Trainor, Laurel J. "Are There Critical Periods for Musical Development?" *Developmental Psychobiology* 46 (2005): 262–78.

Transactions of the American Gynecological Society by the American Gynecological Society, published by The Society, 1911. Item notes: v.36 (1911); original from Harvard University, digitized May 25, 2007.

Trevathan, Wenda. *Human Birth: An Evolutionary Perspective.* Aldine Transaction, 1987.

Tucker, Robert C. *The Soviet Political Mind: Stalinism and Post-Stalin Change.* New York: W. W. Norton & Company; rev. ed., 1972.

Van Dijken, S. *John Bowlby: His Early Life—a Biographical Journey into the Roots of Attachment Theory.* New York: Free Association Books, 1998.

Warner, Judith. *Perfect Madness: Motherhood in the Age of Anxiety.* New York: Riverhead, 2005.

Wattenberg, Laura. *The Baby Name Wizard: A Magical Method for Finding the Perfect Name for Your Baby.* New York: Broadway Books, 2005.

Wright, Robert. "Go Ahead—Sleep with Your Baby." Slate.com, March 28, 1997.

About the Author

SAM APPLE's first book, *Schlepping Through the Alps*, was a finalist for the PEN/Martha Albrand Award for First Nonfiction. Apple lives in Brooklyn with his family. Visit the author's website at samapple.com or contact him at samapple@gmail.com.